Awakening to Wholeness

Awakening to Wholeness

On Pilgrimage with Dante

KERRY WALTERS

CASCADE *Books* • Eugene, Oregon

AWAKENING TO WHOLENESS
On Pilgrimage with Dante

Copyright © 2026 Walters, Kerry. All rights reserved. Except for brief quotations in critical publications or reviews, no part of this book may be reproduced in any manner without prior written permission from the publisher. Write: Permissions, Wipf and Stock Publishers, 199 W. 8th Ave., Suite 3, Eugene, OR 97401.

Cascade Books
An Imprint of Wipf and Stock Publishers
199 W. 8th Ave., Suite 3
Eugene, OR 97401

www.wipfandstock.com

PAPERBACK ISBN: 979-8-3852-4551-2
HARDCOVER ISBN: 979-8-3852-4552-9
EBOOK ISBN: 979-8-3852-4553-6

Cataloguing-in-Publication data:

Names: Walters, Kerry S. [author.]

Title: Awakening to wholeness : on pilgrimage with Dante / by Kerry Walters.

Description: Eugene, OR: Cascade Books, 2025 | Includes bibliographical references.

Identifiers: ISBN 979-8-3852-4551-2 (paperback) | ISBN 979-8-3852-4552-9 (hardcover) | ISBN 979-8-3852-4553-6 (ebook)

Subjects: LCSH: Dante Alighieri, 1265–1321. Divina commedia. | Spiritual life. | Spirituality in literature. | Dante Alighieri, 1265–1321—Religion. | Poets, Italian—To 1500—Criticism and interpretation.

Classification: PQ4416 W35 2025 (paperback) | PQ4416 (ebook)

VERSION NUMBER 01/05/26

For Kim and Jonah,
Always

Come si vede qui alcuna volta
l'affetto ne la vista, s'elli è tanto,
che da lui sia tutta l'anima tolta

Paradiso XVIII, 22–24

Contents

Introduction: Voyages of Discovery | 1

Part I: Inferno | 12

Part II: Purgatorio | 58

Part III: Paradiso | 120

Works Cited | 223

Introduction
Voyages of Discovery

(1)

The French philosopher Gabriel Marcel once said that to be a human is to be *homo viator*.[1] We're wayfarers, pilgrims, explorers, always stretching forward, forever in search of what lies beyond the horizon. There's a deep restlessness in us that keeps us on the move. We're uncomfortable remaining in place for very long. We have the aroma of the sea in our nostrils. We dream of embarking on voyages of discovery.

Our wayfaring nature has led us to explore the entire globe, and in recent years fueled ambition of doing the same in outer space. The same restlessness that inspired Neanderthal clans to cross the Alps, Polynesian sailors to brave the unknown ocean, or European explorers to venture forth into the New World animates today's astronauts.

Of course, most of us will never launch into space in a rocket, any more than most of our ancestors sailed to all those unexplored places left tantalizingly blank on maps of the time. We won't set out in search of far distant El Dorados. But for all that, there's a voyage of discovery available to everyone, and it promises the greatest treasure of them all. It's not a search for places on land or sea or space, but for deep meaning and personal wholeness.

For each and every *homo viator*, this is the undiscovered country toward which our restlessness pulls us. I suspect that all other voyages of discovery, important as they may be, are sublimations of it.

---

1. Marcel, *Homo Viator*.

(2)

In the upper left corner of a painting widely considered to be his masterpiece, Paul Gauguin enigmatically scrawled three questions:

> D'où venons-nous? Que sommes-nous? Où allons-nous?
> "Where do we come from?" "What are we?" "Where are we going?"

These questions, and others very much like them, simmer in the heart of every human being. They're not simple requests for geographical locations—"Where are we now? What's the shortest route to our destination?"—much less about getting ahead in the world—"What class backgrounds must we come from to succeed in the world? What career trajectory best leads to success?" No, they're Big Questions about Ultimate Meaning whose answers, we hope, will shed light on this mysterious, wonderful, and tragic enterprise we call life. Along the way, we've most likely caught occasional flashes of what we're looking for. Sometimes the clouds break open just enough to let a sudden ray of illumination shoot through, a kind of revelatory disclosure of the kind Virginia Woolf once called a "moment of being." Although it disappears quickly enough, we're left with a soul-stirring hint of what lies behind the cloud and a deep, deep yearning for more.

In his *Walden*, Henry David Thoreau described these moments of being as beautifully as anyone ever has:

> I long ago lost a hound, a bay horse, and a turtledove, and am still on their trail. Many are the travelers I have spoken concerning them, describing their tracks and what calls they answered to. I have met one or two who had heard the hound, and the tramp of the horse, and even seen the dove disappear behind a cloud, and they seemed as anxious to recover them as if they had lost them themselves.[2]

When we venture forth as wayfarers into the undiscovered country, it's because our yearning for meaning, fed by peripheral glimpses of Thoreau's wonderful creatures, has awakened us to the fact that the world is unimaginably resplendent. All we need do is pierce its veil.

---

2. Thoreau, *Walden*, 16.

(3)

The first stage of a voyage in search of deep meaning requires travel to a place that for many of us is murky and unfamiliar: our interior landscapes. If we would follow the allusive trail of Thoreau's animals, we must begin there.

But why? Doesn't this risk turning the whole enterprise into a subjective mind-game, a fruitless exercise in navel-gazing? Isn't the meaning we want better sought in the *outer* world of solid facts? After all, evolution can answer Gauguin's first question, neurology his second, and geriatrics his third.

The problem is that this approach misunderstands both the intent of the questions and the restless yearning for meaning that lies at the heart of *homo viator*. We're not looking for a physical explanation of our origins, important as that is, so much as an answer to the question of why we, or everything else for that matter, exist at all. We're not focused on brain states and biochemistry (again, important stuff) when we wonder about the sorts of beings we are. Instead, we want to know what it means to be a creature aware of both its sobering fragility and its exhilarating promise—even more urgently, what it means to be *me*. And longing to know where we're going is about ultimate purpose, not gerontology.

Questions about meaning can't be adequately addressed by factual responses alone. Facts are always important. But in the voyage of discovery proper to *homo viator*, they're cargo and ballast, not vessel. What we're after is the *why*, not the *what*: the *quia*, not the *propter quid*.

(4)

Exploring our interiors offers us the opportunity to discover the deep meaning we desire in at least two ways.

First, it clears the ground by helping us ferret out all those psychological hang-ups and spiritual anxieties that prevent us from making progress in our journey. Old maps of the world used to quaintly warn travelers who ventured into unknown seas that "there be dragons here!" But there be dragons in our own uncharted subterraneans too, dragons of vice, confusion, anger, impatience, timidity, insolence, willful ignorance, and so on, and all of them distort the way in which we see ourselves and the world. We need to find and confront them, either girding ourselves for battle or negotiating a truce, if we hope to escape or at least neutralize their influence.

It's an indisputable psychological and spiritual principle: If you want to go up, you must first go down. To ascend, you must descend. That's the initial step in any interior voyage of discovery.

Second, the working assumption behind *homo viator*'s search for meaning is that humans are the creatures par excellence gifted with the ability to ask questions about ultimate meaning. But how is this possible unless, as Thoreau reminds us, we already have some connection to that which we seek?

The answer seems to lie in the fact that we humans are microcosms of the macrocosm. We are little universes, carrying within us a reflection of the ultimate meaning that pervades reality and that gives rise to us in the first place. The Judeo-Christian tradition accounts for this innate connection by asserting that humans are made in the likeness of God and hence infused with an at least dim awareness of cosmic meaning. Hindus speak of the atman, that spark of the divine that constitutes the true self and connects it to the Whole. The seventeenth-century mystic Blaise Pascal says it would never occur to any of us to search for God had we not already found Him.[3] However it's understood or expressed, we're connected at our deepest core with the meaning we seek. When we explore our interior landscape, we grow increasingly aware that what we seek already has a foothold within us. It's closer than we think.

Socrates speaks for this view when he gives but one strong bit of advice to seekers: *gnothi sauton*, "know thyself." In knowing our self—our *true* self, the one connected to deep meaning, not the false one spawned by psychological and spiritual insecurities—we begin to learn whence we came, where we go, and who we are.

At some point along the way, we wayfarers begin to move back and forth between our interior landscapes and the outer world. Realizing that we carry within us an awareness, ever blossoming, of the meaning we seek, we look more ardently for traces of it in the world around us. Our microcosmic exploration has prepared us to explore the macrocosm. Facts about the world, hitherto viewed, perhaps, as little more than isolated bits of information, now begin to display themselves as tiles in a great mosaic, each of which derives its meaning from the whole of which it is a part. Our pilgrim head and heart turn to the world's wisdom

---

3. Pascal, *Pensées*, 279.

traditions—its philosophies, theologies, poetry, sacred writings—to add polyphony to the *cantus firmus*, the underlying melody of meaning, that is now heard within us and outside of us.

(5)

Explorers of land, sea, and space don't venture forth on voyages of discovery out of idle curiosity. Too much effort is required, too much is at stake. All of them hope to discover something that will fundamentally change their lives. For some, the goal is untold riches. For others, scientific fame. Still others aim for conquest and power.

Seekers of meaning likewise hope for treasure, although we may not be quite sure what it looks like at the beginning of our journey. But as we clear away the inner demons that so often fracture and fragment life and steadily awaken to the fact that our microcosmic identity offers a portal to ultimate meaning, we begin to experience a harmonious *integritas*, a transformative coming-together of what earlier was disjointed and disruptive. In rhythm with the order of things—joyfully running, if you will, with Thoreau's three creatures instead of passively pining for them—we see that we're not the same person at journey's end as at its start. The treasure we discovered is rebirth. We see ourselves and the world differently than we did before we set out on the voyage of discovery. We act differently too. We've become whole persons.

(6)

Foolish explorers set out with neither map nor guide, believing that their untested sense of direction is good enough to get them where they think they want to go. But no ship can sail effectively without a pilot; uncharted water needs at least a compass by which to steer.

That's where the fourteenth-century Florentine poet Dante Alighieri comes in. His epic work the *Divine Comedy*, one of the world's truly great poems, is tailor-made for *homo viator*'s pilgrimage.

It's a perfect guide to the transformation of self that takes place as we travel in search of deep meaning. What could be more fitting for this kind of voyage of discovery than a poem, since the very word itself—*poiesis*—means "a making" or "a creating."

As he journeys through the three regions of hell (Inferno), purgatory (Purgatorio), and paradise (Paradiso), Dante the pilgrim is recreated. From his initial lostness in a dark wood, unsure of who he is or where he should be going—sound familiar?—he emerges whole after an intense unitive encounter with Ultimate Meaning. Heeding the twists and turns of his voyage—the monsters he encounters, the moral lessons he learns, the importance of spiritual discipline, the insights into what it means to be a human, and the culminating *integritas* he obtains—can further our own journeys to transformation as well.

More specifically, here's what Dante the poet and the pilgrim offers us.

Psychodrama. On the surface, Dante is journeying through "hell," "purgatory," and "paradise." That's undeniable. But beneath the surface, he's tunneling deep within his own psyche, exploring its sometimes terrifying depths as well as its brilliant heights. Like Dante at the beginning of his journey, all of us find ourselves at one time or another lost in a dark wood. His own trek into the interior of self in search of a clearing in the tangled forest (a *lichtung*, as the philosopher Martin Heidegger puts it)[4] offers a vantage point and roadmap for us.

Life Lessons. Along the way, Dante invites us to think about the qualities of character and modes of behavior that either maximize or minimize our chance of awakening to a rich, fulfilling life. There's a lot of moral instruction in the *Divine Comedy*, and it's presented, thank goodness, in a memorable and non-pedantic way. If I had to sum up in a single phrase Dante's overall life lesson, it might be *age quod agis*: "Do what you're doing." Be mindful. Focus on the task at hand. Remember your best self in every endeavor you undertake. Don't sleepwalk through life. *Be* there.

Love. Dante makes clear that love is the common denominator that links all human activity. In fact, it's the divine pulsation that sustains and animates all of reality. There is nowhere, even in the deepest pit of hell, where some trace of it isn't found. Those who fall into wickedness do so not because they cease to love but because they love badly, in the sense that their objects of love are unworthy of love. The ultimate human goal, and achieving it takes a lifetime if not more, is learning to love well. Dante's poem is a primer in how to do that.

---

4. Heidegger, "Origin," 176–203.

Spiritual Value. You needn't be a Christian—or even a religious believer of any stripe—to profit from Dante's reflections on the deep human longing for Ultimate Meaning which transcends yet illuminates the here-and-now. And it's to his credit that he refuses to offer easy, canned answers. Of course he writes in a Christian idiom. But there's no mawkish Sunday School simplicity in his poetic struggle to say something about the wholeness for which we yearn. Quite the contrary.

Horizon-Broadening. Who wouldn't want to read as many of the great literary classics as possible before death forever takes away the opportunity? Dante's *Divine Comedy* is indisputably one of them. Even if few of us would go so far as T. S. Eliot's claim that "Dante and Shakespeare divide the world between them. There is no other,"[5] it's undeniable that Dante is one of the world's truly great artists. And because he's so erudite, but at the same time user-friendly once one gets into his rhythm, reading him can be a real education in theology, philosophy, history, and spirituality.

Beauty. The erudition of Dante's poem, its life lessons, its spiritual value, its prodding us to think deeply, and its capacity for giving voice to our yearning for transcendence all are conveyed in verse that is simply quite beautiful. Even in translations (most of them, anyway), it's possible to savor the poem's fluid tones. If you ever hear a native Italian read a bit of untranslated Dante, you can't but be struck by the beauty of the language even if you don't understand it. And who doesn't need more beauty in their life?

(7)

I've lost count of the number of people who've told me they want to read Dante's *Divine Comedy*, but either were too intimidated to begin or, once started, eventually gave up because they got bogged down.

Of the first group, those who never start, the usual reason is that the poem strikes them as alarmingly erudite. How can anyone without a PhD in Italian literature possibly understand, much less fully appreciate, it? The second group, those who begin but don't finish, typically throw in the towel for a couple of reasons. Either in their innocence they pick up a wooden or clumsy translation that quickly turns them off, or the

---

5. Eliot, "Dante," 265.

sheer tedium of flipping back and forth between poem and translator's explanatory notes defeats them.

The pity is that both groups miss out on the experience of exulting in some of the most beautiful verse ever written. They also lose the opportunity to have their intellects and wills stimulated and challenged by the moral, political, religious, philosophical, and social insights Dante so generously offers. (The *Comedy* is also, believe it or not, hilarious in places; Dante has a genius for both sarcasm and, occasionally, slapstick.) Finally, and most importantly, they pass over a guide who can help steer them on their own voyages of discovery in search of wholeness. Because in addition to being great literature, the *Comedy* is a penetrating source of psychological and spiritual wisdom.

This book is for both groups. My aim is to make the spiritual direction Dante offers perfectly accessible without in any way sacrificing the beauty of his language or the depth of his insights. This is neither a Dante-for-Experts nor a Dante-for-Dummies book. It's a Dante-for-Pilgrims one.

(8)

Dante divides his journey into three separate but related treks. The first is through hell (Inferno), where he descends into his and humanity's darkest corners; the second is through purgatory (Purgatorio), where he teaches us how to exorcise our self- and other-destructive tendencies; and the third is in paradise (Paradiso), where the wholeness, the integrity, the harmony, and the joy, which is his goal—and ours!—is achieved.

Along the way our guide Dante is steered by three guides of his own, each symbolizing a mood or attitude essential for the journey. The Roman poet Virgil, his first guide, represents reason or intellect. Beatrice, his second guide, represents love or the heart. And his final guide, St. Bernard, represents reverence or the soul. If we would find the answers to Gauguin's questions, we must follow the promptings of head, heart, and soul.

There's a noticeable and delightful stylistic progression throughout the century of cantos that speaks to Dante's skill as a poet. His verses mirror in tone what they describe in words. It's as if Dante is presenting us with a kind of performance art.

As his voyage of discovery brings him closer and closer to God, for example, his Paradiso cantos become richer, more lavish. That's because God is the Fullness of Being. God is the Supreme and Unsurpassable Plenitude, the *Ipsissima Esse*, the That Than Which Nothing Greater Can Be Thought, the I Am Who I Am, the Infinite and Eternal, the Alpha and the Omega.

It only stands to reason that as Dante draws nearer to God, the text exponentially proliferates with allegory, symbolism, metaphor, theology, and imagination. Its sometimes dizzying fulsomeness mirrors the Divine Plenitude. Accordingly, my commentary on Paradiso is the lengthiest in the book. There's just so much there to mine. (Yet another reason why it's sad that most readers never get beyond the Inferno.)

By way of contrast, consider the Inferno's style. In it, Dante offers us some hair-raising scenes. No doubt about it. And because of that, they tend to lodge in the memory. But when you reflect upon them, their descriptions are surprisingly minimalistic. That's Dante's way of underscoring the Nothingness that characterizes hell. Everything there is the opposite of the Divine Plenitude, and Dante's way of writing about it mirrors its tragic emptiness, just as his verse in the Paradiso mirrors blessed Fullness.

Finally, in the Purgatorio, the style moves steadily away from the stark cantos of the Inferno to ones with more color, allegory, and symbolism. It's as if the tone is preparing us slowly and carefully—a perfect purgative stratagem for the bedazzling explosion to come in the Paradiso.

(9)

Each of the *Divine Comedy's* three sections is divided into stanzas or three-lined "cantos." There are one hundred of them, thirty-four in Inferno and thirty-three each in Purgatorio and Paradiso. The average length of a canto is around 140 lines, expressed in a number of three-lined verses or tercets. In Italian, each of the three lines has eleven syllables, making thirty-three syllables in each tercet.

The recurrence of threes clearly gestures at the Trinity. God's perfect presence is everywhere in the *Comedy*, written into the very structure of the poem just as, believes Dante, it's written into the text of the universe itself.

For each one of these one hundred cantos, I've focused on its single-most important spiritual, psychological, philosophical, or moral insight, selected appropriate lines (usually fewer than ten) from it, and then offered a brief commentary, pulling from philosophy, theology, literature, history, current events, and my own experiences, that both explores the canto's relevance for the contemporary wayfarer's journey and sheds some light on Dante the poet and pilgrim.

(10)

A final word.

As I mentioned earlier—although it scarcely needs saying to anyone with even the slightest idea of what the *Comedy* is all about—the roadmap Dante offers us for our own voyages of discovery is steeped in Christian imagery. But the genius of his masterpiece is that it speaks to people from all faith traditions as well as those who are spiritual but not religious, on the one hand, or humanistic, on the other. Speaking personally, I think the worst way to read Dante is to see him as simply a Christian apologist. This too narrowly confines him, too domesticates his wonderfully universal vision.

So, regardless of whether you believe that the proper culmination of your journey is mystical union with God or simply an integrated self attuned to what really matters in life, Dante is worth reading and pondering. You may not agree with everything he has to tell you. As you'll discover, there are moments (although not many) when his guidance either baffles me or leaves me cold. Yet my trust in his wisdom far outweighs any quibble I might have with this or that part of his counsel. With each re-reading of him, I find more to admire.

The ominous sign over his Inferno may be "Leave all hope, ye that enter," but the overall message of the *Comedy*, the one Dante wants us to take away, is beautifully expressed toward its end when he writes about the Deep Meaning he sought and found, and that he hopes we will too:

> *Within its depths I saw ingathered,*
>   *Bound by love in one volume,*
>   *The scattered leaves of all the universe.*
> *I feel that I rejoice!*

A Note on Translations

Throughout the text, I've drawn upon the so-called Carlyle-Okey-Wicksteed translation of Dante's *Divine Comedy*. The work of three different men: John Aitken Carlyle (Inferno, 1849), Thomas Okey (Purgatorio, 1901), and Philip Henry Wicksteed (Paradiso, 1899), it's a good rendering of Dante's Italian into easily understandable English.

There are several excellent recent translations of the *Comedy*, complete with helpful reference notes. In my estimation, Mark Musa's and Robert and Jean Hollander's are the very best. Both Musa and the Hollanders separate their translations into three separate volumes. The Hollander translation has the additional advantage of offering a bilingual text.

>Mark Musa
>*Inferno*. New York: Penguin, 1984.
>*Purgatory*. New York: Penguin, 1985.
>*Paradise*. New York: Penguin, 1986.
>
>Robert and Jean Hollander.
>*Inferno*. New York: Vintage, 2002.
>*Purgatorio*. New York: Vintage, 2004.
>*Paradiso*. New York: Vintage, 2008.

Inferno

*... in which Dante and we begin
the inward journey ...*

Inferno, Canto I, Part 1: A Dark and Hollow Landscape

> *In the middle of the journey of our life*
>   *I came to myself in a dark wood,*
>   *Where the straight way was lost.*
>
> *Ah me! how hard a thing it is to tell*
>   *What a wild, and rough, and stubborn wood this was,*
>   *Which in my thoughts renews the fear.*
>
> *So bitter is it, that scarcely more is death.*

Like so many other dark human experiences, we seem to be incapable of talking seriously about midlife crises. Spurred on largely by cinematic stereotypes, but also by our self-protective drive to deflate threats to our well-being, we crack jokes about facelifts and tummy tucks when it comes to women or sports cars and extramarital affairs when it comes to men. The assumption is that a midlife crisis is purely and simply sparked by the fear of growing old.

Once we learn to accept our balding heads and sagging physiques, so conventional wisdom says, we get over the crisis and return to normal life.

But Dante pushes through such shallowness to get to the genuinely dark heart of a midlife crisis: when our taken-for-granted world comes across as alien and threatening. Here, our well-trodden landscape loses its familiar features, becoming a "dark wood," "wild, and rough, and stubborn," whose gnarled canopy shuts out sunlight.

Sometimes an abrupt misfortune topples our world. Divorce, illness, financial ruin, loss of reputation: these can all collapse the houses of cards we mistake for safe fortresses. Our values and hopes, our relationships, and even our very self-image get buried under the rubble.

But more commonly the process is an incremental disillusionment with our lifestyle that reaches the point of asking, "Is this all there is?" What worldly success we've managed to achieve takes on the stale taste of dust and ashes. We feel empty, played-out, directionless, burdened with a despairing sense of lost time, feeling that our manner of living over the years betrayed the ideals and dreams of our youth. Looking back over the trajectory of our life, we see that somewhere along the line we strayed off the "straightforward path" and now drift rudderlessly.

T. S. Eliot surely must have had this fate in mind when in one of his poems he has a chorus of lost souls, likewise lost in the forest dark, proclaim themselves "hollow."[1]

To make things even worse, we hollow men and women can be so lost in the dark wood that we can't see our way out. Dante is correct. Living like this is a kind of death in which the past becomes an empty regret, the future disappears, and nothing remains but the bleak present.

Inferno, Canto 1, Part 2: Sleepwalking

> *I cannot rightly tell how I entered it,*
> *So full of sleep was I about the moment*
> *That I left the true way.*

Homer offers us a chilling parable in Book IX of *The Odyssey*. Odysseus and his men, storm-tossed for days on the wine-dark sea, finally spy an island on which to take refuge. Odysseus sends a reconnoitering team ashore, but when they don't return he goes looking for them. When found, the lost men, surrounded by the rinds of a strange fruit, lie languidly under trees.

Odysseus immediately senses the danger. His men have eaten of the lotus, whose "sweet delicious fruit" induces spiritual sleepiness. Now, having "forgotten home," they want "only to stay there." But "I dragged

---

1. Eliot, "Hollow Men," 77.

them back in tears," says Odysseus, "forced them on board the hollow ships, pushed them below the decks, and tied them up!"[2]

What's the deep-down reason for the midlife crisis? What's the foundational cause of so losing our way that we wind up in a forest dark? We eat of the lotus fruit. We become, like brave Odysseus's men, sleepwalkers, slipping into spiritual slumber and forgetting—or, as Dante says, abandoning—our yearning for home.

To sleepwalk one's way through life is to become so befogged that we lose sight of what's really important for attaining a genuinely good life. Our culture offers us all sorts of tailor-made soporific drugs to shoot up: sensual gratification, vaulting ambition, wealth accumulation. But perhaps the most potent sleeping draught of them all, and certainly the most prevalent one, is the mechanical tedium of day-to-day living.

In one of his sermons, John Donne marvels at our somnambulism. "Was there ever any man seen to sleep in the cart between Newgate and Tyburn? Between the prison, and the place of execution, does any man sleep? Yet we sleep all the way; from the womb to the grave we are never thoroughly awake."[3]

Our English word "awake" comes from the Old English *wacan*. It carries the same meaning as "awake": to be roused from slumber. But an older and richer meaning is "to be born" or "to come into being." To sleepwalk through life is to fail to become a full human. It's to be stillborn. To be jolted in some way out of complacency long enough to see that one is in a bad place: this is the beginning of the transformative pilgrimage.

Inferno, Canto 1, Part 3: Gods of Sleep

> *And behold, almost at the commencement of the steep,*
>   *A leopard, light and very nimble,*
>
> *So impeded my way,*
>   *That I had often turned to go back.*
>
> *I feared at the sight*
>   *Which appeared to me, of a lion.*

---

2. Tennyson, "Lotos-Eaters," 24.
3. Quoted in Rundell, *Super-Infinitie*, 295.

He seemed coming upon me with head erect,
  And furious hunger.

And a she-wolf, that looked full of all cravings;

  She brought such heaviness upon me
  That I lost the hope of ascending.

As somnambulists who drowse our way through life, we genuflect before gods of sleep who discourage us from wakefulness. They work hard at waylaying us should we happen to shake off our grogginess long enough to venture onto the pilgrim's path. Dante the pilgrim lists the three most powerful: lust (the leopard), pride (the lion), and greed (the she-wolf).

These gods induce sleepwalking by addicting us to immediate gratification, witless self-satisfaction, and unquenchable avarice.

The first two deaden our sensibilities, enslaving us to pleasure and encouraging a lazy complacency. These are genuine lotus-effects. The third afflicts us in a different way. Its incessant drive to accumulate keeps us scrambling at such a frenetic pace that we have no time to pause long enough to think about what we're doing with our lives.

Worshiping at the altars of lust and pride makes us too muddled to awaken. Pledging our troth to greed keeps us too trapped in somnolent dreams of more and More and MORE. At the end of the day, it's the most powerful of the three gods of sleep because the frantic pace it sets continuously accelerates. As Dante warns, the wolf

  Has a nature so perverse and vicious,
  That she never satiates her craving appetite;
  And after feeding, she is hungrier than before.

Remember the iconic line "greed is good" from Oliver Stone's 1987 film *Wall Street*? It's spoken by Gordon Gekko, the cutthroat broker, during a shareholders meeting of a company he plans to seize and dismantle. "Greed is good," he reassures his audience. "Greed is right, greed works. Greed clarifies, cuts through, and captures the essence of the evolutionary spirit."

This is the delusional and ultimately self-destructive credo of worshipers of the wolf. No wonder Dante finds that avarice is the chief obstacle preventing him from journeying to transformation. It inflicts a spiritual "heaviness" that makes it hard to keep one's eyes open.

Inferno, Canto 1, Part 4: Pilgrims, Not Wanderers

> *I to him: "Poet, I beseech thee*
> *By that God whom thou knowest not:*
>
> *Lead me!"*

Scholars tell us that the word "Hebrew" is derived from the Akkadian *habiru*, which means "nomads," people in search of a home. (In the ancient world, it tended to have a negative connotation, mainly because people looking for a home might threaten yours.) It fit the ancient Israelites perfectly, who were pilgrims in both a literal and spiritual sense. They sought the geographical land promised them by God, and they sought to rest in God's favor. Both were places to call "home."

Pilgrims aren't wanderers. The latter are folks who roam without an itinerary or destination. They're motivated largely by restlessness or curiosity. They get antsy if they stay very long in one place, or they have an irresistible itch to see what's around the next bend or just over the horizon. But when they do, they can't rest content. Before long, they're on the move again.

Pilgrims, on the other hand, have a destination in mind, a haven they'll be able to call home, a place of transformation and fulfillment. The problem is they're not entirely sure how to get there. There is a space, be it geographical or spiritual, between them and their destination, and it is unfamiliar territory. To venture into it without any kind of guidance is both foolhardy and daunting.

That's why, like Dante, we need an experienced guide, someone who can steer us in the right direction, keep our eyes on the prize, comfort us when we drop with weariness or cower with fear, scold us when we get lazy, bull-headed, or self-pitying, and in general remind us that we're pilgrims, not wanderers.

Virgil, the pre-Christian Latin poet (that's why he "knowest not" God) is the guide who helps Dante escape the three gods of sleep and begin the arduous journey to personal transformation.

Inferno, Canto II: Take Courage and Begin!

Virgil speaks:

> "Thy soul is smit with coward fear,
>
> which oftentimes encumbers men,
>   so that it turns them back from honored enterprise;
>   as false seeing does a startled beast."
>
> As flowerets, by the nightly chillness
>   Bended down and closed, erect themselves all open
>   On their stems when the sun whitens them;
>
> Thus I did, with all my failing courage,
>   And so much good daring ran into my heart,
>
> That I entered on the arduous and savage way.

Make no mistake about it: entering on the transformative pilgrim's path takes courage. Dante, like the rest of us, isn't sure that he has the right stuff to go the full length. So Virgil his guide tells him to buck up instead of being like an animal frightened by its own shadow. The way ahead is fraught; there's no denying it. But our imaginative anticipation of hardship is nearly always worse than the reality turns out to be. There's no sense in allowing our souls to be tainted by cowardice.

This talking-to inspires Dante, and he feels "good daring" coursing through his heart.

Dante is punning here, which comes through beautifully in the original Italian: *al cor mi corse*. "Heart" and "courage" share the same Latin stem, *cor*. To be courageous is to have strength of heart. It's to be motivated and sustained by love, devotion, and a dedication to perform deeds that otherwise would seem too daunting to undertake.

This is a significant point in our journey toward transformation. Our culture encourages us to think of courage as brawny daring-do in combat, and this sort of physical courage is surely a reality. But there's also moral courage, in which, longing to uphold the good, we dare to take unpopular stands, and spiritual courage, in which our longing to become the sort of person God intends us to be gives us the fortitude to plumb and exorcise the dark recesses of our souls.

Physical courage alone, much less a mere intellectual commitment to morality or self-improvement, is unable to fuel and sustain acts of moral or spiritual courage. Only a commitment born of yearning love can do that.

You say you don't feel that love? Nonsense. You wouldn't be on the pilgrim's trail if that were true. The love is there, motivating you, even if you don't yet fully realize it. But as you progress, it becomes more apparent.

Inferno, Canto III: Those Who Play It Safe Get Nowhere

LEAVE ALL HOPE, YE THAT ENTER!

These words of color obscure,
  Saw I written above a gate.

Strange tongues, horrible outcries,
  Words of pain, tones of anger,
  Voices deep and hoarse, and sounds of hands among them,

Made a tumult, which turns itself
  Unceasing in that air forever dyed,
  As sand when it eddies in a whirlwind.

This miserable mode
  The dreary souls of those sustain,
  Who lived without blame, and without praise.

These have no hope of death,
These unfortunates, who never were alive.

Everybody, including those who've never opened the *Comedy*, knows the baleful warning inscribed above the entrance to hell. It's become one of our culture's iconic phrases. Yet the first souls Dante encounters aren't actually in hell proper, but only in its vestibule. They no more deserve hell than they do paradise. They're exactly where they belong: nowhere.

Why? Because they avoided making choices, taking stands, affirming or denying, accepting or rejecting. Embracing neither goodness nor wickedness, they settled for being passive spectators in life. Their neutrality wasn't principled, as neutrality sometimes can be, but simply an expression of moral and spiritual torpor. They preferred to sit on the sidelines because it was safer than getting in the game and mixing it up. "Nothing ventured, nothing lost" was their motto.

This kind of passivity avoids committing to other persons, calling out injustice, dedicating to a cause, or taking account of the differences between truth and falsehood, beauty and ugliness, virtue and vice. In his short story "Bartleby," Herman Melville offers an unforgettable portrait of this way of living—or, of unliving, as Dante says—in the eponymous character. A drab and listless figure, Bartleby's catchphrase response to any request made of him is "I prefer not to."

Dante gives us no inscription tailor-made for the vestibule of avoiders. But the author of Revelation gives us one in Jesus's terrible words to the church at Laodicea: "I know your works; I know that you are neither cold nor hot. I wish you were either cold or hot. So, because you are lukewarm, I will spew you out of my mouth" (Rev 5:15–16).

Inferno, Canto IV: Scorn Not Worldly Wisdom

> *"O thou, that honorest every science and art;*
> *Who are these who have such honor,*
> *That it separates them from the manner of the rest?"*
>
> *And he to me: "The honored name,*
> *Which sounds of them, up in that life of thine,*
> *Gains favors in heaven which thus advances them."*
>
> *People were there with eyes slow and grave,*
> *Of great authority in their appearance;*
> *They spoke seldom, with mild voices.*

In the late second century, a debate raged between two of the period's greatest theologians, Clement of Alexandria and Tertullian, about the relationship between pagan philosophy and Christianity. Clement believed that pagan philosophy was a helpmeet to the faith. Tertullian strongly disagreed, scornfully asking (although it's more a statement than a question!): "What has Athens to do with Jerusalem?"[4]

---

4. Tertullian, *Prescription*, 246.

The debate is still alive today, with the fault line frequently but not inevitably dividing Protestant and Catholic Christians. For my part, I think Thomas Aquinas settled the disagreement by pointing out that truth is one. Consequently, truth—wherever it is found and from whomever it is encountered—can only enrich the faith.

It follows that Athens has a lot to do with Jerusalem, and it's a smugly self-imprisoned faith or a self-destructively disdainful secularism that denies it.

Dante the poet owed a lot to pagan thinkers. It's no coincidence that he chose Virgil, a pre-Christian Latin poet, as his guide through the underworld. Relishing the greatness of ancients such as Homer, Hesiod, Democritus, Thales, Heraclitus, Ovid, Seneca, Cicero, Averroes, and Virgil himself, just to name a few he mentions, Dante can't bring himself to consign them to hell simply because they weren't Christians. So he places them in Limbo, the First Circle, a well-lit region where they are held, as Virgil tells him, for no other reason than that they died unbaptized.

> *For such defects, and for no other fault,*
> *Are we lost, and only in so far afflicted,*
> *That without hope we live in desire.*

To condemn, even if gently, people who lived in pre-Christian times clearly sticks in Dante's craw, just as, I suspect, it sticks in ours today. From the very get-go, then, his poetic descent into hell invites us to reflect on justice.

Inferno, Canto V: Contrapasso of Lust

> *I came to a place void of all light,*
> *Which bellows like the sea in tempest,*
> *When it is combated by warring winds.*
>
> *The hellish storm which never rests*
> *Leads the spirits with its sweep;*
> *Whirling, and smiting it vexes them.*
>
> *I learnt that to such torment*
> *Are doomed the carnal sinners,*
> *Who subject reason to lust,*

> *And as the wings of starlings bear them on*
> *In the cold season in large band and full,*
> *So doth that blast the spirits maledict;*
>
> *Hither, thither, down, up, it leads them.*

The ancient Greeks, recognizing that sexual desire can be an all-consuming fire, called it *theia mania*, a "divine madness" inflicted by Aphrodite and Eros. Desire or lust is one of the driving forces of human behavior. To deny this is a symptom of deep repression or outright dishonesty. For all our potential for grandeur, even the noblest of us can be derailed when we're blown "hither, thither, down, up" by the hot sirocco of *theia mania*.

We saw in Canto IV that the inhabitants of the limbic first Circle are pagan teachers of wisdom whose innocent fault is that they died unbaptized and unshriven. The Second Circle is reserved for those who allowed lust to overpower their reason, consume their attention, scatter their resources, fragment their integrity, and stymie their life journey.

Given the faux-puritanism of much of American Christianity, it's important to note that lust, in the grand scheme of things, is a relatively minor offense. Dante is absolutely not condemning sexual intimacy, but only out-of-control and hence destructive lust, which, like all the other violations chronicled in the Inferno, prevents us from leading rich and fulfilling lives. That's why the souls of those who courted *theia mania* during their lifetimes are in the second instead of a deeper level of hell.

We see in this canto Dante's signature use of what's called contrapasso: the consequences of a destructively sinful act imitate—or, perhaps, mock—it. Just as the souls in the Second Circle were pulled hither and yon by their insatiate lust when they were alive, so they're now blown in all directions here by "a hellish storm which never rests." Contrapasso is a perfect expression of the dictum that we eventually reap what we sow.

Inferno, Canto VI: Eating Ourselves to Death

> *I am in the third circle.*
> *That of the eternal, accursed, cold, and heavy rain;*
> *Its law and quality is never new.*
>
> *Cerberus, a monster fierce and strange,*
> *With three throats, barks dog-like*
> *Over those that are immersed in it.*

> *His eyes are red, his beard greasy and black,*
> *His belly wide, and clawed his hands;*
> *He clutches the spirits, flays, and piecemeal rends them.*

In Chinese Buddhism and folk religion, hungry ghosts, possessed of spindly thin limbs and bloated, out-sized bellies, roam the world, insatiably famished but never satisfied. No matter how much they gorge themselves, they're unable to fill the empty feeling that drives them ever onward.

Hungry ghosts are the souls of people who, when alive, refused to control their appetites but instead allowed themselves to be enslaved by them. Their voraciousness led them to eat and eat and eat, but all the while they themselves were being devoured by their undisciplined hunger.

I suspect that what we might call "hungry ghost syndrome" is one of our cultural malaises. Our appetites are enormous, and it's not simply food on which we glut ourselves, but on any other commodity that we see as desirable—or that we've been assured is so by marketers, whose business is to keep us hungry.

We know that over-eating is a contributing cause of many physical illnesses: diabetes, heart disease, high blood pressure, and so on. What we too often fail to recognize is that it also leads to the spiritual illness of enslavement.

You probably know what it feels like to be genuinely hungry, so much so that you can think of little else than filling the emptiness inside. Imagine what it must be like to be a perpetually hungry ghost, how the hollowness occupies every moment of existence to the exclusion of any other thought or motive. Out-of-control craving sucks all the oxygen out of the room.

In Dante's Third Circle, the souls of gluttons pay for their inordinate appetites. Lying pig-like in filthy muck, they're ripped apart by the avatar of gluttony, the hideous three-headed dog Cerberus, who rapaciously "flays, and piecemeal rends them" just as their own insatiable appetites did to the things they devoured when alive. To remain perpetually hungry, but to be food rather than fed, is their dismal lot.

Inferno, Canto VII, Part 1: Hell's Babel

> *"Pape Satàn, pape Satàn aleppe!"*
> *Began Plutus, with clucking voice.*

In the New Testament, the devil is referred to as *ho diabolos*, "the diabolical one." It comes from the verb *diabellein*, which means both "to deceive" and "to cast through or scatter." The distinctive function of evil or wickedness is to disrupt the natural rhythm of things by sowing confusion and dissension—in short, chaos. That's why St. Augustine famously called evil a deprivation of being.[5] He knew that it's a rip or hole in reality's fabric.

As they prepare to enter hell's Fourth Circle, the one reserved for those who misuse money, Dante and Virgil are blocked by Plutus, classical mythology's god of wealth. In the Inferno, he's a harsh-voiced malicious imp who has more bark than bite. In a high-pitched voice, he screams *"Pape Satàn, pape Satàn aleppe!"* at the two travelers—and, by implication, at us.

This phrase is never translated, and for good reasons: it's nonsense. For centuries scholars have tried to discern meaning in it, but it simply defies all efforts. *Pape* may signify "pope," and *aleppe* is the Italian form of aleph, the first letter of the Hebrew alphabet, leading some to interpret the phrase as "Pope Satan, pope Satan god!" But this makes no more sense than the original.

So what's the point here? I think Dante wants to get across the truth that evil seeks to confuse. Above all, Satan and his minions are liars intent on stirring up chaos. So the poet has the imp Plutus shouting sheer gibberish, cacophonous nonsense words, to remind us of this.

All of us know, though, that the lies wickedness spreads, cloaking themselves as they do in patinas of reasonableness and virtue, can be pretty seductive. But discerning hearts and clear minds can sense that, like Plutus's gibberish, they're nonsense.

Inferno, Canto VII, Part 2: Drink It Yourself!

> *That gentle Sage, who knew all,*
>
> *Turned himself to that inflated visage,*

---

5. Augustine, *Enchiridion*, 40–42.

> And said: "Peace, cursed wolf! consume
> Thyself internally with thy greedy rage!"
>
> As sails, swelled by the wind,
> Fall entangled when the mast breaks:
> So fell that cruel monster to the ground.

I have an acquaintance who once told me that whenever he feels himself being overpowered by a temptation to dark thoughts, he shouts—literally, not mentally—"Drink your own poison, Satan!"

One needn't believe in the actual existence of Satan to appreciate the psychological acuity of this strategy for confronting and challenging one's own inordinate desires. To vocalize a rebuke to passions that threaten to run amok throws out a powerful counterpunch. It forces the temptation out into the open instead of allowing it to burrow deep inside one's psyche to fester.

Virgil calls out Plutus, the swollen avatar of avarice, by telling him to "consume" himself: to drink his own poison rather than infect others with it. This unafraid defiance is too much for Plutus. It robs him of his power; he collapses in on himself, as temptations do when they're named and shamed.

Inferno, Canto VIII: Don't Look Back

> Above the gates I saw more than a thousand
> Spirits, rained from the Heavens, who angrily exclaimed:
> "Who is that, who, without death,
>
> Goes through the kingdom of the dead?"
>
> Then they somewhat shut up their great disdain,
> And said: "Come thou alone; and let that one go,
> Who has entered so daringly into this kingdom.
>
> Let him return along his foolish way;
> Try, if he can!"
>
> Judge, Reader, if I was discouraged
> At the sound of the accursed words;
> For I believed not that I ever should return hither.

Confronting Plutus is one thing. Although he's an agent of corruption, he's also a bit buffoonish. But now Dante and his guide Virgil come up against spirits of a different caliber.

The two of them stand at the gates of Dis, entrance to the deepest and most nightmarish circles of hell. Angelic demons, condemned to guard the gates because of their failed rebellion against heaven, mock and threaten them. They tell Virgil to continue if he wishes; he's a proper citizen of the kingdom of the dead, although why anyone would want to visit the dreadful inferno puzzles them. It's not exactly a tourist spot. But Dante they will *not* allow to enter. He's an outsider, an interloper. He's alive.

Menacingly, they dare him to try to proceed: "Try, if he can!" Their implicit threat is that they'll stop him.

This is bad enough. But Dante is doubly terrified because in that moment of danger all his pent-up anxieties overwhelm him. He panics, becoming convinced that he'll never be able to find his way back to the land of the living if he tries to retrace his steps. He'll be stuck in the underworld forever, a homeless refugee in this horrible land of shadows.

There reaches a point, and it may come sooner than later as it does with Dante, when wayfarers wish they'd never left home. Their pilgrimages seem foolhardy if not downright dangerous. Their reasons for venturing forth in the first place no longer feel as convincing as they once did. They can see nothing but hardships and danger ahead of them.

But then they realize that they can't turn back. There's no going home again. Even the slight distance they've traveled, the few things they've experienced, have changed them. They're no longer the persons they were. Consequently, the home for which they pine no longer suits them. There's nothing for it but to go on, putting one foot in front of the other.

So Dante, knowing he can't turn back but that he needs help going forward, turns to Virgil. "O my loved Guide, leave me not undone!" he cries. "Fear not," Virgil replies. "For our passage none can take from us."

Inferno, Canto IX: Look Away from Medusa

All at once had risen up
  Three Hellish Furies, stained with blood.

"Let Medusa come, that we may
  Change him into stone," they all said.

> "Turn thee backwards, and keep thy eyes closed:
> For if the Gorgon shew herself, and thou shouldst see her,
> There will be no returning up again."
>
> Thus said the Master, and he himself turned me,
> And trusted not to my hands,
> But closed me also with his own.

Freud famously argued that we humans have a Thanatos instinct: a fascination with and attraction to death. It's in tension with the Eros instinct, the drive on the part of our bodies and psyches to live. But sometimes Thanatos is in the ascendance and drives us to life-denying acts of destruction against others as well as ourselves.[6]

People who push the envelope, who court danger, the thrill-seekers and risk-takers in our midst, may be acting out of the thanatoic impulse. So may adventurers who embark on voyages of discovery. Their willingness to risk everything could be a disguised urge, unarticulated even to themselves, to embrace death.

That's why the Medusa myth is so intriguing. To gaze upon her in all her serpentine-locked hideousness is to die, to be turned instantly and irrevocably into a thing, an object, an inert stone. Yet the temptation to look at her is nearly irresistible. Even here, when the Furies call on Medusa to attack the two wayfarers, Virgil senses that Dante won't be able to resist the allure of thinghood. He turns his ward's head aside and covers his eyes with his own hands.

The desire to sink into the comforting solidity of thinghood rather than endure the unpredictability of subjectivity is, perhaps, the greatest temptation of all. When you think about it, each of the condemned souls in hell succumbed to that temptation. They all acted during their lives as if they craved to gaze upon Medusa. They willfully chose behavior—betrayal, cruelty, deceit, and so on—that slowly ossified their humanity. They ceased living fully long before they actually died.

Throughout the *Comedy*, Virgil is the personification of reason. In shielding Dante from gazing upon Medusa, he testifies to the saving fact that our Thanatos tendencies can be overridden by reason. There may always be some part of us that yearns for thinghood. But our reason counteracts it by reminding us that life, with all its ups and downs, is a far preferable state.

---

6. Freud, *Beyond Pleasure*.

Inferno, Canto X: The Threat of Nothingness

> *"Like one who has imperfect vision,*
> *We see the things," he said, "which are remote from us;*
> *So much light the Supreme Ruler still gives to us.*
>
> *When they draw nigh, or are,*
> *Our intellect is altogether void; and except what others bring us,*
> *We know nothing of your human state.*
>
> *Therefore thou mayest understand that all our knowledge*
> *Shall be dead from that moment when*
> *The portal of the Future shall be closed."*

Once through the gates of Dis, Dante encounters a shade who tells him that the dead are myopic: they can remember the past and see the future—"see the things which are remote" both backward and forward—but can't focus on the present. Consequently, when the final judgment comes and their futures as well as their pasts once and for all evaporate, they'll sink into profound blindness. Inky, dark nothingness will engulf them. They'll cease, for all practical purposes, to be. The second death.

I think there's a grim warning here for those of us who sacrifice the present by nostalgically clinging to the past or moonily dreaming about the future. Both are modes of denial or escapism which prevent us from being fully alive to each experience on life's journey. As such, we come to dwell in a kind of spiritual twilight in which the sharp edge of reality, both its joys and its sorrows, are obscured. Or perhaps a better analogy would be spiritual macular degeneration: we grow blind to what should be the center of our focus—the present—and can see, although increasingly dimly, only the peripheral remnants of past and future.

Whatever metaphor we choose, the point is that when we ignore the present, we shed substance. We become shades in danger of losing both the safely abstract memories and dreams to which we cling as well as the concrete here-and-now reality that we avoid.

Inferno, Canto XI: Is There a Special Place in Hell for Blue-Nosed Puritans?

Virgil speaks:

> "They all are filled with spirits accurst;
> But that the sight of these hereafter may of itself suffice thee,
> Hearken how and wherefore they are pent up."

> And I: "Master,

> But tell me: Those of the fat marsh;
> Those whom the wind leads, and whom the rain beats;
> And those who meet with tongues so sharp,

> Why are they not punished in the red city
> If God's anger be upon them?"

> And he said to me,

> "Rememberest thou not
> How incontinence less offends God,
> And receives less blame?"

In hell there are two distinct regions: the upper depths, the "fat marsh," reserved for those who allowed their passions—lust, gluttony, sloth, and so on—to rule them, and the lower depths, Dis, the "red city," in which those guilty of violence and fraud are consigned. The first group is guilty of incontinence, or what Aristotle called *akrasia*, weakness of will. But the second is overtly and deliberately malicious, guilty not simply of lack of will but of wicked acts of will. Hence, they're more culpable.

I think Dante's distinction here is psychologically and morally astute. There surely is both a psychological and moral difference between failing to do what's right because of the torpor of habitual self-indulgence (weakness of will) and intentionally inflicting harm or deception on others (malice). They feel different from a psychological perspective, and they surely carry different weight from a moral one.

One of the worst excesses of some versions of American evangelical Christianity is a failure (or refusal) to recognize this difference. Offenses of incontinence, especially sexual ones, are obsessively assigned way too much weight, while acts of violence and fraud, particularly in the political arena, are too frequently given a pass. If there is a hell, it will hold some surprises for blue-nosed puritans.

Inferno, Canto XII: Who's the Real Monster Here?

On the top of a broken cleft
  Lay spread the infamy of Crete.

And when he saw us he gnawed himself,
  Like one whom anger inwardly consumes.

As a bull, that breaks loose, the moment
  When he has received the fatal stroke,
  And cannot go, but plunges hither and thither:

So I saw the Minotaur do.

Oh blind cupidity both wicked and foolish,
  Which so incites us in this short life,
  And then, in the eternal, steeps us so bitterly!

Dante and Virgil prepare to descend into the Seventh Circle of Hell, reserved for those who committed violence in life. Canto XI told us that there are three classes of violence: against others, against oneself, and against God and nature. Accordingly, there are three corresponding rings in this circle. Canto XII describes the first one, the prison of souls who inflicted violence on others.

It's appropriate that the entrance to the ring is guarded by the Minotaur, the "infamy of Crete." Half man and half bull, he symbolizes the bestial impetuosity, cruelty, and destructiveness of violent rage. The link between violence and bestiality is further symbolized in the canto by centaurs, half-human and half-horse, who serve as sentinels in this first ring, shooting arrows at the damned souls who seek to escape their torment.

Violence really is a kind of madness, an explosion of wrathful mayhem that bespeaks a terrifying rupture in reason and compassion. It's unsurprising that Dante portrays the Minotaur in such an antic frenzy that he bites at his own flesh.

Of course, we know that ascribing this sort of behavior to wild animals is largely a canard. Only the human creature is capable of such out-of-control destructiveness. It's not his bull half that makes the Minotaur a monster. It's his fallen human side.

Inferno, Canto XIII: Suicide

We moved into a wood,
  Which by no path was marked.

Not green the foliage, but of color dusky,
  Not smooth the branches, but gnarled and warped;
  Apples none were there, but withered sticks with poison.

Here the unseemly Harpies make their nests.

Wide wings have they, and necks and faces human,
  Feet with claws, and their large belly feathered;
  They make rueful cries on the strange trees.

I heard wailings uttered on every side,
  And saw no one to make them.

Then I stretched my hand a little forward,
  And plucked a branchlet from a great thorn;
  And the trunk of it cried: "Why dost thou rend me?"

It had grown dark with blood.

No other scene in the Inferno disturbs me more than this one. Dante and Virgil are in the second ring of the Seventh Circle, reserved for suicides, those who commit violence against themselves. Their souls are transformed into thorny bushes, forever tormented by the Harpies.

My only two male cousins on my mother's side both took their own lives. One's death was shocking but unsurprising. The other came as a total surprise, and hence colossal shock, to the family. Both of these men lived tormented lives, the one openly and the other secretly. Both of them reached the point where they simply couldn't go on.

Christian tradition condemns self-killing as a mortal sin, and popular opinion frequently disdains suicides as weaklings. That's why Dante reserves a place in hell for those who commit this violence against themselves. But surely our default response to anyone desperate enough to kill themselves ought to be compassion, not condemnation. Surely the peace they were unable to find in this world is owed them in the next. And if there is no next world, at least their suffering is ended.

In the non-Christian ancient world, suicide was frequently seen as an honorable way out of a life that had become intolerably burdensome. In our own time, people suffering from incurable and agonizing illnesses who opt to end their lives are increasingly, thank goodness, looked upon with understanding. And people who automatically scorn suicides either for "taking the coward's way out" or for committing a "mortal sin" are, I hope, on the decline.

None of this is to deny the pain and grief that friends and families of suicides experience, especially when, as in the case of my one cousin, the death comes unexpectedly. But it is to say that people who take their own lives deserve something better than condemnation.

If hell actually exists, and if it's anything like the place Dante describes, and if God is as merciful as we like to believe, the Seventh Circle's second ring surely will be empty.

Inferno, Canto XIV: Better to Reign in Hell . . . ?

"Master," began I,

"Who is that great spirit who seems to care not
  For the fire, and lies disdainful and contorted,
  So that the rain seems not to ripen him?"

And he himself, remarking
  That I asked my Guide concerning him,
  Exclaimed: "What I was living, that am I dead.

Though Jove

Hurl at me with all his might,
  Yet should he not thereby have joyous vengeance!"

Then my Guide spake:

"O Capaneus, in that thy pride remains unquenched,

> *Thou art punished more;*
> *No torture, except thy own raving,*
> *Would be pain proportioned to thy fury."*

Dante and his guide Virgil are in the Seventh Circle's third ring, reserved for blasphemers. It's a horrible place of burning sand where gobs of flame perpetually rain down upon the tormented souls.

Unsurprisingly, most of the third ring's inhabitants are miserably broken. But Virgil encounters one of them, Capaneus, who seems unbowed by his sorry fate. In Greek mythology, he was a mighty warrior who, while attacking the city of Thebes, boasted that even Zeus (Jove) himself couldn't stop him—whereupon the peeved god promptly struck him down with a lightning bolt.

The fascinating thing about Capaneus is that he continues his defiance in hell: "What I was living, that I am dead!" He reminds me of other figures in Western literature who refuse to bend to divine will. Think, for example, of Prometheus, the Titan who bestows fire (and civilization) upon humans; John Milton's Lucifer, brought low in the heavenly war but disconcertingly appealing even in sullen defeat; or Albert Camus's Sisyphus, refusing to allow his absurd punishment in hell to break his spirit.

These archetypal stories suggest that our culture is somewhat ambivalent about blasphemy. Sometimes, when it's malicious or petty, it's unanimously declared worthy of condemnation. But when it's born out of what some consider to be heroic hubris, as was Capaneus's, the case isn't so clear cut.

Similarly with those times when it smacks of despairing hopelessness: think of the biblical Job's wife's bit of advice for him to curse God and die. And especially difficult are those cases that suggest a kind of noble resistance to fate, even in characters like Lucifer and Sisyphus, who have clearly crossed a moral line but who nonetheless decide, as Milton's fallen angel famously remarks, "Better to reign in hell, than serve in heaven."[7]

Very few things in life are simple. Defining blasphemy is no exception. I suspect that Dante's focus on Capaneus is his homage to that truth.

---

7. Milton, *Paradise Lost*, 1.263.

Inferno, Cantos XV & XVI: Love That Can't Be Named?

"Were my desire all fulfilled,"
  Said I to him, "you had not yet
  Been banished from human nature:

For in my memory is fixed, and now goes to my heart,
  The dear and kind, paternal image of you,
  When in the world, hour to hour

You taught me how a man makes himself eternal." (XV)

Ah me! What wounds I saw upon their limbs,
  Recent and old by the flames burnt in!
  It pains me yet, when I but think thereof.

Had I been sheltered from the fire,
  I should have thrown myself amid them below. (XVI)

We're still in the Seventh Circle's third ring, where we've already witnessed the fate of blasphemers, or those who commit violence against God. Now we encounter in the same Burning Desert sodomites, those who commit violence against nature—although, curiously, nowhere do the words "sodomites" or "sodomy" appear.

In both cases, given the background of the desert, the implication is that their acts are sterile. In Canto XV, we meet with clerics and men of letters; in Canto XVI, statesmen and warriors. It's hard to know what to do with these two cantos for at least three reasons.

First and most obviously, my guess is that everyone reading this most likely agrees with me that "sodomy" is not a sin. Like all sexual acts, it can be abused. But same-sex relations are not in themselves wicked, nor need they be "sterile." Some Christians may declare homosexual acts "intrinsically disordered," but this blue-nosed judgmentalism increasingly grates on well-ordered moral sensibilities.

Second, Dante speaks of the sodomites he encounters with great pity and respect. There's not a shred of disdain or condemnation in his description of them. Quite the contrary. One is a past teacher of his to whom he is affectionately grateful (Canto XV). Others are men he so admires that only fear of the fire raining upon them prevents him from jumping from his place of safety to physically embrace them (Canto XVI).

Third, as we'll discover when we come to purgatory, many souls there guilty of sexual sin, including homosexuals, are being prepared for paradise. This is strange, because Cantos XV and XVI suggest that sodomy is a mortal sin (all souls in the inferno's lower depth are mortally guilty), while Canto XXVI of the Purgatorio clearly implies that it's merely venial.

The mixed message suggested by these two latter points leads some commentators to surmise that Dante may have been gay, and that Inferno Cantos XV and XVI are just reluctant homages to the moral conventions of his day.

I have no opinion about this. But I'm very impressed, especially given the acerbic and even violent discourse in which our culture today is steeped, by the graceful, respectful, and affectionate way Dante the pilgrim interacts with the men he meets in these two cantos. I can't help but wonder if he's not conveying a message of tolerance and even, perhaps, acceptance.

Inferno, Canto XVII: A Terrifying Descent on a Terrifying Monster

> *Behold the savage beast with the pointed tail,*
> > *That passes mountains, and breaks through walls and weapons;*
> > *Behold him that pollutes the whole world.*
>
> *And that uncleanly image of Fraud*
> > *Came forward and landed his head and bust,*
> > *But drew not his tail upon the bank.*
>
> *The face was the face of a just man,*
> > *So mild an aspect had it outwardly;*
> > *And the rest was all a reptile's body.*
>
> *In the void glanced all his tail,*
> > *Twisting upwards the venomed fork,*
> > *Which, as in scorpions, armed the point.*

There's absolutely nothing I can say here that comes close to capturing the cinematic horror of this canto. But in brief, here's what's going on: Virgil and Dante encounter the final inhabitants of the Seventh Circle's Burning

Desert: the usurers, those who commit violence against human skill and industry by making money from money, another sterile activity. The two are now ready to descend to the inferno's Eighth Circle. But to do so, they have to lower themselves into an immensely deep abyss. They'll do so on the back of Geryon, described above in the quoted snippets. He's the personification of the sin of fraud, which souls in the next hellish circles have all committed in one way or another.

Geryon is a perfect symbol of fraud: a benevolent face that hides a poisonous intent to sting, one whom neither "walls" nor "weapons" can withstand. He's frightening enough. But the description of the descent to the Eighth Circle is equally so. Geryon, his scorpion tail undulating like an eel, descends into the deep in a slow circular motion, allowing plenty of time for Dante to catch glimpses of flames and snatches of moaning from the damned souls they pass.

Inferno, Canto XVIII: Frozen by the Other's Look

There is a place in Hell called Malebolge.

In the ditch beneath,
  I saw a people dipped in excrement,
  That seemed as it had flowed from human privies;

And whilst I was searching with my eyes,
  Down amongst it, I beheld one with a head so smeared in filth,
  That it did not appear whether he was layman or clerk.

He bawled to me: "Why are thou so eager in gazing at me,
  More than the others in their nastiness?"

After descending into the abyss on the back of Geryon, Dante and Virgil are in the Eighth Circle, otherwise known as Malebolge or "Evil Pockets." It's the region of hell reserved for fraudsters. (I'll leave to your judgments which American politicians and televangelists might dwell there one day.) It's so named because it consists of ten ravines or ditches connected by stone bridges and descending in a spiral into the very lowest pit of hell. In each of these ditches are the tormented souls of those guilty of one form or another of fraudulent deception.

In this canto, we meet the souls in the initial two ditches. In the first are the panderers, those who procured sexual partners for third parties, and seducers, those who pretended love to lure others. In the second are flatterers who used honeyed and false words to manipulate their victims. The first are tortured by whips; the second are sunk up to their eyes in excrement.

What's so terrible about these fraudsters is that they treated other people as objects, using them and then casting them aside as soon as they got what they wanted from them. They denied the personhood, the subjectivity, of their victims.

And so, in typical contrapasso form, they themselves have been reduced to objects. In the passages I quoted above, we see two of the souls recoiling at being seen by Dante. This reminds me of the philosopher Jean-Paul Sartre's famous category of "The Look." To be scrutinized by another, says Sartre, is to be reminded that one is an object for another, and this realization is both threatening and demeaning, particularly if we're caught—or "looked at"—when we're doing something shameful.[8]

Perhaps one of the worst things about hell is being "looked at" continuously for the shameful thing one willingly became in life. No wonder the souls in the first and second bolge can't bear to be scrutinized by Dante.

I suppose a moral lesson to be drawn from this is that we oughtn't to do anything in private which would cause us shame if Looked At by another person—or God.

Inferno, Canto XIX: Christianity, Inc.

O Simon Magus! O wretched followers of his!

From the mouth of each hole emerged
   A sinner's feet, and legs up to the calf;
   And the rest remained within.

The soles of all were both on fire:
   Wherefore the joints quivered so strongly.

"Stay thou there, for thou art justly punished,

For your avarice grieves the world,
   Trampling on the good and raising up the wicked.

---

8. Sartre, *Being and Nothingness*, 347–408.

Ye have made you a god of gold and silver!

Ah, Constantine! To how much ill gave birth,
  Not thy conversion, but that dower
  Which the first rich Father took from thee!"

In the Acts of the Apostles (8:9–24) we're told that Simon the magus (magician) offered to buy some Christian "magic" off John and Peter. The word "simony," born from this episode, narrowly refers to the buying and selling of church privilege and office.

Because those church leaders guilty of it have fraudulently betrayed their baptismal vows, their contrapasso punishment in Canto XIX's third bolgia is to be shoved headfirst into pits that resemble baptismal fonts. Instead of cool water on their heads, they're eternally tormented with flames on their feet.

In a wider sense, simony refers to the way in which corrupt Christians suck up to political and economic power brokers in order to acquire wealth, social standing, and worldly influence. Beginning in the late 1970s with Jerry Falwell's toxic Moral Majority and most recently in the shamefully simoniac support of Trump's MAGA movement by self-proclaimed Christians, we've endured an explosion of this sin rivaling the worst excesses of medieval and Renaissance popes.

Dante suggests that the perennial Christian temptation to sell out for wealth and power was sparked by Constantine's "dower," or the Roman emperor's fourth-century recognition, subsidization, and institutionalization of the Christian community into an increasingly top-heavy and rulebound behemoth. With very few exceptions—Quakers as well as Anabaptists come to mind—this act set the stage for the ossification of all three branches of Christianity.

Throughout the centuries there have been spring times in which reformers strove to return to the innocence of the earliest Christian communities. But the Constantinian virus with its simoniac symptoms inevitably resurfaces.

Inferno, Canto XX: Marching Forward Blindly

When near at hand I saw our image
  So contorted, that the weeping of the eyes
  Bathed the hinder parts at their division.

Certainly I wept, leaning on one of the rocks
  Of the hard cliff, so that my Escort said to me:
  "Art thou, too, like the other fools?

Here pity lives when it is altogether dead;
  Who more impious than he
  That sorrows at God's judgment?"

"You shall be like gods!" So the serpent promised Adam and Eve (Gen 3:5), thereby initiating the primordial temptation which has resurfaced in each successive generation. In the fourth bolgia, Dante and Virgil encounter soothsayers who succumbed to it. Because they claimed to be able to tell the future, their contrapasso punishment is having their heads turned around, so that they always face backward, their tears wetting their buttocks.

Soothsaying isn't the real crime here, just the mode in which the crime gets expressed. The true crime is the attempt to usurp the divine will—to bend it, as Dante says, to human will. It's a species of fraud (remember, the entire Eighth Circle of hell is reserved for fraudsters) because trying to be godlike is simply pretending to be something one isn't.

If there's a single place in hell that I think most of us would easily fit in, it's this one. Our individual and cultural behavior suggests that we have grand illusions. We fancy ourselves the unquestionably superior species. We arrogantly dominate the natural world, and in the process are quickly destroying it. Our sciences produce horrible weapons of mass destruction. We reckon ourselves to be the final arbiters of right and wrong and truth and falsity. And interpersonal relations too often reduce to a struggle for dominance.

So, like the backward looking soothsayers in the fourth bolgia, we march blindly forward, fancying ourselves invulnerably and omnipotently godlike, smugly insisting that we're furthering progress, but wickedly ruining everything. Virgil is right. There's no occasion for crocodile tears of pity here, only ones of remorse and shame.

Inferno, Canto XXI: Hellish Hijinks

They struck him with more than a hundred prongs,
  And said, "Covered thou must dance thee here;
  So that, if thou canst, thou mayest pilfer privately."

Not otherwise do the cooks make their vassals dip
  The flesh into the middle of the boiler with their hooks,
  To hinder it from floating.

They lowered their drag-hooks, and
  Kept saying to one another: "Shall I touch him on the rump?"
  And answering: "Yes, see thou nick it for him."

But the Demon who was speaking
  With my Guide turned instant around,
  And said: "Quiet, quiet, Scarmiglione!"

By the sinister bank they turned;
  But first each of them had pressed his tongue between
  The teeth toward their Captain, as a signal;

And he of his rump had made a trumpet.

It would be convenient to discuss the twinned Cantos XXI and XXII together. But they're each just so damn funny that I don't want to cram them together.

That's right. I said funny. Whenever I read these two cantos I hear Mussorgsky's weirdly festive "Night on Bald Mountain" playing in the background.

It's startling to find humor in hell, isn't it? But a bit of comic relief helps us endure the genuine horror of the Inferno. I suspect that these two cantos serve the same function as the figure of the fool in Shakespeare's tragedies.

Dante and Virgil have reached the fifth bolgia, where political grifters and frauds are boiling in ditches of fiery pitch. If they dare to rise to the surface to ease their torment, winged Malebranche ("Evil Claws") devils seize and rip them to pieces. In life, they connived behind the scenes. In death, they're immersed in sticky, scalding pain.

When these devils see Dante, they yearn to torment him too. But Virgil, who for once seems properly frightened, warns them off, telling them that his companion has a get-out-of-hell-free card from The Big Guy Himself. So instead of going on the attack, they back off and agree—perhaps just a bit too eagerly—to guide Dante and Virgil to a bridge leading to the next bolgia.

Their boss Malacoda ("Evil Tail") selects ten wonderfully named devils like Scarmiglione, "the ruffled hair one," as escorts and off they march in high spirits, almost like an infernal troop of fraternity brothers intent on mischief. Malacoda lives up to his name by giving them a farewell salute-fart.

But Malacoda and his imps are lying, as we'll soon discover. Their duplicity seems more than appropriate in a canto about political fraud.

Dante's genius at creating scenes in this and the following canto that are both terrifying and hilarious is genuinely astonishing.

Inferno, Canto XXII: Double and Triple Cross

> *"If you wish to see or hear Tuscans or Lombards,"*
> *The frightened sinner said,*
> *"I will make them come.*
>
> *Let the Malebranche hold back a little,*
> *That they may not fear their vengeance."*
>
> *The Navarrese selected well his time;*
> *Planted his soles upon the ground, and in an instant*
> *Leapt, and from their purpose freed himself.*
>
> *Thereat each was stung with guilt.*

The dark humor that broke the horror in Canto XXI continues in this one. Dante and Virgil, led by the ten Malebranche or clawed demons, are still in the bolgia where political grifters are given the sad choice of boiling in burning pitch or, if they surface for some relief, getting ripped apart by the demons.

Ciampolo, one of the damned grifters, a native of Navarre, decides to call upon his skills of deception to get himself out of a tight spot. Surfacing from the pitch, he makes a deal with the demons. If they won't tear him asunder, he'll deliver several of his "Tuscan or Lombard" companions to the demons by falsely promising them safety. The imps agree—well, sort of, because having no intent on honoring the deal, they hide behind some rocks, waiting on their quarry. But Ciampolo double crosses *them* by diving to safety beneath the pitch and away from their claws before they can double cross *him*!

It's a wonderfully slapstick scene which exemplifies the crime—fraud, betrayal, deception—that is the specialty of the inferno's Eighth Circle.

But Dante quickly yanks us back to the sober truth that this is, after all, hell. The demons, furious that they've been tricked, begin to squabble among themselves. Two in particular go at it, dive-bombing each other into the boiling pitch, and when they resurface, their peeved companions

> stretched their hooks towards the limed pair,
> who were already scaled within the crust.

Hell is full of anger, malevolence, and cruelty, notwithstanding these two cantos of dark humor. If demons can't vent their spleen on damned souls, they'll turn on one another. A bit like the world we live in, come to think of it.

Inferno, Canto XXIII: Father of All Lies

> The Friar said: "I once heard at Bologna
> Many of the Devil's vices told; amongst which,
> I heard that he is a liar and the father of lies."

This canto concludes the drama of the previous two—although, unlike them, there's nothing darkly humorous or slapstickish about it.

Keep in mind that we're still in the Eighth Circle, the region in hell reserved for those who commit some species of fraud. Cantos XXI–XXIII don't just talk about fraud; they exemplify it. In the first two, clawed demons or Malebranche who are "safeguarding" Virgil and Dante are actually just waiting for an opportunity to rend them. Their boss, the demon Malacoda, lied to the two travelers about a bridge to the sixth bolgia. Ciampolo, the condemned grifter politician, lied to the demons about offering them up more victims. The demons lied to one another about not fighting among themselves if Ciampolo's promise proved false. Deception, lies, fraud: such is the cloying atmosphere of these three cantos—and, indeed, of the entire Eighth Circle.

Now, in Canto XXIII, Virgil and Dante escape the Malebranche by the skin of their teeth, tumbling into the sixth bolgia just out of their murderous reach. Once there, they encounter the condemned souls of hypocrites whose contrapasso punishment is to wear heavy gowns gilded and fancy on the outside but weighed down with dull, heavy lead on the inside. "O weary mantle for eternity!" sighs Dante when he sees them.

It's in this bolgia where one of the souls famously tells Dante that the devil is the "father of lies." Evil is incapable of truth-telling, of honesty, of open-heartedness. These qualities are alien to its narcissistic mania for manipulation, enslavement, and destruction. In a day and age such as ours in which truth is under constant attack, this canto's bottom line is especially noteworthy. Dante's *Divine Comedy* may have been written eight centuries ago. But its insights remain utterly relevant today.

Inferno, Canto XXIV: Time to Remember What We're Doing

> *Were it not on that precinct the ascent*
> *Was shorter than on the other, I know*
> *Not about him, but I certainly had been defeated.*
>
> *"Now it behooves thee thus to free thyself from sloth,"*
> *Said the Master: "for sitting on down,*
> *Or under coverlet, men come not into fame;*
>
> *And therefore rise! Conquer thy panting*
> *With the soul, that conquers every battle,*
> *If with its heavy body it sinks not down.*
>
> *A longer ladder must be climbed."*

Cantos XXIV and XXV feature the seventh bolgia, where the souls of thieves are held. But before describing their punishment, Virgil offers Dante a pep talk, excerpted above, worth taking some time to consider. Later, I'll write about both cantos. But as a kind of prelude, I want to concentrate on Virgil's counsel in XXIV. It's an important bit of advice for pilgrims.

Here's the context. The two travelers have discovered that the bridge over the sixth bolgia is shattered. You'll remember that yesterday they slid down its rubble just in the nick of time to escape the malevolent Malebranche, the winged and clawed demons. Today they're struggling up the other side of the ditch to reach the bridge that spans the seventh bolgia. It's an arduous climb, and even with Virgil's help an exhausted and dispirited Dante is ready to throw in the towel.

So I think that a breather and a refresher on what we're about is appropriate here.

Remember that I said at the beginning of our search for wholeness that Dante's infernal journey can be understood on several levels. One of them is that the *Divine Comedy* is an allegory of self-exploration. On this reading, Dante is traveling into the very heart of who he is, and the nightmarish scenarios he encounters are actually dark places within himself.

Anyone who honestly and authentically undertakes the journey within will encounter similar horrors. We all carry our personal hells inside us and, all too often, spew them out onto the people we meet. Like Dante, there may well come a time when emotional and spiritual weariness at what we're discovering risks paralyzing us. We feel as if it's impossible to go on. All we want is to forget about the distressing truths we've been shown so that we can return to our old uncomplicated selves.

But once we sally forth into the soul wilderness, we can't turn back. Vestiges of what we've encountered will always haunt us. The complacency we once enjoyed is forever shattered. Shall we simply stop where we are, cover our eyes, and pretend that everything's okay? If we try that, we're stuck, as Dante suggests, in the sixth bolgia of hypocrisy.

No, there's nothing for it but to "conquer thy panting" and push forward. We have to go down, all the way down, to go up. Finish the race, as St. Paul would say. Be grateful for any guides we have, past and present, who can uphold us with their own resolve, wisdom, and strength. And even though the journey's been rough and is likely to get rougher, hang onto the intuition that something glorious awaits at its end. It's this promise of fulfillment, vague and amorphous as it may have been, that summoned us to the inward journey to begin with.

Inferno, Canto XXV: FUCK YOU, GOD!

Whilst I kept gazing on them,
  Lo! a serpent with six feet darts up
  In front of one, and fastens itself all about him.

With its middle feet it clasped his belly,
  With the anterior it seized his arms;
  Then fixed its teeth in both his cheeks;

> *The hinder feet it stretched along his thighs,*
>   *And put its tail between the two, and*
>   *Bent it upwards on his loins behind.*
>
> *Ivy was never so rooted*
>   *To a tree so, as round the other's limbs*
>   *The hideous monster entwined its own.*
>
> *Then they stuck together, as if they had been of heated wax*
>   *And mingled their colors; neither the one*
>   *Nor one nor the other seemed what it was at first.*

Holy cow! Anyone who's frightened of snakes (here complete with six arms and legs) needs to steer clear of larceny, because the seventh bolgia, reserved for thieves, is crammed full of serpents with names—Chelydri, Jaculi, Phareans, Cenchres, Amphisbenes—as hideous in sound as the creatures are in appearance.

These serpents bite their victims, instantly setting them afire and reducing them to ash. Or, as described in the quoted selection, they merge into the victim's humanity, creating an utterly nightmarish monstrosity. Or they bite and suck the humanity out of their quarry, hideously morphing into them.

No wonder poor Dante moans (XXIV):

> *"Power of God! O how severe,*
>   *That showers such blows in vengeance!"*

For eight centuries commentators have speculated about why snakes and morphing are the punishments in this bolgia. The consensus is that thieving souls, in good contrapasso fashion, have their very essences stolen from them just as they stole riches from others when they were still alive.

Perhaps. But I think something more horrible is going on.

At the very beginning of Canto XXV, a thief introduced in the previous canto "raised up his hands with both the figs," shouting: "Take them, God, for at thee I aim them!"

Now, shaping fists into figs means to thrust the thumb between the first and second fingers while making a fist. It's still a common gesture today, and it means, not to put too fine an edge on it, "fuck you!"

So this particular thief is defiantly cursing God.

I think that this is a clue about the meaning of the serpents. Go back to Genesis. The Evil One, in the form of a serpent, robs humanity of innocence, and in so doing figuratively shouts, "Fuck you!" to God and God's plan. All thieves, from the petty to the grandly scheming ones, follow in his footsteps. It's only appropriate, then, that their torment be snake-filled, and especially that one of the wretched punishments meted out to them is to have their essence merged with a serpent's. In life, they imitated the thievery in the Garden. In death, they suffer the consequences. They acted like the Serpent. Now they're transfigured by serpents.

Inferno, Canto XXVI: A Dark Don Quixote?

Ulysses speaks:

> *"When I*
>
> *departed from Circe,*
>
> *Neither fondness for my son, nor reverence*
>   *For my aged father, nor the due love*
>   *That should have cheered Penelope,*
>
> *Could conquer in me the ardor*
>   *That I had to gain experience of the world,*
>   *And of human vice and worth;*
>
> *I put forth on the deep open sea,*
>   *With but one ship, and that small company*
>   *Which had not deserted me."*
>
> *"O brothers," I said, "who through a hundred thousand*
>   *Dangers have reached the West,*
>   *Deny not, to this the brief vigil*
>
> *Of your senses that remains, experience*
>   *Of the unpeopled world behind the sun."*

The sheer beauty of this canto takes my breath away. To my mind, it's the poetic high-water mark of the Inferno. And yet the figure through whose mouth Dante speaks so eloquently is a damned soul: wily Ulysses, the Homeric trickster famous for coming up with the idea of the wooden horse that brought proud Troy down, not by honorable combat but by subterfuge.

He's in the eighth bolgia, the subject of this canto, because it's the region of hell reserved for deceivers, givers of false counsel.

Ulysses tells Virgil and Dante about his life following the fall of Troy. (Dante invents it whole cloth, by the way; there's no analogue to it in Homer.) On the surface, it's a noble tale of human longing for knowledge, the desire to see what's on the other side of the horizon, to explore the unknown, despite the dangers in doing so, to discover, before this "brief vigil of senses" ends, as much as we can. As Ulysses says to his crew,

> *"Consider your origin: ye were not*
> *Formed to live like brutes*
> *but to follow virtue and knowledge."*

Noble sounding? Absolutely. "Dreaming the impossible dream," as the musical *Man of La Mancha* reminds us, sounds a deep chord within us all. But there's a dark underbelly here to Ulysses's words. Remember, this is the bolgia of the deceivers. Ulysses's declamation conceals his careless abandonment of his family, his disregard for the safety of his crew, and his own hubris. The best that can be said for him is that his motives are mixed. His beautiful words, therefore, are deceptive. He's disguising his own selfish ambition in the dress of noble-sounding aspiration.

Perhaps, ironically, he's deceiving himself as well as his men about his true motives. His deceit spells disaster this time around, like it did for the Trojans at the end of the fabled war. Just as Ulysses's ship sails beyond charted waters and discovers a never before discovered land, disaster strikes. As his shade sadly tells Dante and Virgil,

> *"We joyed, and soon our joy was turned to grief:*
> *For a tempest rose from the new land,*
> *And struck the forepart of our ship.*
>
> *Three times it made her whirl round with all the waters,*
>
> *Till the sea was closed above us."*

I suspect most of us have tendencies to disguise less than noble motives with deceptively highfalutin talk. But few of us pull it off as poetically, or as tragically, as Ulysses does in Canto XXVI.

Inferno, Canto XXVII: Demonic Logic Meets the Psychology of Sin

> *Saint Francis afterwards, when I was dead,*
>   *Came for me; but one of the black Cherubim*
>   *Said to him: "Do not take him; wrong me not.*
>
> *He must come down amongst my menials,*
>   *Because he gave the fraudulent counsel*
>   *Since which I have kept fast by his hair;*
>
> *For he who repents not cannot be absolved,*
>   *Nor is it possible to repent and will a thing at the same time,*
>   *The contradiction not permitting it.*
>
> *Maybe*
> *Thou didst not think that I was a logician!"*

We're still in the eighth bolgia, where deceivers or givers of false counsel are punished.

After listening to Ulysses's confession, Dante and Virgil hear out a soldier who in old age sought to atone for his martial sins by taking religious vows. But his subsequent behavior suggests that his vow-taking and atonement weren't genuine. As the poet tells us, he still willed to do actions he'd supposedly repudiated on becoming a Franciscan monk. Consequently, he's guilty of the sin of deceit.

As the "black Cherubim" who wrested him out of St. Francis's hands to drag him to hell says, it's a logical contradiction to repent of X while simultaneously willing X.

But alas! As all too many philosophers sadly discover, human psychology refuses to be constrained by the rules of logic. Our motives are almost always mixed, and frequently those motives contradict one another. That we're able to hold them simultaneously attests to how well we can compartmentalize our desires and intentions, sealing them off from one another when doing so suits us. So I think that from a psychological perspective it's perfectly possible to will that which one also repents. St. Augustine's famous prayer, "Lord, make me chaste—but not yet!" perfectly illustrates this.[9]

---

9. Augustine, *Confessions*, 145.

Such compartmentalization is, I suppose, yet another species of deceit—in this case, self-deceit.

And speaking of deceit: Dante begins this canto with a reference to the tyrant Phalaris's bull, a hollow bronze statue in which a person could be imprisoned. When the statue was slowly heated, roasting its unfortunate occupant, his ensuing screams, because of an inserted mechanical acoustic contraption, sounded like the bellowing of a real bull. This tale is appropriate for the eighth bolgia because it is, of course, a parable of deceit. The noise coming from the statue sounds as if it's made by a bull. So listeners are deceived.

As Dante notes, Perillus, the bull's artisan, was its first victim. Yet another example of deception, since Phalaris surely promised Perillus that he'd be richly rewarded once his task was completed, all the while planning to use Perillus as the guinea pig who would test his own hideous device.

Inferno, Canto XXVIII: Ensanguined Splintering

The hideous mode of the ninth Bolgia:

Even a cask, through loss of middle-piece or cant,
    Yawns not so wide as one I saw, ripped from the chin
    Down to the part that utters vilest sound:

Between his legs the entrails hung;
    His pluck appeared and the wretched sack
    That makes excrement of what is swallowed.

While I stood all occupied in seeing him,
    He looked at me, and with his hands opened
    His breast, saying: "Now see how I rend myself!

And all the others, whom thou seest here,
    Were in their lifetimes sowers of scandal and schism;
    And therefore are they thus cleft."

The images are bloody and the language coarse in this canto. Hell is getting more terrible as Virgil and Dante approach its dead center of gravity, and so the horrors they witness are described in increasingly repulsive ways.

Contrapasso is hideously played out here in the ninth bolgia. Those whose malicious gossip and lies sowed dissension have their tongues perpetually ripped out. Schismatics are forever being split in two—or, worse, must rip themselves apart. One resident of the bolgia holds his severed head in his hand because in life he set a son against his father, the paternal "life force."

Therefore, he is separated from his own "life force," his torso.

It would be easy to be so stunned by the bloodiness and butchery described here that one forgets the very real crime that gives rise to it. That would be tragic. In our own time, we're witnessing just how destructively splintering malicious talk and falsehoods can be.

What else are cries of "fake news," "rigged elections," "ballot dumps," "perfect phone call," "biggest crowd ever," "alternative facts," "RINO," and so on but deliberate—and shockingly successful—strategies to split social and moral order asunder from stem to stern? Blues against reds, "wokes" versus "traditionals," urban sensibilities sparring with rural ones: it's as if the entire nation has fallen into the ninth bolgia.

Dante's Inferno is timeless because it warns us about human failings that are as real today as they were in his own time. It chauffeurs us in a dizzyingly downward spiral through all the wickedness humans are capable of so that we, as Virgil says of Dante, "may have full experience" of it. Without a consciously mindful awareness of our darker propensities, we can never hope to surmount them.

Thankfully, the inferno is only a partial reckoning of what humanity is about. Soon, we'll leave the nether regions to begin an upward climb through purgatory to paradise, an ascent that will remind us of humanity's promise.

But until then, we still have to get through the darkest pit of hell, the deepest, most demon-infested dungeon of our psyche. So strap in.

Inferno, Canto XXIX: It's Enough to Make You Puke

When we were above the last cloister
Of Malebolge, so that its lay-brethren
Could appear to our view,

Lamentations pierced me, manifold,
Which had their arrows barbed with pity;
Whereas I covered my ears with my hands.

> Such pain as there would be,
>> If the diseases in the hospitals
>
> Were all together in one ditch:
>> Such was there here; and such stench issued
>> Thence, as is wont to issue from putrid limbs.

Dante and Virgil have arrived at the tenth and very lowest level of the Malebolge. Curiously, it seems to be a grab-bag of fraudsters, either because their transgressions don't fit nicely in any of the other levels or because their acts of deception are unspeakably worse and hence deserving of the lowest one. I don't know which is more likely. But I do know that the torment they endure is telling.

Think of Oscar Wilde's character Dorian Gray who remains remarkably young and comely despite the passage of years. But his portrait, secreted away in an attic, mutates horribly, not just because of the ravages of chronological age but also from the moral disfigurement brought about by Dorian's behavior.[10] Wickedness causes the beauty with which we're born to become repulsive and afflicts our natural spiritual health with loathsome corruption.

So it's fitting, although completely disgusting, that the souls in this final bolgia suffer from hideous sicknesses. Two of them, for example, afflicted with leprosy, try to ease their suffering in a way that sets the reader's teeth on edge:

> Each of these plied thick the clawing
>> Of his nails upon himself, for the great fury
>> Of their itch which has no other succor.
>
> And so the nails drew down the scurf,
>> As does a knife the scales from a bream
>> Or other fish that has them larger.

Ghastly.

Dante describes the tenth bolgia as a place emitting a stench that makes one want to vomit. This detail is so significant, isn't it? We too often sanitize wickedness (especially our own) by thinking too abstractly about it, removing it from the concrete ugliness it spawns and thereby deceiving ourselves into thinking it's not so bad after all.

---

10. Wilde, *Dorian Gray*.

But Dante refuses to let us get away with that. He forces us, in a visceral way, to acknowledge that wickedness is a putrid rotting of the soul, and the spiritual place in which it lands us is a cesspool. Don't romanticize evil or what it does to one's character. It stinks to high heaven—or, as the case may be, to low hell.

Inferno, Canto XXX: Hell's Social Media

> "To thee be torture the thirst that cracks
>   Thy tongue," the Greek said, "and the foul water which makes
>   That belly such a hedge before thy eyes."
>
> Then the false-coiner: "Thus thy jaws gape wide,
>   As usual, to speak ill."
>
> I was standing all intent to hear them,
>   When said the Master to me: "Now keep looking,
>   A little longer and I quarrel with thee."
>
> When him I heard speak to me in anger,
>   I turned towards him with such shame, that it comes
>   Over me again as I but think of it.

This final description of the tenth and lowest bolgia is the verbal equivalent of one of Bosch's paintings of hell. It's a madhouse, with damned souls pursing one another in homicidal rages, tearing at each other's throats, lashing out with fists at hideously distorted bodies, and endlessly, poisonously bickering.

Two of them, a counterfeiter and a Greek who was instrumental in deceiving the Trojans with the wooden horse ploy, are especially engaged in hurling insults at one another, as you can see from the snippet I've quoted.

Reading the toxic exchange between them reminds me of the vicious sparring that goes on in social media, where invective, lies, and point-scoring submerge civility and truth. Social media can indeed be useful. But it can also set loose the very worst in us by allowing us to rant and slander and strut our alleged superiority.

And here's the thing: You and I are drawn to these purple outbursts and unhinged verbal fights, aren't we? We may tsk-tsk over such displays, shaking our heads sadly or disdainfully, but we tend not to turn away when they show up on our screens. There's something perversely appealing about them that turns all of us into media rubberneckers. "Can you believe what he/she/they said?!" we gleefully ask our friends, eager to scandalize them with the latest juicy bit of media poison.

If you doubt this, just reflect on how easy it is to become disgusted and outraged but fixated on the latest Tucker Carlson or Sean Hannity tweet; the latest bit of dangerous idiocy from the hideously misnamed Truth Social; the latest celebrity imbroglio; dueling pundits on network and cable outlets; furious podcast hosts; or simply the latest nasty exchange on Facebook. It's so hard to look away.

Dante succumbs to the same temptation in this bolgia. In fact, he becomes so intrigued by the bickering between the Greek and the counterfeiter that his guide, Virgil, angrily chastises him—this, by the way, is the only time in the entire Inferno in which Virgil is irritated by Dante—warning him that "the wish to hear it is a vulgar wish!" It damages one's character, coarsening one's sensibilities as well as one's ability to relate honestly and openly to others.

To his credit, Dante immediately feels shame at having his voyeurism called out. Would that we might do so too.

Inferno, Canto XXXI: Pride Does Indeed Come Before the Fall

On the round wall,

With half their bodies, the horrible giants
  Turreted the bank which compasses the pit.

Nature certainly, when she left off the art
  Of making animals like these, did very well.

And if she repent her not of elephants and whales,
  Whoso subtly looks, therein
  Regards her as more just and prudent:

For where the instrument of the mind
  Is joined to evil will and potency,
  Men can make no defense against it.

Having worked their downward way over the ten ditches that make up the Malebolge, the Eighth Circle of Hell, Dante and Virgil now stand on the cusp of the lowest and Ninth Circle known as Cocytus (Greek for "lamentation"). This icy, dead place is reserved for those who commit treachery.

The rim is guarded by four giants, three Titans from Greco-Roman mythology and one, Nimrod, from the Bible. The Titans exemplify treachery because they rebelled against the gods by trying to storm heaven. Nimrod is portrayed as a mighty hunter and the chief architect of the Tower of Babel, the purpose of which was likewise to storm heaven. (Although Nimrod is indeed a biblical character—Gen 10:8–12—his gigantic stature and involvement with the Tower are post-biblical traditions.)

The primordial sin that lies beneath all treachery is pride: the assumption that I'm better than you and therefore have a right—no! a duty!—to betray you and take your place.

Treachery and pride are the worst kinds of failings because, as Dante says in what I've quoted above, they combine intellect with an evil will. The fraudsters in the Malebolge are there because they wouldn't tame their appetites. But the inhabitants of Cocytus are a different matter entirely. They deliberately and maliciously chose wickedness.

The giants are awful because they add brute force to intellect and wicked will. Thank goodness, Dante exclaims, that the only giants left on earth are creatures like whales and elephants, who are benign and even gentle behemoths, lacking both human intellect and evil intentions. But that doesn't mean that the trifecta of force, intellect, and wicked will isn't present, albeit in lesser degrees, in humans. We'll meet some examples of them in the concluding three cantos of the Inferno.

And of course we'll also meet the fallen angel who is the absolute epitome of all three, the one who sullenly and impotently serves as hell's very foundation.

Inferno, Canto XXXII: When Hell Freezes Over

> *To describe the bottom of all the universe,*
> *Is not an enterprise to be taken up in sport,*
> *Nor for a tongue that cries mamma and pappa.*

> *I turned myself and saw before me and beneath*
> *My feet a lake, which through frost had*
> *The semblance of glass, and not of water.*
>
> *Livid, up to where the hue of shame appears,*
> *The doleful shades were in the ice,*
> *Sounding with their teeth like storks.*
>
> *Each held his face turned downwards.*
>
> *We were going towards the middle,*
> *At which all weight unites, and I was*
> *Shivering in the eternal shade.*
>
> *I saw a thousand visages, made doggish*
> *By the cold: whence shuddering comes over me, and always*
> *Will come, when I think of the frozen fords.*

I've always been struck by Dante's description of the very lowest region of hell, upon which all the universe's weight rests, as a frozen landscape. It's a far cry from the lurid portrayals of a fire-festooned wasteland we usually associate with hell, and which we encountered in the earlier Malebolge cantos.

But I think it's sheer brilliance on Dante's part. The deepest part of hell is reserved for those who've been treacherous to family members, to the state, to guests, or to God. There was no human warmth within them—no compassion, no love, no tenderness—when they were alive. So their contrapasso punishment is to be trapped up to their necks in ice, their heads bent downward so that they forever stare at their icy prison (and perhaps see their reflections in its glass-like surface), their tears forever freezing on their cheeks.

There's so little movement in these lowest regions because the spiritual deadness of the imprisoned shades is mirrored, as we'll see when we conclude our journey through the inferno, in the spiritual deadness of Satan himself.

To lose an awareness of the values that make life worth living—loyalty, decency, honesty, love, and altruism—is to give oneself over to the stasis of spiritual death. To imprison oneself in a cold heart is truly to waste one's life. And what better metaphor for that tragedy than being imprisoned for all eternity in ice.

Inferno, Canto XXXIII: The Walking Dead

Such privilege has this Ptolomaea,
  That oftentimes the soul falls down hither,
  Ere Atropos impels it.

Know that forthwith, when the soul betrays,

As I did, her body is taken from her
  By a Demon who thereafter rules it,
  Till its time has all revolved.

The lowest depth of hell, where those who commit treachery are punished, is one huge ice-lake with four regions. The outermost one, Caina (named after the biblical Cain), is reserved for those who betray their kin; the next, Antenora (named after a traitorous Trojan soldier), holds those who betray their country; the next, Ptolomea (named after Ptolemy, who murdered his father-in-law as he supped with him), imprisons those who betray their guests.

And still we haven't yet arrived at hell's very center of gravity.

Dante meets and speaks here with a soul in Ptolomea, one Friar Alberigo (who speaks in the quoted passage). But to his amazement, Dante discovers that the soul's body still walks the earth, to all appearances like a perfectly healthy living man. Alberigo's sin is so horrendous—he murdered his own brother and nephew as they dined with him—that he died spiritually. Every bit of goodness, any final streak of humanity, dissolved away, and emptiness, the non-being of wickedness took its place. His body became a zombie-like thing, his soul thrown into hell before Atropos, or fate, wrapped Alberigo in death.

This is a chilling image, but one that I think is morally astute. Surely every wicked act we perform, especially horrific ones like those which land us in the region of Ptolomea, chips away at our substance. If we're not careful, we become organic automatons, resembling humans but having lost along the way any semblance of humanity.

Of one thing we may be sure: the dead do indeed walk among us. Let's hope we're not one of them.

Inferno, Canto XXXIV: Hell Is Not to Love

I had come (and with fear I put it into verse)
  Where the souls were wholly covered,
  And shone through like straw in glass.

It pleased my Guide to show to me
  The Creature which was once so fair.

The Emperor of the dolorous realm,
  From his mid-breast stood forth out of the ice.

If he was once as beautiful as he is ugly now,
  And lifted up his brows against his Maker,
  Well may all affliction come from him.

In this final canto of the Inferno, Dante enters into the deepest and most frozen region of hell. It's called Judecca, after Judas Iscariot, and it holds the souls of those who betray God. At its center is Lucifer, the once beautiful angel whose lightning-like plunge from heaven punched a great chasm in the earth, which subsequently became the prison of damned souls.

Lucifer is encased waist-deep in ice. As a former member of the angelic order of the cherubim, he has three sets of wings which he flaps incessantly, presumably trying to break free. But of course the cold wind that the flapping generates only imprisons him even more solidly in the frozen lake's grip. Wickedness always traps its perpetrators.

Lucifer has three faces, the mouths of which devour Judas, Cassius, and Brutus. These unholy three visages are a perversion of the Trinity, and it reminds us that everything about Lucifer is a dark counterpart of God. One of the most striking contrasts only becomes clear in the third part of Dante's epic. Here, Lucifer is grossly gigantic; his batlike wings are as huge as windmills. But in the Paradiso, God is described as a single brilliant point of light, undivided, pure, and perfect.

Most significantly, Lucifer, God's opposite—as well as the souls scattered like straw beneath the ice—is unable to love. Consequently, he who was once so fair is now foully misshapen. He who strove to be God has become a nightmarish caricature of the divine because, unlike the God who is love, Lucifer can only hate. Hatred is often thought of in terms of heat and fire. But Dante has it right. Hatred freezes the spirit, encasing hope and compassion in an icy prison of despair and resentment. It paralyzes our better natures.

Ultimately, it seems to me, Dante's understanding of hell is similar to the description Dostoevsky puts into the mouth of Father Zossima, one of his fictional characters: hell is being unable to love.[11] Whether because of careless self-indulgence, as in the upper regions, or deliberately willed evil, as in the lower, the inferno's denizens are there because of their failure to love. And loveless Lucifer is both their infernal king and their supreme exemplar.

Having explored the hells buried deeply within our psyches, an exploration that invites us to suss out our own failings, Dante and Virgil make their way back to the earth's surface. They gratefully breathe in the clean air and exult in the starry sky above them, welcome signs that they've escaped the claustrophobic confinement of hell. They're ready to ascend the seven storied mountain of purgatory, the next stage of the journey. It's there that they, and we, will remember what it is to love. The nearer we draw to the Source of love, the more the ice of hatred melts.

The purgatorial thaw is nigh.

---

11. Dostoevsky, *Brothers Karamazov*, 322.

Purgatorio

. . . in which Dante and we begin the painful process of liberation . . .

Purgatory, Canto I: For Freedom's Sake

I will sing of the second realm,
   Where the human spirit is purged,
   And becomes worthy to ascend to heaven.

I saw near me an old man solitary,
   Worthy of such great reverence in his mien,
   That no son owes more to a father.

"Who are ye that against the dark stream
   Have fled the eternal prison?" said he.

Virgil said:

"He hath never seen the last hour,
   But by his madness was so near to it
   That very short time there was to turn.

I was sent to him to rescue him
   And no other way there was
   But this along which I have set me.

I have shown him all the guilty people,
   And now do purpose showing those spirits
   That purge them under thy charge.

He seeketh freedom, which is so precious."

The final three cantos of the Inferno reminded us—as if we didn't already know as much from personal experience—that wickedness imprisons us in an icy lake of hopeless despair.

Who wouldn't long to break free from this spiritual stasis?

Purgatory, into which Dante and Virgil have emerged just as dawn is about to break, is an opportunity for still redeemable souls to purge themselves of guilt in search of freedom, "which is so precious."

I think it's a mistake to think of "purge" as "punitive." Far better to see it as ascetic discipline. Whenever we struggle to break a bad habit, we suffer. The more we've allowed the bad habit to enslave us, the harder it is to get free of it and the more pain we endure in the process. To drag in a trite but sometimes apropos expression, "no pain, no gain."

And what's the gain that the pain of purgation promises? Full humanity, supreme fulfillment, the joy of being in the presence of That Than Which Nothing Greater Can Be Experienced.

Purgatory is a place of preparation, not punishment. It's a school for confused souls, a hospital for those yearning for health, a rehabilitation center for spiritual addicts.

Dante evidently believes that some people have so exiled themselves from the Source of light and life that they've willfully fallen into eternal darkness. Perhaps. But there's also the possibility (a very good one, in my estimation) that C. S. Lewis is more correct when he writes that the lonely cells in which we imprison ourselves open from the inside. People can leave if they so choose. It's just that most may not, or that it takes them a helluva long time to want to do so.[1]

But God's mercy, as we'll discover in the journey through purgatory, is inexhaustible.

Dante envisions purgatory as a seven-storied mountain looming up from an island. At each of the seven levels a different category of sinners work out their salvation. Right now, in Canto I, Dante and Virgil stand at the mountain's base where they encounter Cato, guardian of purgatory's antechamber. It's he to whom Virgil speaks in the quoted passage.

Recall that in the very first canto of the Inferno, Dante tells us that he'd lost his way and was in the midst of a spiritual crisis:

> *In the middle of the journey of our life*
> *I came to myself in a dark wood,*
> *Where the straight way was lost.*

1. Lewis, *Great Divorce*.

But it's only now that we discover just how perilous his situation really was. As Virgil tells Cato, Dante was close to the edge of despair and lostness when he began his journey. No wonder the hell through which he wandered was so terrifying. It mirrored his chaotic spiritual condition.

Purgatory, Canto II: Fellowship Is a Sign of Salvageability

On the stern stood the celestial pilot,
  Such, that blessedness seemed writ upon him,
  And more than a hundred spirits sat within.

In exitu Israel de Aegypto!
  They chanted all together with one voice.

Dante describes the arrival to the purgatorial island of a shipload of blessed souls. In perfect harmony, chanting "with one voice," the souls sing Psalm 114, "when Israel came out of Egypt"—given their circumstances, an appropriate song of liberation.

The crucial point here is that they sing with one voice. They're in fellowship with one another. Although they must undergo purification before arriving in Paradise, their essential God-given goodness is still so alive that they're able to connect with other people. They haven't been imprisoned in greedy, suspicious, and antagonistic egos. They haven't perverted their humanity with wickedness to the point where selfish desires have become their centers of gravity.

Contrast this with the arrival in hell of the damned in Canto III of the Inferno. Ferried by Charon, each condemned individual is snarlingly locked inside him or herself. Their wickedness has broken all human (much less humane) connection. Disdaining the well-being of others in life, fixated as they were on themselves, so they remain in death. Even huddled together in Charon's boat, sharing the same horrible fate, they remain isolated from one another. They don't sing in harmony. Instead, "these unfortunates who never were alive," are cacophonous in their cries:

"Strange tongues, horrible outcries, words of pain,
  Tones of anger, voices deep and hoarse.

> *They blasphemed God and their parents;*
> *The human kind; the place, the time, and origin*
> *Of their seed, and of their birth."*

Wickedness corrupts and ultimately severs our relations with fellow humans because it corrodes our own humanity. Fellowship is a sign of salvageability, redeemability, and eventually a recovery of full humanity.

Purgatory, Canto III: Virgil's Rebuke of the Philosophers Rebuked

Virgil speaks:

> *"Mad is he who hopes that our reason*
> *May encompass that infinitude which*
> *One substances in three persons fills.*
>
> *Be ye content, O human race, with the quia!*
> *For if ye had been able to see the whole,*
> *No need was there for Mary to give birth;*
>
> *And ye have seen such sages desire fruitlessly,*
> *Whose desire had else been satisfied,*
> *Which is given them for eternal grief.*
>
> *I speak of Aristotle and of Plato,*
> *And many others"—and here bent his brow,*
> *And said no more, and remained disturbed.*

In purgatory's antechamber, two groups of late repentants are encountered: excommunicants in this canto and the indolent in the next. All of them were late in repenting their sins while they were still living. But because they do, they escape hell and make it to purgatory.

Dante seems conflicted in this canto about the authority of the church. (Although I confess that I may be projecting my own robust aversion to churchianity onto him.) In writing about one of the repentant excommunicants, he insists that God's mercy always outweighs the church's interdictions.

> *"By curse of Church man is not so lost*
> *That eternal love may not return,*
> *So long as hope retaineth aught of green."*

You'd think this would be obvious. Yet when church and God get conflated, such reminders are important.

But what really intrigues me in this canto is Virgil's rebuke of the philosophers who yearn to plumb the depths of reality through reason. They ought, he says, to be satisfied with *quia*, an explanation of the "whats" of the world—the bare facts, ma'am, so to speak—and not seek for the *propter quid*, an explanation of their "whys." In other words, stick to description of what is and forego trying to figure out how it came to be.

As a member of the peculiar tribe of philosophers, I'm well aware of the limits of reason and language. (As fellow-philosopher Wittgenstein warned, we ought to remain silent about that which can't be spoken.)[2] But I'd offer two mild rebukes of Virgil's rebuke.

The first is a technical but important distinction, offered by none other than Thomas Aquinas. We absolutely can understand "infinite" things. We just can't comprehend them. We can rationally understand and demonstrate, for example, that God, the Infinite, does indeed exist. But our reason can't stretch wide enough to comprehend (*com* + *prehendere* = "completely catch hold of") God.

Secondly, in a God-created world, surely the profoundly human yearning for deep meaning can't be blameworthy. It seems to be a trace memory of our divine origin indelibly stamped on our spiritual DNA. And since we're also rational creatures, it's surely perfectly appropriate that reason should explore the contours and wellspring of this yearning. We simply can't be satisfied with *quia* description; we'll always search, and rightfully so, for *propter quid* explanation.

Virgil wants Dante (and us) to make room for faith, something that his pre-Christian mind can't do. (That's why he bends his head in this canto, caught up in anguished thoughts.) I no longer quite know what faith is, or at least I'm no longer willing to speak as glibly about it as I once did. Now I prefer to speak of "mystery."

There are dimensions of human existence—consciousness, love, beauty, an experience of transcendence—which seem to defy our best efforts at rational explanation. They're profoundly meaningful, but

---

2. Wittgenstein, *Tractatus*, 108.

profoundly mysterious as well. Their richness bring us up against the limits of reason: a boundary, it should be noted, discerned by reason itself.

So mystery isn't beyond the purview of rational appreciation. The wise philosopher takes seriously the human yearning for deep meaning, explores the uncharted waters into which it takes us, celebrates the usefulness, limited thought it may be, of reason, and silently bows before those depths of human experience that lend richness to life but are ultimately and mysteriously immune to analytical dissection. This isn't a situation that, contrary to Virgil, breeds hopeless, painful longing. It's one that gives rise to humility, awe, and gratitude.

Purgatory, Canto IV: The Complexity of "Laziness"

> *One of them, who seemed to me weary,*
> *Was sitting and clasping his knees,*
> *Holding his face low down between them.*
>
> *"O sweet my Lord," said I, "set thy eye*
> *Who shows himself lazier*
> *Then if Sloth were his very sister."*

After an exhausting initial climb upward from Mount Purgatory's base, Virgil and Dante encounter the souls of those who were too lazy to get right with God for most of their lives. So they're condemned to languish outside the gate of purgatory for as many years as they put off repenting. Only then can they begin the purgative ascent up the mountain.

I'm fascinated but perplexed. The Italian word Dante uses, *pigrizia*, is variously rendered as "sloth," "indolence," and "laziness" in English translations of this canto. This is confusing, because these three words have quite different meanings. They're not at all synonymous.

In ordinary language, "laziness" simply designates an unwillingness to perform even the slightest task. It's lying in a hammock when the grass needs mowing or couch-potatoing as your significant other vacuums around you. A lazy person is a shiftless loafer.

"Indolence" is subtly different. It stems from the Latin *indolentia* = "freedom from pain" or "insensibility." This suggests that, unlike laziness, it has an explicit motive: to escape situations deemed unpleasant. Laziness seems to be an inactivity entered into mindlessly. But indolence is more of a defense mechanism. True, habitual indolence eventually may display as laziness. But it doesn't start out that way.

"Sloth" is still more different. Termed *acedia* in antiquity, it's generally understood as a volitional paralysis inflicted by despair. Desert ascetics frequently called it the "noontime devil" because sufferers from it feel drained of all physical, mental, and emotional energy, just as if they're languishing under a burning sun. Sloth is also associated with boredom or indifference, two conditions that often suggest an underlying quiet desperation.

Note that the three carry intuitively different moral weights. Laziness is annoying, but a relatively minor offence. Indolence suggests a sort of timidity that's at least a cousin to cowardice. But sloth, if we're careful not to confuse it with psychological depression, is a state of the soul traditionally labeled as one of the seven deadly sins, seen as a repudiation of God and God's gifts.

So, is it laziness, indolence, or sloth that keeps souls waiting at the gate of Mount Purgatory? My guess is that it can't be sloth—this is a pretty heavy-duty sin—but is most likely a mash-up of laziness and indolence. Modern English translators might see the three as synonymous. But Dante, steeped in ancient and medieval thought, absolutely wouldn't have.

Purgatory, Canto V: Lust for Life & Recognition

Meanwhile across the mountain slope
Came people a little in front of us,
Singing the Miserere verse by verse.

When they perceived that I gave no place,
Because of my body, to the passage of rays,
They changed their chant to an "Oh!" long and harsh.

"O soul, that goest to be glad
With those members which thou was born with,"
They came crying, "Arrest a while thy step.

Look, if ever thou sawest any one of us,
So that thou mayest bear tidings of him yonder:
Ah, wherefore goest thou? Ah, wherefore stayest thou not?"

When Odysseus visits the underworld, he brings a gift of blood with him, knowing that the insubstantial shades of the dead have a ravenous lust for the elixir of life.[3] And when Jean-Paul Sartre writes his twentieth-century play *No Exit*, he suggests that the dead only really die when the last person on earth who remembers them likewise dies.

Both of these come to mind here. Virgil and Dante are still in antepurgatory. They've just encountered the souls of those who died violently but repented at the last moment. When the souls realize that Dante is alive (he casts a shadow and light doesn't beam through his solid frame), they quickly rush him, begging to be remembered to their loved ones when he returns to earth.

On the surface, the souls flock around Dante with their request because they want to be remembered so that relatives and friends can pray for them; such prayers can ease the length of their stay in purgatory. But at a deeper psychological and spiritual level, I think this scene gestures at Homer's and Sartre's insights.

Part of the shades' attraction to Dante must be the sheer fact that he, unlike they, pulses with life. (By the way, some of the condemned souls in the inferno were drawn to him for this reason too.) As Homer knew, we humans have a lust for life, even when our personal existences are unpleasant or downright miserable. Bodiless souls, even those on their way to paradise, surely rue the fact that they no longer feel vitality coursing through their veins, no longer can exult in the sheer sensuality of enfleshment, no longer can sink their teeth—figuratively and literally—into the marrow of life.

But we don't just lust for life. We lust, as Sartre knew, for recognition as well. We want to be seen, noticed, and remembered. This needn't be a narcissistic yearning for glory or adulation, but simply a very human desire to have our existence confirmed and ratified. The playwright Eugene O'Neill was once accused of vanity. "You can't pass a mirror without looking into it," a friend of his teased him. "No," replied O'Neill, "I want to make sure I'm alive."[4]

We all want to make sure we're still here, in the midst of life. The recognition of others helps assure us of that.

---

3. Homer, *Odyssey*, 249–70 (bk. XI).
4. Gelb and Gelb, *O'Neill*, 273.

Purgatory, Canto VI: A Purgatorial Reminder of Hell

Ah Italy, thou slave, hostel of woe
  Vessel without pilot in a mighty storm,
  No mistress of provinces, but a brothel!

Now in thee thy living abide not without war,
  And one doth rend the other of those
  That one wall and one fosse shuts in!

Search, wretched one, around thy seacoasts
  By the shores, and then gaze in thy bosom,
  If any part of thee enjoy peace.

In the midst of Canto VI, while still among the late repentants outside the gate of purgatory, Dante breaks through the fourth wall of his narrative to mourn the political and civil strife ripping his homeland apart. Neighbors lunge at one another's throats, verbally and sometimes literally. Nowhere is peace to be found. The state is a fragile, tempest-tossed vessel.

If you substitute USA for Italy, you not only retain Dante's meter; you also, alas, pretty well describe the current state of affairs in our own nation. Sometimes Dante's relevance is mind-boggling.

Purgatory, Canto VII: Landscape Messiness

Gold and fine silver, cramoisy and white,
  Indian wood bright and clear,
  Fresh emerald at the moment it is split,

Would each be surpassed in color by the grass
  And by the flowers placed within that fold,
  As the less is surpassed by the greater.

Not only had Nature painted there,
  But of the sweetness of a thousand scents
  Made there one, unknown and indefinable.

I suspect that Dante intends this description of a valley on one of ante-purgatory's ledges to be enticing. But I find it chillingly artificial, unreal, as if it's a set straight out of *Westworld* or *The Truman Show*.

I suppose my aversion to it hearkens back to my Canto V reflection in which I celebrated what I called the human lust for life. I don't want a landscape so sterilely perfect, so pristinely blemishless—and so lifeless—that it can only be described by comparing it to glittering but inert gemstones. Nor do I want a steady state fragrance that drowns out specific aromas. I want the palpable feel in my nostrils and mouth of both the pleasant and the odiferous. I want to breathe in all of life's undulating odors.

What's beginning to slip in here is the Platonic assumption, widely held in antiquity and embraced by Dante, that the messiness of change belongs to the lower realms while pristinely unchanging perfection characterizes the higher ones. Dante means this purgatorial valley to be an intermediate landscape that falls between the constantly changing one of earthly existence and the unchangingly perfect one of paradise.

But I don't know. It feels to me more like a china shop in which I'd be forever worried about breaking something—but also, if I'm honest, secretly wanting to.

Purgatory, Canto VIII: Illuminative Darkness

> "... Him, who so hideth his first purpose
> That there is no ford to it ..."

In the middle of a rather tedious canto, in which a mock confrontation between two angels and a serpent take place—in, by the way, a fake Garden of Eden—one line stands up and demands attention. It speaks of the ultimate and unresolvable mystery of things divine. God's "first purpose," we're told, is unfathomable: "no ford to it," no navigating it.

By "first purpose," Dante probably means at least three things.

First, God's origin lies in mystery. I've often heard people ask, "If God is the creator of everything, what created God?" It explains nothing to offer the traditional response that God is *sui generis*, self-caused. And yet what else can one possibly say? To posit an antecedent cause for the First Cause means that God is no longer God.

Second, God's reason or purpose for creating everything that is, what theologians call providence, remains mysterious. The ultimate purpose or final cause of creation is beyond our ken, despite sophomoric (and soporific) catechetical explanations. ("Why did God create us?" "To love and serve Him and be happy with Him forever in heaven." *Yawn*.)

Third, the nature of God remains inscrutable. In the twentieth century, Paul Tillich famously said that all our language about God is necessarily symbolic. But Pseudo-Dionysius the Areopagite and Thomas Aquinas anticipated this claim by centuries.[5] We can use metaphors and similes in talking about God, they insisted, but not straightforward description. Theology, at the end of the day, is really poetry—or at least *good* theology is.

If all this is true, if God is too deep a ford for us to traverse, how do we know anything about God to begin with? I've always thought that a throw-away line in Ecclesiastes (3:11) is worth pondering in this connection. Old Qoheleth tells us that God has placed *olam* in our hearts. *Olam* is a curious noun. It can mean "eternity" but also "enigma," "darkness," "hiddenness," or "obscurity."

The suggestion is that we're born with an awareness of something that utterly transcends "normal" knowledge, completely defies our efforts to nail it down with ordinary language, and yet insists on ceaselessly tugging at the sleeves of our imaginations. This awareness is, if you will, an unknowing knowledge, an illuminative darkness, a tantalizing surd whose very inaccessibility seduces us. This is how and why we have even the vaguest awareness of God. We sense the depth, even though we're incapable of delving it.

Purgatory, Canto IX, Part 1: Rehabilitating Shame

> *There where we came, at the first step*
> *Was white marble so polished and smooth*
> *That I mirrored me therein as I appear.*
>
> *The second darker was than perse,*
> *Of a stone, rugged and calcied, cracked*
> *In its length and in its breadth.*
>
> *The third, which is massy above,*
> *Seemed to me of porphyry so flaming red*
> *As blood that spurts from a vein.*

---

5. Tillich, *Dynamics of Faith*; Pseudo-Dionysius, *Divine Names*; Thomas Aquinas, *Summa Theologica* I.I.q.13.

> *Upon this God's angel held both his feet,*
> *Sitting upon the threshold.*

Canto VIII, except for that one intriguing line about the hiddenness of God's "first purpose," was uninspiringly tedious. But Canto IX is anything but.

Dante and Virgil are now at the gate of purgatory. (Dante's been wafted there, while he slept, by St. Lucia.) Before the gate is an angel of the Lord. As we'll soon discover, it's his job to allow or delay entrance to penitents. He sits at the top of three steps, the colors of which symbolize the three stages of repentance or purgation.

The first step, marble, so polished that one can see one's reflection in it, stands for honest self-scrutiny. We can't repent our faults if we refuse to face them. The second step, black and rough, symbolizes the painful sorrow that besets us once we acknowledge our own brokenness. The blood-red third step reminds us of the need for genuine penance, of making right, as best we can, the wrongs we've committed.

Our culture today is uncomfortable with the language of repentance. We tend to subjectivize moral discourse, don't we? But the logic of repentance maintains that certain actions are objectively wrong, that we incur guilt if we commit them, and that the proper response from us at that point is shame. Without a sense of shame, repentance and a resolution to be better is impossible.

(Remember, by the way, that the souls in the inferno appear not to display shame so much as anger, fear, and lamentation over their fate. They're aware of what sins landed them in hell, but seem not to actually own them.)

Feeling an appropriate sense of moral shame oughtn't to be confused, as it too often is, with the pernicious act of "shaming": inflicting an unnecessary burden of humiliation upon others whose actions in reality are quite innocent. To "guilt-trip" another person is always an unacceptable power-play. But this shouldn't cast doubt on the moral and spiritual value of experiencing shame when we've done something wicked.

One final point. The angel guarding the entrance of purgatory is wearing dull, ash-colored robes. Ashes are, of course, a traditional sign of repentance. A good confessor, a wise spiritual mentor, is someone who acknowledges his or her own failings rather than assuming a position of moral superiority. Henri Nouwen famously noted that all of us carry our own wounds, and that if we hope to empathetically mentor others, we've got to acknowledge and deal with them. It's to Dante's credit that he gestures at this truth by dressing the angel, the judge of the souls who wind up in purgatory, in the clothes of a penitent.

Purgatory, Canto IX, Part 2: Excelsior!

The angel speaks:

> "From Peter I hold these keys; and told me to err
> Rather in opening than in keeping it locked,
> If only the people fell prostrate at my feet."
>
> Then he pushed the door of the sacred portal,
> Saying: "Enter, but I make you ware
> That he who looketh behind returns outside again."

The angelic keeper of purgatory's gate offers Dante and anyone else who has embarked on a journey of self-discovery a note of reassurance as well as two sound bits of counsel.

The reassurance is that God prefers to err on the side of merciful generosity when it comes to aiding those of us who, like Dante, find ourselves lost in a dark wood but genuinely, even desperately, hope to find our way through to the other side. Admit too many, rather than too few: that's the standing order.

But God won't (I'm tempted to say *can't*) magically fix us. God's not a genie in the bottle. It's our task to persevere until we reach the pinnacle of Mount Purgatory. To give up the quest, to turn back to our old unfulfilling lifestyles because going ahead just seems too hard, is to squander the opportunity to attain wholeness. Single-minded commitment—or, in more traditional terms, humble and grateful cooperation with grace—is the ticket.

I'm struck by how archetypal this warning against looking back is. Think of the story of Lot's wife at the destruction of Sodom (Gen 19:26) or of Orpheus's loss of Eurydice.[6] Think of Jesus's caution about keeping a steady hand on the plow (Luke 9:62). All underscore the importance for the spiritual pilgrim of courage and resolve.

Joseph Campbell famously demonstrated that what he called the hero's journey is a common trope in folklore and literature. The first stage

---

6. Ovid, *Metamorphosis*, 383–86.

in the journey, leaving the comfort of home to venture into the unknown, is quite possibly the most difficult. The hero leaves the familiar behind because s/he senses, even if only vaguely, that salvation lies ahead. But the unknown, for all its promise, still remains the unknown, and so is also frightening. It only stands to reason, then, that the hero—and that's you and me—might at times long to return to the old way of life.[7]

But to actually do so—to "look back"—is spiritual regression.

Our way lies forward and upward. We've already descended into the depths. Now it's time to climb.

Purgatory, Canto X, Part 1: "Bad" Love?

> *When we were within the threshold of the gate,*
> *Which the evil love of souls disuses*
> *Because it makes the crooked way seem straight.*

In the final decade of the nineteenth century, C. S. Peirce (pronounced "purse"), one of America's most eccentric and brilliant philosophers, wrote an extraordinary articled entitled "Evolutionary Love." In it, he claimed that evolution can't be exhaustively explained in terms of natural selection or purely material processes.

We must posit, he argued, a third mechanism: a cosmic force of love, what he called agapism, which encourages and cherishes the emergence of new life forms. For Peirce, agapism is also a kind of universal empathy that holds everything together.

Aristotle seems to have held a similar view. In Christian terms (Peirce, by the way, is not a Christian), agapism is reminiscent of grace or providence.

Obviously, then, the notion of love being considered here oughtn't to be confused with the sentiment that popular imagination too often associates with the word. Think of love as a power of unification that strives for flourishing rather than as an emotion.

The very opening words of the canto suggest that Dante likewise holds with a principle of cosmic love. If love is a pervasive force in reality, permeating everything that is, even actions that appear contrary to love are actually distortions of it. They're not acts of "unlove" but of "evil love."

---

7. Campbell, *Hero*.

Evil love reaches out, but not to cherish and sustain others. Instead, the evil lover cherishes his own ego and its gratification, and wishes to sustain himself by using others. Evil love strives for unification and flourishing, but its focus is the evil lover's aggrandizement, not the well-being of others.

Some evil love is so bad, such a perversion of the real article, that there's no way back. At least this is what Dante thinks. That's the justification for his inferno. But most evil love is not of this utterly fallen kind. Hence the usefulness of purgatory. How could it be otherwise in a universe created by and infiltrated with Supreme Love?

Purgatory, Canto X, Part 2: Let's Go to the Movies!

I discerned a circling bank,
  (which, being upright, lacked means of ascent)

To be of pure white marble, and adorned
  With sculptures so that not only Polycletus,
  But Nature there would be put to shame.

He who ne'er beheld a new thing,
  Wrought this visible speech,
  New to us because here it is not found.

In his *U.S.A.* trilogy, John Dos Passos pioneered the literary technique of "cinematic fiction." He wanted to create with the written word the you-are-there feeling of a movie. So he wrote in the present tense, switched quickly to different "scenes" and "sets" throughout his narrative, and created verbal montages to give the impression of fluid immediacy.

In his own way, Dante anticipates this technique in Canto X.

Evoking a well-known biblical image, Dante tells us that he and Virgil enter purgatory by squeezing through a passage as narrow as a needle's eye. Once inside, they find themselves on a ledge bounded by an inner marble cliff wall. On it are marvelous bas reliefs depicting stories that illustrate the virtue of humility.

But there's something uncanny and wonderful about the sculptures: they seem to somehow move and shimmer. Groping for a way to express their aliveness, Dante calls them "visible speech." They're neither cunning but nonetheless static images, such as the Greek sculptor Polycletus created, nor are they quite like naturally vital objects in motion. They belong to a category of their own.

Whenever I think of Dante's description, what comes to mind is a cinematic storyline projected onto a flat white screen. It's one-dimensional but appears three-dimensional. It's artificial but comes across as palpably real. It's the product of a huge amount of anterior forethought and artistic manipulation, but is experienced as a series of events taking place here-and-now in real time.

How wonderful that Dante's rich artistic imagination anticipated by centuries the art form of cinema. The white marble wall bounding the first ledge of Mount Purgatory is the screen against which he projects his "visible speech." In reading this canto, and with just a slight effort on our parts, we're at the movies.

Purgatory, Canto X, Part 3: Genuine Humility

> *O ye proud Christians, wretched and weary,*
> *Who, sick in mental vision,*
> *Put trust in backward steps,*
>
> *Perceive you not that we are worms,*
> *Born to form the angelic butterfly*
> *that flieth to judgment without defense?*
>
> *Why doth your mind soar on high*
> *Since ye are as 'twere imperfect insects,*
> *Even as the grub in which full form is wanting?*

How fitting it is that in our kick-ass, remorselessly take-no-prisoners culture, "humiliation" is an opprobrious word. To humiliate someone is to publicly scorn, shame, or disgrace him or her. Sometimes, we say, a person deserves to be humiliated; at other times, especially when we're the target, we judge humiliation to be an undeserved affliction.

But in either case, no one wants to be humiliated.

What a strange reversal of meaning! For two millennia of Christian tradition, humility was considered a desirable virtue, not a mortification to be avoided. It was thought, in fact, to be the proper attitude for human beings. Even the very etymology of the word "humility," along with its cognate "humble," attests to this. Both are derived from the Latin *humus* = earth. To be a human is to be a creature of the earth.

To be a creature of the earth is to gratefully acknowledge that one's existence depends upon something greater than oneself. This, not public mortification, is the true meaning of humility. But too often—again, particularly in our cutthroat age—we arrogantly fancy that we're the total masters of our fate and captains of our soul. So we bestride the world like colossi, insisting that others keep out of our way. Our "mental vision," an awareness of our true identity, becomes "sick."

After viewing the "visible speech" sculptures that showcase the virtue of humility, Dante and Virgil spy a crowd of penitents who walk crouched over, their faces turned to the ground, because they carry upon their backs huge stones. These are the haughty colossi who forgot their humble origins and thus forsook the gratitude, proper to humans, for the sheer gift of life. Their purification consists in keeping their faces close to the ground as a reminder of who they are.

The mystery of our human existence, Dante learns in this canto, is that we must embrace our earthen humanity, comporting ourselves with humility, so that we can grow into our destiny. The metaphor that Dante uses here is one that appears again and again in literature to signify rebirth or metamorphosis: the life cycle of a butterfly. The butterfly must first be a caterpillar. There's simply no way around that. To try to skip the process or to accelerate it is to thwart the birthing process.

That's what the penitents in this first ledge on Mount Purgatory are learning. It's a hard lesson for them. But as Dante reminds us,

> "Heed not the form of the pain;
> Think what followeth, think that at worst
> Beyond the great judgment it cannot go."

Purgatory, Canto XI: Vanity of Vanities

> O empty glory of human powers!
>
> Earthly fame is naught but a breath of wind,
> Which now cometh hence and now thence,
> And changes name, because it changes direction.
>
> What greater fame shalt thou have, if thou strip thee
> Of thy flesh when old, than if thou hadst died
> Ere thou wert done with pap and chink,

> *Before a thousand years are past? which is shorter*
> *Space to eternity than the twinkling of an eye.*
>
> *Your repute is as the hue of grass*
> *Which cometh and goeth.*

All humans crave recognition. We want to be seen, acknowledged, and affirmed by others. There's nothing inherently pernicious about this desire. Quite the contrary. It's this kind of mutual recognition that helps create the reciprocity that binds together a community.

But the craving can veer out of control if we're not careful. A desire for fame both blights individual character and diminishes the possibility of healthy community. It's a demand for adulation that puts the ego front and center of any other consideration: "ME, ME, ME: Look at ME!"

No surprise that two of the three wilderness temptations resisted by Jesus had the allure of fame at their core (Luke 4:1–13).

Sometimes it seems as if we live in a culture where the craving for fame is in hyperdrive.

It frequently manifests itself in relatively banal ways. How many clicks can I get on my latest TikTok or YouTube post? How many likes on my FB page? How many times is my written work cited by others? Have my latest antics generated the amount of buzz I think they should?

But at other times, the craving is genuinely dangerous. Think of the politicians who so lust for glory that they'll indulge in just about any lie, slander, or hypocrisy to attain it. Think of the professionals—physicians, attorneys, professors, clergypersons—so intent on making a name for themselves in their chosen fields that they neglect the very people they should be serving.

Think of you and of me.

In Canto XI, Dante and Virgil are still in the first round of purgatory, where the proud and the haughty who allowed their craving for fame to overtake them are taught to be humble. In both their words and their purgative discipline (carrying heavy stones that bend them double), they remind Virgil of how fleeting worldly fame is, and how utterly foolish it is to place a lot of stock in it.

Dante has to bend down to hear what the crouching souls have to say to him. Since we know from his own mouth that one of his moral weaknesses is pride, he's at least symbolically participating in the purgation of the proud.

As a demonstration of how psychologically astute Dante the artist is, he at one point in this canto tells us that the weighted down slowness of the burdened souls was "like that whereof we sometimes dream."

Has anyone *not* experienced this unsettling phenomenon of dream paralysis in which we desperately try to escape danger but feel as if we're fleeing through an ocean of molasses? I think Dante's point here is that an inordinate craving for fame cloys our spiritual progress in much the same way. We may think we're making great strides—"Wow! Look at how many FB friends I've racked up!"—when in point of fact we're stuck in our gluey egos.

Purgatory, Canto XII: Seven-Step Program

> *Now were we mounting up the sacred steps,*
> *And meseemed I was exceeding lighter,*
> *Than meseemed before on the flat.*
>
> *Wherefore I: "Master, say, what heavy thing*
> *Has been lifted from me, that scarce any*
> *Toil is perceived by me in journeying?"*
>
> *He answered: "When the P's which have remained*
> *Still nearly extinguished on thy face shall,*
> *Like the one, be totally erased out,*
>
> *Thy feet shall be so vanquished by good will,*
> *That not only will they feel it no toil,*
> *But it shall be a delight to them to be urged upward."*

Why is Thomas Merton's autobiography entitled *The Seven Storey Mountain*? Simple. Because Merton envisions his pre-monastic life as an ascent up the seven storeys (or terraces, rounds, or ledges) of Dante's Mount Purgatory.

And why are there seven storeys? Because each represents one of the seven capital sins that must be purged before penitents can enter paradise. These sins are pride, envy, wrath, sloth, greed, gluttony, and lust. As penitents are cleansed, they climb the Mount, storey by storey. On ascending to each storey, they're greeted with music and with solemnly chanted Beatitudes that signal the opposite of the particular sin to be expiated.

Now, Dante enters purgatory as a living human. But like all humans, he carries his own weight of sin. In Canto IX, at the beginning of his purgatorial journey, an angel carved seven "P"s on Dante's forehead. P is for *peccatum* = sin. The seven "P"s stand for the seven cardinal sins.

As Dante works his way up Mount Purgatory, in symbolic ways sharing the purgation of the penitents he encounters, the "P"s will be removed, one by one, by the brush of an angel's wing. The removal of the first is described in this quoted passage.

All this reminds us that Dante's journey through the three realms is a form of spiritual therapy—in purgatory, it's a seven-step program—in which the soul sickness from which Dante suffers, and which, by implication, afflicts us all, is gradually healed.

Dante undertook his journey in the first place because he was regretfully aware of his soul sickness and desired to recover the straight path. This suggests he's every bit as much a penitent as the souls in purgatory. Awareness of sinfulness and desire for cleansing, necessary conditions for entering into the seven-step program of spiritual healing, is something souls trapped in the inferno are incapable of.

Purgatory, Canto XIII: Let There Be Light!

As to the blind the sun profits not,
   So to the shades there where I was now speaking,
   Heaven's light will not be bounteous of itself;

For all their eyelids an iron wire pierces,
   And stitches up, even as a wild hawk
   Because it abideth not still.

I turned to them and began: O people
   Assured of seeing the Light above, which alone
   Your desire hath in its care;

So may grace quickly clear away
   The scum of your conscience.

Like about 2 percent of Americans over the age of fifty, I suffer from macular degeneration, a disease of the retina that eventually results in near blindness. The center of one's vision dims and blurs until only peripheral clarity remains.

It's a bleak prospect. As Aristotle noted centuries ago, and as common experience attests, vision is the dominant physical sense in humans. To lose it is tragic.

But as Dante suggests in today's canto, there may be a vision loss that's even worse. It's the self-imposed spiritual blindness of envy, the refusal to look at and celebrate the good fortune of other people.

This kind of blindness, like macular degeneration, is progressive. Before long, it so corrupts the envious that they're unable to bear or "see," much less share, the joy of others. They sink into a darkly shuttered room of poisonous spite. Smugly fancying that their spiritual vision is 20/20—superior, in fact, to anyone else's!—they're pitiably blind. Their envy, as Dante tells us in the quoted passage, is a "film" that "clouds" their consciousness.

Because they refused to see in life, the penance of the envious is to have their eyes sown shut until divine grace opens them again. This is a terrible scourging. But as they lean against the cliff wall of this second storey of purgatory, weeping in contrition, they're reassured of ultimate salvation by softly chanted words from scripture that speak of kindness and generosity, the two virtues they scorned in life but now ardently long for.

And well they might long for them. Because the spiritual blindness of envy is horrible.

Purgatory, Canto XIV: Is Dante Mocking Himself?

Guido said:

"Virtue is driven forth like an enemy
  By all, even as a snake, either because of the ill-favored
  place, or of evil habit which incites them;

Wherefore the dwellers in the wretched vale
  Have so changed their nature that it seems
  As if Circe had them in her pasturing

Among filthy hogs, more worthy of acorns
  Than of other food made for use of man."

Then Virgil said:

> "You mortals take in the bait so that the old adversary's
> Hook draws you to him, and therefore
> Little avails bridle or lure."

This canto has always mystified me, from the first time I read it nearly forty years ago to the present day. But I'd like to offer a tentative interpretation.

Virgil and Dante are still in purgatory's second storey, the place reserved for those penitents who were envious in life. To suffer the vice of envy, according to Dante, is (1) to resent the success of others; (2) to bear them ill-will because of their success; (3) to hope that their success collapses; and (4) to exult in Schadenfreude when it does. This dynamic came through loudly and clearly in Canto XIII.

In the present canto, Virgil and Dante encounter two shades. One of them, Guido del Duca, launches into a vitriolic denunciation of the people who inhabit the Arno Valley. They're more swinish than human, he proclaims. They're subhuman. And he goes on and on and on decrying them in breathtakingly bitter tones.

What's going on here? One way to interpret this is to see it as another one of Dante's personal criticisms of his contemporaries, a smuggled-in commentary on the incredibly hate-fueled feud between Guelphs and Ghibellines. Dante's peers would've immediately gotten all his current event allusions that somewhat mystify us today.

But I'm not so sure that this is the best or at least the only way to read this canto. What if Dante is mocking *himself* here?

From earlier cantos, we know that Dante considers his own abiding sin to be pride. In this canto, he alludes to this by insisting with false modesty (and a hint of resentment) that the shades with whom he's speaking wouldn't know his name because he's not famous. Only a proud person suffering from frustration at not being immediately recognized and admired would say something like this.

But this kind of pride inevitably spawns envy, doesn't it? If I lust after celebrityhood, I can't abide others achieving what I haven't been able to. So I wonder if the vitriol spewed by Guido is meant by Dante to be a sly confession, put in the mouth of one of his poem's characters, of the poet's own prideful envy of others, his ill-will toward them, and his Schadenfreude at their misfortunes.

Guido, in other words, shrieks the envious poison Dante senses in himself but can't quite bring himself to openly acknowledge. But he's deeply aware of his failing, and so he mocks both his envious pride and his cowardly failure to own up to it by letting Guido be his stand-in.

The final lines of the canto further persuade me that Dante is mocking himself—or, in more purgatorial terms, that he's making, even if only backhandedly, a contrite confession. Virgil offers a judgment on humanity's continuously succumbing to vice, despite the many lifelines to virtue offered by God. Can it be that in this concluding judgment on humanity, Dante is implicitly chiding himself for his pride/envy and, in doing so, once again implicitly confessing his guilt?

Purgatory, Canto XV, Part 1: In Praise of "Wimps"

> *My Leader, who could see me acting like a man*
> *Who frees himself from sleep, said:*
> *"What aileth thee, that thou canst not control thyself?*
>
> *I did not ask, 'What aileth thee?' for that reason*
> *Which he asks who looks but with the eye that seeth*
> *When senseless the body lies,*
>
> *But I asked to give strength to thy feet;*
> *So must the slothful be goaded who are slow*
> *To use their waking hour when it returns."*

A few years ago, disturbed by the pugilistic will-to-power American ethos that places a high value on cutthroat competitiveness and a proportionately low value on "wimpy passivity," I wrote a book, *Merciful Meekness*, in defense of the countercultural biblical value of meekness.

We pay lip service to meekness when we're in church or trying to appear pious in front of the pastor. But in the "real world," we too often scorn meek people as losers, pushovers, milquetoasts who are just begging to be taken advantage of by stronger people like us.

This Nietzschean-inspired devaluation of meekness is given the lie by the biblical description of Moses as a meek man (Num 12:3) and Jesus as the paragon of meekness. No person who knows even the slightest thing about these two would describe them as milquetoasts. Quite the contrary.

In the New Testament, the Greek word translated as "meek" (in Matt 5:5, for example) is *praus*. It means gentleness combined with strength—the genuine strength that comes from gentleness and the gentleness that comes from true strength. A meek person possesses a stalwart and disciplined character that allows her to face hardship with equanimity. She controls her emotions, never allowing herself to explode in rage, wallow in poisonous envy, or pickle in arrogant pride.

In Canto XV, Dante and Virgil ascend to the third storey of Mount Purgatory, where penitents atone for their earthly wrathfulness, the opposite of meekness. Just prior to the lines quoted above, Dante experiences three visions extolling meekness that leave him confused. Apparently he, like so many of us today, has been taught by his culture to devalue meekness as spinelessness. But he's about to be awakened from sleep. His blind eyes are about to be opened to the fact that genuine strength isn't a display of kick-ass wrath but a gentleness that is ultimately fueled by the indomitable power of love.

Purgatory, Canto XV, Part 2: Magnetic Love = Koinonia

> *That infinite and ineffable Good,*
> *That is on high, speedeth so to love*
> *As a ray of light comes to a bright body.*
>
> *As much of ardor as it finds, so much of itself*
> *Each other, the more there are to love well, and the more*
> *Love is there, and like a mirror one giveth back to the other.*

Still on the third storey of Mount Purgatory, Virgil offers Dante a short but absolutely intriguing lesson about love. Virgil speaks here specifically of love in paradise. But I think his words also apply to earthly love.

Remember what Jesus once said (Matt 13:12) about knowledge of the kingdom of God? Whoever has much will be given more and whoever has none will lose even the teensy bit they have. Virgil applies that same formula to love.

People who love are like spiritual magnets. They attract love to themselves, much like a shining surface attracts light rays. The more love they possess and radiate (the shinier they are), the more love they draw in. Additionally, love both absorbs and multiplies the love it attracts, thereby creating deeper, richer, and broader streams of love than previously existed.

Love, in other words, is generative. When a light ray hits a shiny surface, the union creates an even more intense brilliance.

So, the more we love, the more we attract and amplify love. And the more people we draw into the circle of our love, the more love all of us experience. Each of us becomes a mutually mirroring mirror, reflecting and intensifying one another's love but also—and this is crucial—absorbing and reflecting the Supreme Goodness, Love Itself, Who is immediately attracted to our shiny surfaces.

The more people who share love with one another and with God, the more each is personally enriched. There is no law of diminishment here. Love doesn't get spread thinner and thinner. Instead, it becomes deeper, richer, more fulfilling for everyone—and, I believe, for all of creation.

This mutual mirroring is what we may call *koinonia* or communion. Its perfect expression, as Virgil tells Dante, is in paradise. But we get tastes of it in this life.

All this may sound too Christian-y for some. Fair enough. But just spare a thought for how transformative and fecund your own experience of love is. Surely it's the case that in your personal life you've seen how love attracts love, whereas wrath, hatred, envy, and so on repel it. Even if you have reservations about Dante's Christian idiom, you can't help but admire the psychological astuteness of his description.

Purgatory, Canto XVI: I Want What You Want— Especially If You're Rich and Famous!

> *From his hands who fondly loves her*
> *Ere she is in being, there issues, after the fashion*
> *Of a little child that sports, now weeping, now laughing,*
>
> *The simple, tender soul, who knoweth naught*
> *Save that, sprung from a joyous maker, willlingly*
> *She turneth to that which delights her.*
>
> *First she tastes the savor of a trifling good;*
> *There she is beguiled and runneth after it,*
> *If guide or curb turn not her love aside.*
>
> *Wherefore the people, that see their guide aiming*
> *Only at that good whereof he is greedy,*
> *Feed on that and ask no further.*

> *Clearly canst thou see that evil leadership*
> *Is the cause which hath made the world sinful,*
> *And not nature that may be corrupted within you.*

René Girard, the twentieth-century philosopher, argues that we humans are basically imitative creatures when it comes to our desires.[8] We desire what we see other people desiring.

Our imitative desire is even more pressing when we heed what the beautiful people, the movers-and-shakers, the cultural celebrities of our day, desire. We want to be like them. We too want to be special. So we ooh and ah and drool with desire over the latest outfit our favorite pop singer wears, the automobile our favorite movie star drives, the books our favorite politician says are on her nightstand, or the commodity the latest trendsetting influencer hypes.

Internet clickbait, ads, product networks, and glossy celebrity magazines feed and thrive on our mimetic tendencies.

This is an incredibly insightful account of what motivates us. We don't simply desire in a vacuum, or even desire because the object of our desire is intrinsically desirable. No, our desires are imitative. We want what we see other people wanting.

In this canto, Dante anticipates Girard's mimetic account of human desire. One of the shades he encounters assures him that humans are born innocent and good. But our very innocence also make us extremely gullible and hence easily manipulable by the people whom we look up to and admire. So the flock will fall into line with whatever they see their shepherds desiring. If cultural, religious, and political leaders desire worldly goods (wealth, power, prestige) instead of genuine ones, we, their imitators, become corrupted.

This doesn't mean that humans lack free will, the shade assures Dante. Were that so, it would be unjust, or at least beside the point, to reward or punish any deed.

A final observation. This exchange takes place on Mount Purgatory's third storey, where penitents are purged of wrath. But it strikes me that mimetic desire better fits with the second storey, devoted to purging envy. If we desire what we see others, especially celebrities, desiring, surely this encourages envy. In fact, Girard insists that mimetic desire is the source of interpersonal as well as social rivalry.

---

8. Girard, *Deceit*.

Purgatory, Canto XVII: The Heart of the Matter

Virgil said:

"Nor Creator nor creature, my son,
  Was ever without love, either natural or rational;
  And this thou knowest.

The natural is always without error;
  But the other may err through an evil object
  Or through too little or too much vigor.

While it is directed to the primal goods,
  And in the secondary moderates itself,
  It cannot be the cause of sinful delight;

But when it is turned awry to evil,
  Or speeds towards the good with more or less care
  Than it ought, against the Creator his creature works.

Now inasmuch as love can never turn its face
  From the weal of its subject,
  All things are safe from self-hatred.

It follows, if I judge well in my division,
  That the evil we love is our neighbors'."

Canto XVII is the midpoint in Purgatorio, and consequently the midpoint of the entire *Divine Comedy*. It's no surprise, then, that it's also the thematic core of both.

That core is love. Love is the heart of the matter.

Virgil and Dante leave the terrace of the penitential wrathful and stand at the entrance to the fourth storey, where the slothful are purged. It's here that Virgil takes the opportunity to discourse on love, the substance of which I quote above. It amazes me that Dante is able to pack so much dense philosophy into verse. The only other person I can think of who successfully does this is Lucretius in his *De rerum natura: On the Nature of Things*.

Virgil says that love is at the substratum of every kind of action, good or ill. There are two kinds of love, natural and rational. Natural love is our default position, our "natural" inclination, instilled in us by virtue of our being made in the likeness of Love Itself. Rational love is subject to our conscious will and hence is prone to error.

In this canto, Virgil focuses on rational love.

We can, through an error of rational judgment, deliberate malice, or weakness of will, actually love evil. But what is its target? When we love evil, on whom do we wish to see the evil fall?

On ourselves? Do we will our own misfortune? No, says Virgil. We're psychologically incapable of wishing anything but good for ourselves, even though we may be mistaken about what's genuinely in our best interests. Obviously misguided rational love eventually harms us by eroding our character. How else would those guilty of it need to expiate in purgatory? But we don't intentionally wish harm or evil on ourselves.

Do we love evil with God as the target? Again no, Virgil asserts. Inextricably connected with the "First Being" as we are, we cannot, by association, wish evil to befall God any more than ourselves. This doesn't deny, of course, that in loving evil we turn on the Creator. But God is collateral damage, so to speak, not the target.

So the only object left for our evil-wishing is our fellow humans.

> *"It follows, if I judge well in my division,*
> *That the evil we love is our neighbors'."*

This perversion of love, in which we love the evil that befalls others, displays in two general ways: by actively wishing harm upon them through pride, envy, or wrath, or by being either too excessive or too defective in our relations with them via sloth, avarice, gluttony, or lust. These, of course, are the seven capital sins. The first three have already been examined in the purgatory; the other four are still to come.

Back in my reflection on Canto X, I mentioned C. S. Peirce's claim that all of reality is shot through with love; he called this agapism. His basic intuition is mirrored here in Canto XVII. All human actions are either authentic expressions or perversions of love. How could it be otherwise in a cosmos generated by the Creator's outflow of love? Love is woven into the very warp and woof of reality.

Purgatory, Canto XVIII, Part 1: "Of shoes and ships and sealing wax—of cabbages and kings"[9]

> *Now may be apparent to thee how deeply the truth*
> *Is hidden from the folk who aver that every act of*
> *Love is in itself a laudable thing,*
>
> *Because, forsooth, its material may seem*
> *Always to be good; but not every imprint*
> *Is good, albeit the wax may be good.*

It astounds me that in a culture such as ours that puts such a high premium on love, we actually know so little about it. We sentimentalize love into feel-good warm and fuzzy affection. We equate it with romantic passion. We insist that "all you need is love," thereby bestowing upon it the power of a cure-all elixir. We maintain that love, however and wherever it appears, is unquestionably good.

But these moves are all so problematic that we would do well to jettison them, hard as that may be for us, or at least recognize that they do little more than distantly gesture at the essence of love. In his continuation from Canto XVII of his discussion of love, Virgil here takes on the last of these misunderstandings, namely that all love is good. There, he argued that love is the substratum of both good and evil acts. Here, he explains in more detail how that's possible. Our natural inclination to love is inherently good, he says. But the "impressions" made upon it may be flawed.

What's Virgil getting at?

Let's go back to Plato. I think one of his greatest philosophical contributions is his account of love in the dialogue *Symposium*. He argues that even though we tend to evaluate love in terms of its subjective feel, thereby speaking of love as running the gamut between "intense" and "tepid," we really ought to judge it in terms of that to which it directs itself. How objectively lovable is the target of our love? It's this that will determine whether we love well or ill, thereby putting the lie to the notion that all love is equally good.

So, for example, I may "love" boiled cabbage, finely crafted shoes, teak and brass sailing ships, and powerful political leaders. But surely the objective nature of these different love-targets suggests that my gustatory

---

9. This line is taken, of course, from Lewis Carroll's "Walrus and the Carpenter." See *Looking Glass*, 40.

"love" of cabbage is qualitatively inferior to my love of comfortable shoes, much less beautiful sailing ships. Or take my "love" of political leaders. If the leader is virtuous, my love of her is good. But if she's a scoundrel, my love is bad because it's focused on an objectively bad person.

As Virgil says, the sealing wax—love—inevitably takes on the character of whatever is pressed upon it.

The lesson from both Plato and Virgil is pretty clear: be careful about the direction in which your natural inclination to love flows. If it moves toward an unworthy object, it becomes unworthy itself.

But can we ourselves determine what we love? Isn't love spontaneous, something that simply happens to us over which we have no control? This is another misunderstanding about love, which Virgil takes on in Canto XVIII.

Purgatory, Canto XVIII, Part 2: Robot Love?

Virgil speaks:

> *"Every substantial form, which is distinct*
> *From matter and is in union with it,*
> *Has a specific virtue contained within itself*
>
> *Which is not perceived save in operation,*
> *Nor is manifested except by its effects*
> *Just as life in a plant by the green lives.*
>
> *Therefore man knows not whence the understanding*
> *Of the first cognitions may come, nor the*
> *Inclination to the prime objects of appetite,*
>
> *Which are in you, even as the instinct*
> *In bees to make honey.*
>
> *Wherefore suppose that every love which is*
> *Kindled within you arise of necessity,*
> *The power to arrest it is within you.*
>
> *This noble virtue*
>
> *Is the free will."*

There's a question philosophers have pondered for centuries: Do we possess free will?

We know that so much of reality is locked in a deterministic holding pattern, don't we? That includes to a large extent our own physical bodies and even our psycho-chemical dispositions. This determinism, in fact, is what makes science possible. So are we pre-programmed biological robots? Can we be said to be free?

I've come to the conclusion that this question is philosophically unanswerable but functionally demonstrable. It boils down to this: Most of us are deeply confident that we have the capacity to freely choose because we possess an incorrigible inner sense or intuition or experience of doing so. We can't offer an indisputably airtight abstract argument to "prove" free will. But we don't really need to prove what's functionally self-evident.

Just as "life in a plant," according to Virgil, is proved by its greenness, so our possession of free will is demonstrated by our deeply felt capacity for choosing between alternative options.

Here's the conundrum facing Dante in this canto: As already seen in Canto XVIII, we're programmed to love objects worthy of love; that's our innate power. This seems to imply that we're deterministic, pre-programmed robots: we cannot not love, and we can only love worthily lovable objects. Yet it's entirely possible for love to go bad, which seems to fly in the face of our programming.

Dante (through Virgil) doesn't offer a knock-down-drag-out abstract argument in defense of free will. Instead, he offers a functional one that reminds us of what experience already tells us: we manipulate our "certain power," our inherent disposition to love lovable objects, for good or ill. Human reason serves as our "threshold of consent" when it comes to how and what we love, and reason by definition (and experience) is a freely chosen exercise. You can't coerce someone into thinking rationally. Trust me. Thirty-five years of teaching convinces me of this.

So, even if we are programmed to love, we still have the power to "arrest" a bad application of that love. And this "noble power," associated with reason, is freedom of the will.

It may be that in appealing here to reason, Virgil is simply using a mysterious word to explain the equally mysterious faculty of free will. I'm sympathetic to that criticism. But the functional feel of the capacity to exercise both choice and rationality remains, regardless of our difficulty in providing crisp definitions of free will and reason.

An important coda: Virgil tells Dante that there's more to be said about free will, but that he's not competent to do so. Beatrice, who will be Dante's guide through paradise, is. So stay tuned. There's much more to be said about love and free will. But it'll have to wait awhile.

Purgatory, Canto XIX: Russian Doll

> *There came to me in a dream a stuttering woman,*
> *With eyes asquint and crooked on her feet,*
> *With maimed hands and of sallow hue.*
>
> *I gazed upon her; and as the sun comforteth*
> *The cold limbs which night weighs down,*
> *So my look made ready her tongue.*
>
> *"I am," she sang, "I am the sweet Siren*
> *Who leads mariners astray in mid-sea,*
> *So full am I of pleasantness to hear.*
>
> *Whoso liveth with me*
> *Rarely departs, so wholly do I satisfy him."*
>
> *Virgil seized her and rending her clothes,*
> *Laid her open in front and showed me her belly;*
> *That awakened me with the stench which issued therefrom.*

Just as they're about to make their way to Mount Purgatory's fifth storey, the temporary abode of souls repenting of avarice, Dante dreams of a hag who suddenly transforms into a beautiful seductress. She identifies herself as one of the Sirens whose sweet song and comely appearance lures humans to destruction.

But before Dante can succumb to her magic, the vision of a saintly lady prods Virgil into action. He quickly steps in to rip away the Siren's facade of beauty, thus revealing her true grotesqueness. Dante awakens from his dream.

The hag, as Virgil tells us a bit later, is a symbolic road sign to the uppermost three stories of purgatory where the avaricious, the gluttonous, and the lustful rest on their way to redemption. All three of the vices from which they suffer, ones that seem so appealing at the outset, eventually destroy character.

Now, there's nothing spectacularly new about this claim.

What truly intrigues me in this canto is Dante the artist rather than Dante the philosopher. I'm referring to the startling way he makes the membrane separating the dream world and the real world so seamlessly porous.

Dante the pilgrim has this dream of a hag *cum* Siren. He also dreams that a "saintly lady"—the Virgin Mary? Beatrice?—suddenly appears to sound a warning.

Presumably all this is in Dante the pilgrim's head. It is, after all, a "dream." Yet suddenly Virgil is aware of Dante's dream and steps inside it to expose the Siren for the monstrosity she is. And if there's any doubt about this boundary-crossing, if there's any question about whether Dante the pilgrim was really dreaming and Virgil was really "outside" of the dream until he entered it, Virgil says to Dante, "At least three calls have I uttered to thee!"

Three times I tried and failed to wake you from your revery. So at last I had to jump the thin line between dream and reality to rescue you.

There's a delicious Russian doll-like quality to this scene, and, indeed, to the *Comedy* as a whole, isn't there? The entire three-booked epic can be read as an inner journey or vision—as a dream. That's one layer. But events take place in it that seem very real indeed: another layer.

Unrepented sins in the inferno parallel repented sins in purgatory: a third layer. And now, in Canto XIX, yet another subtle layer is exposed, one in which reality slips into a dream which itself embeds in a very real scene which in turn layers into the overall dream of the *Comedy*.

Whew!

In some respects, Dante reminds me of Lewis Carroll or Jorge Luis Borges—not to mention Freud and Jung—who likewise are adept at rendering porous the border between dream and reality.

Purgatory, Canto XX: Affluenza, the She-Wolf's Cub

Accursed be thou, she-wolf of old,
That hast more prey than all the other beasts,
For thy hunger endlessly deep!

Dante and Virgil are still on the fifth storey or terrace of Mount Purgatory, the one reserved for those repenting of avarice. We're told it's the most crowded of all the terraces, and that the mountain knows no harsher penalty.

Avarice, the inordinate desire to own stuff, people, and power, is a dreadful obstacle to human flourishing. And it's a particularly insidious one because it seductively masquerades as innocent ambition: the more you possess, the safer/stronger/sexier you are.

Throughout the Hebrew and Christian Testaments, the sin of avarice is condemned again and again. You'll find the same judgment in all the world's religious traditions and most of its humanistic ones. And, as Dante suggests when he over-crowds the fifth storey, there's good reason for that: avarice is ubiquitous and it's deadly. Pride is generally recognized as the Ur-sin; the serpent appeals to it when he promises the primordial couple that they can be like gods. But avarice surely goes hand in hand with pride.

Each year immediately following Thanksgiving, the chaotic and soul-killing season of holiday shopping officially begins. As a perceptive book pointed out a few years ago, it's also the season of "affluenza," a time in which the continuous and frenetic din of advertising infects us with a nearly irresistible mania to buy, Buy, BUY! But if Dante is correct, the toxin of affluenza is a settled and transmissible mutation in humanity's spiritual DNA. It may especially rear its ugly head in certain seasons, but it's always poisoning us.

We're reminded of this at the She-Wolf's inaugural appearance in the *Comedy's* very first canto as one of the beasts that threatened Dante in the dark wood. Here's a refresher on how he described her then:

> *"A she-wolf, that looked full of all*
> *Cravings in her leanness; and has ere now*
> *Made many live in sorrow."*

Purgatory, Canto XXI: Purgatory Is a Soul-School, Not a Holding Cell

> *The mountain quakes when some soul feeleth herself*
> *Cleansed, so that she may rise up, or set forth,*
>   *To mount on high.*
>
> *Of the cleansing the will alone gives proof,*
>   *Which fills the soul, all free to change her cloister,*
>   *And avails her to will.*

I said a while back that God isn't a genie in the bottle who folds His arms, nods His head, and makes things magically happen. Nor is sojourning in purgatory simply a matter of putting in one's time and keeping one's nose clean until the sentence is up. These misconceptions dishonor both God and human beings.

God is patient enough to allow mortals all the time we need to work through our stuff, repent of our wrongdoing, and jettison the temptations that entrapped us in the first place. God won't suddenly "abracadabra!" us into wholeness. What good would that do? Wholeness, spiritual health, and love have to be freely chosen by us. We have to so want them that we willingly work hard to acquire them.

True, grace is always present. But grace refuses, for our own good, to infantilize us. Jesus may have said "suffer the little children to come to me," but that doesn't mean God wants us to be childish.

In Canto XXI, Virgil and Dante are still on the fifth storey when they feel Mount Purgatory rumble and shake. Startled, they ask one of the shades, who turns out to be the Silver Age Latin poet Statius, what's going on. He replies, in the passage quoted above, that the mountain trembles every time a soul in purgatory explicitly wills to rise to paradise. Such an act of the will is a sure sign that wholeness or purity has been achieved. In celebration of that complete conversion, a momentous and joyful transformation, all of purgatory shakes.

I love this insight. It tells us that purgatory is more like a school than a holding cell. Souls who wind up there are given the opportunity to learn from their mistakes, to rehabilitate, to grow into their True Selves. At first, they may be so burdened by the contrapasso penalties imposed on them that they can't think beyond a longing for relief. But as the years unfold and their self-awareness increases, they move nearer and nearer to the beatitudinal desire to forsake their old selves in order to cleave fully to God.

It's at this point that they ascend to paradise. It's not that God mechanically lifts them out of purgatory on a skyhook or hands them a Get-Out-of-Jail-Free card. "Okay, you've served your time. Now you're sprung." Rather, they self-lift by freely, gratefully, and lovingly conforming their wills to God's perfectly benevolent will. They graduate through the hard work of disciplined self-metamorphosis. They aren't simply given their diplomas. They earn them by learning in purgatory what they should've learned in life: how to be full human beings.

Statius, by the way, joins Virgil and Dante for the rest of their journey through purgatory because the trembling of Mount Purgatory they felt was for him. His time as a student is over. So as he ascends to paradise, they accompany him.

Purgatory, Canto XXII, Part 1: Great Literature Transfigures Us

> *Statius said: "Thou first didst send me*
> *Towards Parnassus to drink in its caves,*
> *And then didst light me on to God.*
>
> *Thou didst like one who goes by night,*
> *And carries the light behind him and profits*
> *Not himself, but maketh persons wise that follow him,*
>
> *When thou saidst: 'The world is renewed,*
> *Justice returns, and the first age of man,*
> *And a new progeny descends from heaven.'*
>
> *Through thee I Poet was, through thee a Christian."*

Virgil and Dante are climbing up Mount Purgatory in the company of Statius, the Latin poet who's being released from purgation. Virgil asks him how he came to be a Christian. (By the way, this is an artistic invention on Dante's part. Although Statius is a real historical figure, there's no evidence of his conversion.)

In responding, Statius relates something well worth heeding. He says he was converted to the faith through reading Virgil, a pagan: specifically, Virgil's *Fourth Eclogue*,[10] a passage from which Statius cites in the above quoted snippet. Through you, he tells Virgil, I became a poet and a Christian.

Great literature offers us a priceless gift. It transports us out of ourselves. It inspires us, with a sense of adventure and courage, to leave the shallows of life and venture into the deep. In reading great literature, we discover a profundity to existence that we may never have suspected before. We come closer to the Divine foundation of all that is, even if traditional dogmatic religion leaves us cold.

---

10. Virgil, *Eclogues*.

I love the Bible. But what initially drew me to it is the same thing that draws me to Homer, Sophocles, Montaigne, Chaucer, Shakespeare, Tolstoy, Dickens, George Eliot, Balzac, R. S. Thomas, Gerard Manley Hopkins, and, of course, Virgil and Dante: sheer beauty. The poetic magic of their words, the subtlety of their insights, the fluidity of their imaginations bestirs appreciative wonder in me at the dazzlingly complex and yet also purifyingly simple essence of life.

Great literature, I think, is a God-inspired instrument designed to help us become fully human, to save us, as it were, from a monochromatic existence by revealing for us truth, beauty, and goodness. Through it, as Statius says, the world is born again, and so are we.

I'm thankful that Dante reminds us of this in Canto XXII. I often fear that heated squabbles about the "canon" forget the transfiguration great literature offers. But I'm comforted by the confidence that its power endures amid the din of academic debate, and that what it offers will always beckon to us.

Purgatory, Canto XXII, Part 2: Prodigality Isn't Generosity

Statius speaks:

> *"Now know that avarice was too far parted*
> *From me, and this excess*
> *Thousands of moons have punished.*
>
> *Then I perceived that our hands could open*
> *Their wings too wide in spending, and I repented*
> *Of that as well as of other sins;*
>
> *How many will rise again with shorn locks,*
> *Through ignorance, which taketh away repentance*
> *Of this sin during life and at the last hour!*
>
> *And know that the offense which repels*
> *Any sin by its direct opposite, here,*
> *Together with it, dries up its luxuriance."*

One of my favorite Shakespeare tragedies is *Timon of Athens*, one of his lesser-known plays. Its theme is the destructiveness of prodigality.

Generosity and prodigality ought not to be confused. The first is the act of benevolent giving in the service of a genuine good. The second is a thoughtless and often selfish display of wastefulness, a careless stewardship of resources.

Timon learns the difference the hard way. He's an incredibly wealthy citizen of ancient Athens who squanders his fortune by thoughtlessly handing it out willy-nilly to parasites and hangers-on, all of whom pretend to be friends but whose only intention is to milk him for everything he's worth. Timon's prodigality injures both their moral characters and his own. They sink ever more deeply into conniving hypocrisy. Timon, once he realizes that he's broke and betrayed, becomes a bitter, hate-filled misanthrope.

Statius, the redeemed shade who accompanies Dante and Virgil on the way to paradise, explains that his abiding sin was prodigality, and that practitioners of it are housed in the fifth purgatorial storey with the avaricious. I think what Dante has in mind here is classic Aristotle.

Famously, Aristotle argued in his *Nicomachean Ethics* that virtue is the mean between two extreme courses of action. The virtue of generosity lies midway between excess (prodigality) and deficiency (avarice). So in Dante's mind, these opposites are really two sides of the same coin, and it makes sense to put practitioners of both together in purgatory.

Christians often use the word "prodigal" to describe God's incredible generosity. God the sower prodigally flings seeds of grace, letting them fall with abandon so that they might take root in as many places as possible. But we should keep in mind that language like this is deliberately hyperbolic. We don't really mean to say in a literal sense that God is prodigal, but that God's generosity is unimaginably expansive. Perhaps we should be more precise with our words.

Purgatory, Canto XXIII: Open My Lips—But Not to Eat

>*And lo! In tears and song was heard,*
> *Labia mea, Domine!*

>*Behind us, moving more quickly,*
> *Coming and passing by, a throng of spirits,*
> *Silent and devout, was gazing upon us in wonder.*

> *Dark and hollow-eyed was each one,*
> *Pallid of face, and so wasted away*
> *That the skin took form from the bones.*

> "*All of this people, who weeping sing,*
> *Sanctify themselves again in hunger and thirst,*
> *For having followed appetite to excess.*"

According to Buddhist tradition, "hungry ghosts," whom we met in an earlier canto, wander the land, forever famished but never satisfied. These are the shades of people who, while alive, glutted themselves on food and drink, never seeming to get their fill. Artists depict the ghosts with shriveled heads and stick-like limbs attached to hideously bloated bellies.

On the sixth storey of Mount Purgatory, where the gluttonous expiate for their self-indulgences, Dante encounters his own version of hungry ghosts. Their penitential discipline is perfectly contrapasso: because they ate and drank inordinately in life, they're condemned to gnawing hunger in purgatory. Because they misused their lips in life by inordinately stuffing their mouths, they penitentially (but also a bit ironically) sing the *Labia mea Domine*, "Lord, open my lips and my mouth shall proclaim your praise," of Psalm 50.

To our modern sensibilities, gluttony doesn't typically come across as a moral failing unless we go on rants about how "undisciplined" obese people must be—which ultimately, of course, says more about our own lack of charity than about gluttony. But gluttony isn't finally about overeating. It's about an unhealthy indulgence that's both self- and other-destructive. This is what makes it a sin or vice.

To be gluttonous is to assume the identity of a giant maw that constantly demands to be fed. In the midst of this perpetual campaign for satiation, one loses a quintessential human characteristic, concern for others.

In practice, this means that because we demand more than we actually need, we deprive others. So we damage our own humanity by subordinating our hearts and minds to our ceaseless cravings, and in the process we mistreat our fellows by assuming that our wants have priority over their needs.

Purgatory, Canto XXIV: Forbidden Fruit

The laden and green boughs of another tree
  Appeared to me.

I saw people beneath it lifting up their hands
  And crying out something toward the foliage,
  Like spoilt and greedy children,

Who beg, and he of whom they beg answers not,
  But to make their longing full keen, holds
  What they desire on high, and hides it not.

Then they departed as though undeceived;
  And now we came to the great tree
  Which mocks so many prayers and tears.

"Pass onward without drawing nigh to it;
  Higher up is a tree which was eaten of by Eve,
  And this plant was raised from it."

At the summit of Mount Purgatory lies the earthly paradise, the prelapsarian (before the fall) abode of innocence and purity from which the primordial couple was driven. Dante explores it beginning in Canto XXVIII.

But for now, we're still on the sixth storey of the Mount, where the gluttons work out their salvation. Virgil, Dante, and Statius come across a tree surrounded by famished, emaciated shades who stretch upward to futilely grasp at its fruit.

This is an offshoot of the Tree of the Knowledge of Good and Evil which grows in the earthly paradise. Its roots have sunk down from Mount Purgatory's pinnacle to the sixth storey and birthed a tree laden with fruit craved by the penitents. This is their ascetic discipline: they gorged themselves on forbidden fruit in life; now they're forced to abstain from forbidden fruit in purgatory.

This offers us, I think, an often overlooked insight into the nature of gluttony. It's not just a matter of inordinately devouring food, drink, power, sex, and so on. Gluttony also, and perhaps essentially, has to do with craving and demanding that which is beyond our remit.

The fruit of the Tree in the primordial Garden was off limits to our ancestors because we humans are simply unable to digest its richness.

We're too fragmented by our individual self-interests and passions to determine on our own steam what's good and what's evil for humanity. Consequently, it's both unseemly and harmful to yearn for the power to do so. History bears out this sad truth again and again.

Ultimately what gluttons need to get in order is the undisciplined appetite that drives them to crave what isn't good for them or anyone else. We humans should desire to soar as high as our natures will allow. But if our desires outstrip the horizons that are proper to us, we, like Icarus who flew too close to the sun, will plummet to earth.

Purgatory, Canto XXV: Mirage-Bodies Are Better Than No-Bodies

When
   The soul frees itself from the flesh,

The other powers, the whole of them mute;
   Memory, intelligence, and will, keener far
   In action than they were before.

Soon as it is circumscribed in place there,
   The formative virtue radiates around, in form
   And quantity as in the living members;

So the neighboring air sets itself into that form
   Which the soul that is there fixed impresses
   Upon it by means of its virtue.

Therefrom it afterwards has it semblance,
   It is called a shade.

In this canto, Dante the poet answers a question that surely puzzles every reader of his *Comedy*: How is it that he can see and speak with disembodied shades or souls? How do they feel pain in hell, regret in purgatory, or bliss in paradise? How is it that the disembodied shades of gluttons actually look emaciated or suffer from hunger?

Dante frequently appeals to Aristotelian philosophy when he wants to explain something. But here he pulls directly from his own artistic imagination. It's an ingenious explanation that he offers, and reminds me a bit of the "ectoplasm" or visible spiritual substance touted by nineteenth-century spiritualists.

When the body dies, says Dante, physical functions such as respiration and digestion obviously cease. But intellectual and volitional ones remain, as does memory, and, in fact, they are "keener far in action" now they're unburdened by the body. They radiate a spiritual force that, when surrounded by air, takes on a spectral shape that reflects the intellectual and volitional makeup of the particular soul. So a shade's spiritual vitality assumes a kind of mirage-body; think, perhaps, of a holographic image. It's this that Dante sees and speaks to in his tour of the three regions.

It's still not clear (to me, at least) how shades can experience pain or pleasure, since these, being sensuous functions, surely require physical bodies. (Although I suppose that memory traces of pain and pleasure might substitute here.) Nonetheless, Dante's account is a fascinating hypothesis about how we humans who rely so much on our bodies can retain our personal identities in a physically disembodied postmortem existence. Dante's Pauline answer is that we're never actually without bodies. Otherwise, how could we possibly continue to be who we are? How would talk about hell, purgatory, or paradise be anything but nonsense?

Presumably, Dante's mirage-bodies are intermediate states that keep our identities intact until the final judgment in which, according to the Christian story, physical (yet somehow better than physical) embodiment will be restored to the righteous.

Purgatory, Canto XXVI, Part 1: Irresistible Craving for Body

> *And with my shadow, ruddier, I made the flames*
> *Appear, and even at so slight a sign, many*
> *Shades I saw, as they passed, give heed.*
>
> *This was the cause which gave them an opening*
> *To speak of me; and one to the other they began*
> *To say: "He doth not seem a shadowy body!"*
>
> *Then certain of them made towards me,*
> *So far as they could.*

A while back I pointed out that in Book XI of the *Odyssey*, we're told that Odysseus, who wishes to speak to his mother Anticleia's ghost in the underworld, is advised to entice her with a bowl of blood. Only after she laps it will she speak to him.

I find this a remarkably dramatic reminder that all of us crave the ensanguined warmth and vitality of bodily life. We know that our physical frames can bring us pain and suffering. But for all that, the sheer pleasure of embodiment is not something we're willing to forego. Similarly, we know that our bodies one day will give out. But this only makes our fleeting possession of them all the more precious.

Even the shades in Homer's underworld, pitiful wraiths who lack corporeal substance, remember and yearn for embodied life. That's why they find blood, the body's elixir, irresistible.

Over and over, in both the Inferno and the Purgatorio, we've seen the shades whom Dante encounters astounded and attracted by the fact that he, unlike them, is very much physically embodied. They are dead, he is alive. They are wraiths, he is flesh-and-blood. We see the same astonishment once more in today's canto. The shades, noticing that Dante casts a shadow, excitedly flock around him.

Now, on the one hand their astonishment is partly the surprise of seeing the unexpected: a living person among the dead. But mightn't it also be the case that they, like Odysseus's mother, so crave the life they no longer have that they're irresistibly drawn to Dante's pulsingly vital embodiment? He still possesses what they've lost. "He doth not seem a shadowy body!" they exclaim, and crowd around him simply to be near, even if only for a second, to the life—the *embodied* life—they crave.

How strange and sad it is that we who are alive so often take our embodiment for granted, forgetting—or, perhaps, never having recognized—what it is to exult over the primordial experience, uncanny and delightful, of possessing and experiencing flesh, blood, vitality, life. Remember what Thoreau says at one point in his *Walden*?[11] He writes that sometimes he thinks he could seize and devour raw a woodchuck. In moments like that, the naked pulsing power of embodied vitality overwhelms him and the only appropriate way of uttering it is with this chthonic image.

It's particularly appropriate that we're reminded of our irresistible attraction to embodiment in Canto XXVI. Dante and his two companions

---

11. Thoreau, *Walden*, 202.

have entered the seventh storey of Mount Purgatory, the terrace of the penitential lustful, those who were especially attracted to bodily experiences. We'll need to proceed carefully here, treading a fine line between properly celebrating human sensuality and acknowledging its misuse.

Purgatory XXVI, Part 2: Straining Out Gnats but Swallowing Camels

> *There I see on either side each shade*
> *Make haste, and one kiss the other without staying,*
> *Satisfied with short greeting:*
>
> *Even so within their dark battalions one*
> *Ant rubs muzzle with another, perchance to*
> *Spy out their way and their fortune.*
>
> *The one passes on, the other comes away,*
> *And weeping they return to their former chants,*
> *And to the cry which most befits them.*

Freud, I think it's fair to say, uttered a good deal of nonsense. But his most astute observation about human nature—one that all of us know deep down in our bones to be true, even if we often balk at admitting it—is that we human primates are profoundly sexual creatures. The sexual itch is never quite absent, is it? It underlies some of our noblest as well as some of our worst intentions and impulses, such that we tend to seesaw between expression, repression, and sublimation.

Too often, Christian sensibility has decried any sexual expression as degrading or unseemly and urged repression. Alternatively, mystics in the tradition sometimes appear to sublimate their sexuality in a Godward direction. One doesn't have to be a Freudian to see this movement in Teresa of Avila's legendarily rapturous orgasmic experience of being pierced by a golden arrow.

A healthier, openly expressive perspective acknowledges and celebrates chaste human sexuality. Chastity isn't identical to celibacy. To be chaste is to resist allowing sexual urges to become the dominant force in one's life or to indulge in sexual activity harmful either to oneself or to others. Chastity acknowledges that sexuality is a good thing, but cautions against its abuse.

The penitents in the seventh storey of Mount Purgatory are being schooled in that prudential truth. Because they allowed their sexual impulses to burn hotly and without discretion in life, their contrapasso discipline is to run along fiery paths shouting out the nature of their specific excesses. When two groups racing in opposite directions encounter one another they pause just long enough to exchange a quick kiss of peace, a gesture of chastity in stark contrast to the behavior in life for which they're atoning.

It's worth pointing out, again in contrast to blue-nosed Christians who seem to think that the worst sins in the world revolve around sex, that the lustful are in the topmost purgatorial ring. The obvious suggestion is that offenses against chastity are in fact the least offensive of transgressions.

Purgatory, Canto XXVII, Part 1: Soul-Mirror, God-Mirror

> "Know, whoso asketh my name,
>   That I am Leah, and go moving
>   My fair hands around to make me a garland.
>
> To please me at the glass here I deck me
>   But Rachel my sister ne'er stirs
>   From her mirror, and sitteth all day.
>
> She is fain to behold her beautiful eyes,
>   As I am to deck me with my hands;
>   Her, contemplation; me, action, doth satisfy."

The twelfth-century theologian and mystic Richard of St. Victor saw the Old Testament figures of Leah and Rachel, wives of the patriarch Jacob, as symbols of two ways of being in the world and relating to God. Leah represents the active way, Rachel the contemplative way.[12] Their New Testament parallels are, of course, Martha and Mary.

After leaving the seventh purgatorial storey but before entering the earthly, an exhausted Dante dreams of a "young and lovely girl" picking flowers in a meadow. This is Leah, who speaks to him about her and her sister Rachel in the passage I've quoted.

---

12. Richard of St. Victor, *Twelve Patriarchs*, 55–56.

Too often we think of act and contemplation as dichotomous. But as Dante insinuates, they're actually both ways of being that invite gazing into a "mirror." What does the mirror signify?

A common motif in medieval mysticism is the *speculum divina*: the soul is a mirror (speculum) which reveals the presence of the divine. The underlying claim is that humans, made as we are in the likeness of God, carry within us God's reflection. If we can wipe away the smears and blears we impose on our mirrors/souls during our lives, we can discern that reflection—and, in so doing, discover our true selves.

Dante connects the active and contemplative ways together through mirror imagery. The creative and beautiful work Leah performs is reflected when she gazes into the mirror/soul. God is the supreme Creator of the beautiful cosmos (Gr. *kosmos* = "ornament"), and when we participate with the divine nature through work/creativity, we discover both God and our true selves.

But God is also the unnameable Ground, the dark, silent Presence, the Plenitude that permeates but remains hidden, and this aspect of the Divine is reflected in the mirror/soul for the contemplative. To contemplatively "wait for God," as the twentieth-century mystic Simone Weil put it, is to participate in the divine stillness, the brilliant darkness, the revelatory mystery.

So, no. There's no opposition between the active and the contemplative paths. They lead to one and the same destination. This will become increasingly clear to Dante and us as the journey continues.

Purgatory, Canto XXVII, Part 2: Love, and Do What Thou Wilt

Virgil speaks:

> *"Here have I brought thee with wit and with art;*
> *Now take thy pleasure for guide.*
>
> *Free, upright, and whole, is thy will,*
> *And 'twere a fault not to act according to its prompting;*
> *Wherefore I do crown and mitre thee over thyself."*

Virgil has been a good guide, but his time is over. It's here, at the earthly paradise, the restoration of Eden atop Mount Purgatory, that he and

Dante must go their separate ways. I for one will miss him. But painful as his departure is, it really is necessary that he leave. We'll reflect on the bittersweet nature of spiritual transitions when we finish Canto XXVII.

But for now, what does Virgil mean by his parting counsel that Dante let pleasure be his guide? On the face of it, this seems shockingly hedonistic.

And it actually is. But not in the way you might suspect.

Dante hasn't been a mere spectator on his climb up Mount Purgatory. He's also been purified along the way. Remember the seven "P"s that were carved on his forehead back in Canto IX? They stood for the seven capital vices or *peccata*. As he ascended the Mount, they were wiped away, one by one, until he was washed clean of them.

This signifies two things.

First, the sins that Dante committed in the past have been nullified. They were purged, step by step, as he climbed upward.

Second—and this is crucial—his will has been purified of any sinful desires. An unclean will, suffering from the myopia of unhealthy self-love, falsely judges that a harmful vice like lust or gluttony is supremely pleasurable. But a purified will sees, with divinely inspired clarity, that other-love is the route to genuine pleasure. To focus our love on the Divine, on our fellow-humans, on God's beautiful creation and all that dwells therein, is to conform our will to God's supremely beneficent will—and thereby to become fully human, as our primordial ancestors were before the fall.

Such a purified will, as Virgil tells Dante, is free, upright, and whole, desiring only that which is genuinely good. Transfigured in this way, humans become lords of themselves, crowned and mitred, rather than slaves to unworthy desires.

In offering his parting words to Dante, Virgil is paraphrasing St. Augustine. In one of his sermons, Augustine famously assures us that if we only love, we can do whatever we will. His point is that if our wills are properly guided by other-love—if they're conformed to the beneficent will of God—whatever we will to do is good and will give us pleasure.[13]

So, yes. This is a type of hedonism. But it focuses us on the genuinely and ever-lastingly pleasurable rather than transitory and destructive faux-pleasures. That's because the seven "P"s etched on our own foreheads have been erased.

---

13. Augustine, "Homily VII," 504.

Purgatory, Canto XXVII, Part 3: Vale!

Virgil speaks:

> "Here have I brought thee with wit and with art;
> Now take thy pleasure for guide."

There's a crucial difference between a wanderer and a pilgrim.

To be a wanderer is to move hither and yon without any clear destination in mind. In fact, the word is derived from an Old English verb, *wandrian*, which means "to roam" or "to stray."

To be a pilgrim, on the other hand, is to journey with a purposeful intention to arrive at a destination. We go "on pilgrimage" to a particular place. We don't aimlessly roam with no sense of direction.

Lest they inadvertently fall into mere wandering, pilgrims need reliable mentors. They require instruction from people who've already traveled the route over which they must go, seasoned guides who can steer them in the right direction if they happen to veer off course. These guides not only help pilgrims navigate their way. They also comfort them when they lose heart, reassure them that their perseverance will pay off, and inspire them by their wisdom, strength, kindness, and patience.

It stands to reason that pilgrims may need more than one guide to help them through these various stages. Each stage along the way may indeed require saying farewell to one master and accepting the guidance of another.

This is what happens in Canto XXVII. Virgil has been a loyal and essential guide for Dante's pilgrimage through the inferno and purgatory. But now that they've reached the earthly paradise atop Mount Purgatory, it's time to hand Dante over to another guide. Virgil will accompany his ward for a few more steps, but he speaks no more. His mentoring has come to an end.

It's impossible to over-estimate Dante's indebtedness to Virgil. Without the Latin poet's guidance, Dante and we would still be lost in the dark wood we found him in at the very beginning of the *Comedy*. Virgil helped Dante discover the courage and honesty to face the deepest and darkest monsters buried in his psyche (inferno) and then, step by step, helped him conquer his attraction to them (purgatory). Under Virgil's tutelage, Dante has rationally disciplined his will to desire and take pleasure in that which is genuinely good. Now he and we are ready for the next stage of the journey and for a new guide.

So, to Virgil, we regretfully but gratefully say *Vale*!

Purgatory, Canto XXVIII: Humanity's Cradle, Humanity's Yearning

> *The highest Good, who himself alone doth please,*
>   *Made man and for goodness, and gave this place to him*
>   *As an earnest of eternal peace.*
>
> *Through his default, short time he sojourned here.*
>
> *In order that the storms,*
>   *Which the exhalations of the water and of the earth cause below it*
>
> *Should do no harm to man,*
>   *This mount rose thus far towards heaven,*
>   *And stands clear of them from where it is locked.*
>
> *And thou must know that the holy plain*
>   *Where thou art is full of every seed,*
>   *And bears fruit in it which yonder is not plucked.*

Societies the world over have chthonic memories of a golden age in which the good earth was abundantly fruitful, humans lived in harmony with nature and one another, and peace reigned supreme.

The details of these memories are culture-specific. The Greeks and the Chinese, for example, inflect descriptions of their golden ages differently. But in the main, the general contours are similar.

In the Hebrew biblical tradition, the golden age is represented by the story of the Garden of Eden, a place of innocence, fecundity, and serenity. This paradise on earth, this "holy plain," is where Dante (and his now silent companions Virgil and Statius) have arrived. For even though our primordial ancestors lost their right to remain in the Garden, it endures.

God has placed it, Dante learns, on the summit of Mount Purgatory, earth's highest peak, closest to heaven and farthest away from human wickedness. Souls destined for the beatific vision pass through this beautiful and pure place on their way to God.

And yet the earthly paradise remains connected to *terra firma*, and its very existence fructifies the rest of the globe. A constant refreshing breeze blows through it from east to west, following the eternal course of the heavenly spheres and scattering seeds from its abundant vegetation onto earth below. Thus vestiges of the earthly paradise are present even today in our lives.

Surely we know what Dante means whenever we turn to nature. Many people, myself included, are refreshed, awakened, and renewed when they open themselves to the beauty of the natural world. It's in the silent groves of ancient forests, along the banks of creeks and rivers, and on the shores of the great oceans that we make contact with the Transcendent that infuses our lives with wonder and meaning. The pregnant silence of a snowfall, the flash of lightning during a thunderstorm, the breathtaking magnificence of dawn and dusk, the fragile beauty of goldenrod, the intricacy of a spider web, the joyful way in which swallows sail through the air: these are all fruits of the earthly paradise's seeding which keep the memory of the golden age alive in us.

We should take this memory seriously. It's not merely a made-up children's story from myth-minded ancestors (as if myth-mindedness is something to be scorned!). No, it expresses the deep yearning of our hearts for a place we can call home.

Purgatory, Canto XXIX: When Words Fall Short

> A little farther on, a delusive semblance
>   Of seven trees of gold was caused by the long space
>   That was yet between us and them;
>
> But when I had drawn so nigh to them,
>
> The faculty which prepares material for reason
>   Distinguished them as candlesticks even as they were,
>   And in the words of the chant, "Hosannah."
>
> Above, the fair pageant was flaming forth,
>   Brighter far than the moon in clear
>   Midnight sky in her mid month.

> *Full of wonderment I turned me to*
> *The good Virgil, and he answered me with a face*
> *Not less charged with amazement.*

There's a scene in the *Bhagavad Gita* that sends a *frisson* up my spine. The Lord Krishna has been disguised as the lowly charioteer of Prince Arjuna. But at one point he reveals his divine identity in a spectacular display. Before Arjuna's astounded eyes, Krishna progressively expands to subsume within himself all of reality. The revelation opens up the meaning of existence for Arjuna in a breathtakingly dramatic way.[14]

In Canto XXIX we're treated to a similarly expansive revelation. (It's the first of two; the second comes in Canto XXXII.) Beginning with the appearance of seven huge candlesticks whose flames illuminate the sky with a band of rainbow colors, Dante and Virgil witness a procession (what Dante's contemporaries would've recognized as a masque, a stylized pageant) that allegorically presents the first half of salvation history.

The seven candles leading the procession represent the seven gifts of the Holy Spirit. They're followed by twenty-four elders (the books of the Old Testament), four Ezekielesque creatures (the New Testament Gospels), a chariot drawn by a griffin (the church and the two natures of Christ), seven female dancers (the virtues), and seven men (the other books of the New Testament).

This lavishly described spectacle delights but also bewilders Dante, and he turns to Virgil for an explanation. But the Latin poet is unable to say a word. Christian faith is beyond his ken, a mystery to the figure who, throughout the Inferno and the Purgatorio, represents humanistic rationality.

Now, what strikes me about this procession as well as Krishna's unveiling in the *Bhagavad Gita* is that even though their worded descriptions are necessarily temporal and linear, the actual experience of them is surely instantaneous. That's because they're theophanies, divinely inspired revelations that burst upon human consciousness in a flash. In an instant the deep-down reality of things is revealed, not at all compressed but displayed in all its manifold richness. Obviously such an extraordinary experience can't possibly be adequately expressed in words. No wonder Virgil is stone-cold mute, and Dante himself must resort to allegory.

When William Blake wrote about seeing the world in a grain of sand, he must've had this kind of theophanous experience in mind. We

---

14. *Bhagavad Gita*, chapter 10.

are the grains of sand in which Eternity reveals itself and thereby forever changes us. The experience is primary. Efforts to describe it come later.

Purgatory, Canto XXX, Part 1: Changing of the Guard

Within a cloud of flowers,

A lady appeared to me.

And my spirit, that now so long a time
  Had passed, since, trembling in her presence,
  It had been broken down with awe,

Without having further knowledge by mine eyes,
  Through hidden virtue which went out from her,
  Felt the mighty power of ancient love.

"Look at me well; verily am I, verily am I Beatrice!"

Virgil went mute a couple of cantos ago. In this one, he completely disappears, giving way to Beatrice, Dante's next guide. In the Paradiso, the third book of the *Divine Comedy*, Beatrice will be Dante's companion until the final three cantos, when St. Bernard will step in to complete the journey.

When Beatrice appears here in Canto XXX, she's dressed in robes whose colors signify the theological virtues of faith, hope, and charity. This gives us a clue as to who she is and why she supplants Virgil as Dante's mentor.

Virgil, the pre-Christian pagan, is the personification of reason and philosophical equanimity. His long tutelage of Dante was intended to train him in the rational control of his desires and discipline of his will. In other words, Virgil taught Dante the cardinal virtues. But Beatrice will now supplement Virgil's instruction by opening Dante up to the theological virtues. The Latin poet focused on cultivating the intellect and will. Beatrice will tutor Dante in spiritual and divine wisdom. This isn't to imply a disconnection between these different spheres, but only that Dante thinks the first logically prepares the way for the second. It's not at all that faith supplants intellect. Rather, it completes it.

Beatrice of course, is the spirit of a maiden with whom the actual poet Dante fell in love on first sight. (I suspect we're talking about courtly love here, the rather stylized adoration-from-afar popular in the Middle Ages and early Renaissance.) We know little about the historical Beatrice.

But in the *Divine Comedy*, as her very name suggests, she's the personification of beatitudinal wisdom, divine love, and even at times Christ himself. It was the spirit of Beatrice who sent Virgil to Dante in the first place to rescue him from the dark, entangling woods of spiritual and mental confusion. It is she who will now take him on the final third of his soul-journey.

But first she'll have to crack open his heart.

Purgatory, Canto XXX, Part 2: When Bitter Fruit Sweetens

> *"How didst thou deign to draw nigh the mount?*
> *Knewest thou not that here man is happy?"*
>
> *So doth the mother seem stern to her child,*
> *As she seemed to me; for the savor*
> *Of harsh pity tasteth of bitterness.*

I'm so struck by Dante the poet's observation that pity, until it becomes mercy, "tasteth of bitterness." The likening of unmerciful pity to unripe (bitter) fruit is so very evocative, isn't it?

The context is this: Dante stands before Beatrice, the personification of divine wisdom and love. The River Lethe (more of this soon) flows between them. Dante, initially overjoyed to see Beatrice, is shocked when he senses from the tone of her greeting that she's disappointed in him and even a bit angry for the way he's lived his life. He feels ashamed, like a child caught in a bit of devilry.

He intuits that Beatrice feels pity for him but not, as yet, mercy.

When we pity others, we're abstractly sorry for the state into which they've fallen. Usually the pity is reserved for those in trouble through no fault of their own, but it can also be directed at people who've brought their troubles on themselves through unwise or even wicked choices. But pity alone doesn't move us to action. It's a passive and often fleeting sort of response that fails to motivate us to do anything to alleviate the pain of the persons we pity. "Yes, yes, the situation in Ukraine/Gaza/Sudan is perfectly dreadful. Now, what's for lunch?"

The passivity of pity is especially obvious when its target is someone suffering the ill effects of his or her wicked actions. The situation of the murderer sentenced to life behind bars may evoke in us a moment or two of pity, but it doesn't move us to reach out to him or her. Quite the contrary. Our pity remains safely abstract and distant. "Well, yes. Life imprisonment is awful. But he brought it on himself, didn't he?"

So pity is an unripe or underdeveloped moral response. The sun that coaxes it to full-bodied maturity is compassion, the empathic identification with the suffering of others or what's often called fellow-feeling. To feel compassion is to move beyond a passive sorry-for response by rolling up one's sleeves and working to alleviate the suffering of others. I'm convinced that the capacity for compassion is hardwired within us by virtue of the fact that we're made in the likeness of a compassionate God, and that pity is a lazy sublimation of it.

When pity is ripened by compassion, one of its expressions is mercy, the act of forgiving and aiding those who justly deserve censure and punishment for their wickedness. The offer of mercy isn't a Get-Out-of-Jail-Free card. It doesn't whitewash guilt. Guilt must be atoned for. But it does say to the guilty that we recognize their humanity, feel compassion for the sorry state to which their actions have brought them, and desire to help them rehabilitate themselves. Mercy assures them that they are not exiled from the human community and that we refuse to exclusively identify them with the worst deed they may have committed.

Mercy is a lifeline to those desperately in need of a bit of forgiveness. And here, in Canto XXX, that's Dante.

Purgatory, Canto XXX, Part 3: The False Contrition Trap

> *The ice which had closed about my heart*
> *Became breath and water, and with anguish*
> *Through mouth and eyes issued from my breast.*

Beatrice speaks:

> *"My [purpose] is*
> *That he who yon side doth weep may understand me*
> *So that sin and sorrow be of one measure."*

Beatrice is accompanied by a band of angels who seem to be taken back by her rebuke of Dante. They begin singing a hymn in which the pilgrim senses

> *In their sweet harmonies their compassion*
> *On me, more than if they had said:*
> *"Lady, why dost thou so shame him?"*

Dante bursts into tears, behavior that suggests contrition on his part. But Beatrice isn't buying it. She chides the angelic host, warning them that their misplaced pity does Dante no good. Button it, she tells them.

This seems harsh. But Beatrice's experience of the ways in which we humans can deceive ourselves (not to mention others!) gives her an edge over the angels when it comes to seeing what Dante's tears actually signify.

Genuine contrition must include three elements: an acknowledgment of the truth that one has sinned, a humble acceptance of guilt or culpability for one's transgressions, and genuine grief over having offended God and others in committing them. If any one of these elements is missing, the contrition is less than authentic. It's false.

Beatrice senses that Dante hasn't yet arrived at authenticity. His tears at this point seem to be mostly self-pity at being rebuked by her, an ego-focused feeling-sorry-for-himself encouraged by the angels' misplaced pity. He may indeed be experiencing anguish, but not over his sins.

Many of us likely know from personal experience (at least I do!) how easy it is to shed the crocodile tears of false contrition. We refuse to face the full truth about our sinfulness. ("C'mon! I may've gone a bit too far, but it wasn't really all that bad, was it?! I'm basically a good guy.") Our fear of secret misdeeds going public masquerades as guilt. ("Oh god, please don't let this come to light! I absolutely swear I won't do it again if I can just get away with it this one time!") And our grief is the same kind of self-pity Dante wallows in if we *do* get caught out. ("Now everyone knows what I did! How will I ever recover from this? My life is ruined!")

This is the trap of false contrition Dante is enmired in. Beatrice wants to release him from it. But she knows that getting free will be painful for him.

You may be perplexed at this point. We've seen that Dante the pilgrim was purged of the cardinal sins, one by one, as he ascended the seven-storey Mount of Purgatory. So why is it that Beatrice is giving him such a hard time now? Isn't he free of sin?

I'm perplexed too. But perhaps one explanation is that Dante's progressive purgation was just pro forma. As penitential souls climb the Mount, they slowly and painfully repent of their sins. Each stage of their ascent represents progress in holiness. But Dante's ascent was streamlined; he was a visitor, not a penitent. He got automatically rubber-stamped at each stage of the journey, not because he was contrite but simply because he was being moved along the pipeline. So now, when confronted by Beatrice, he finally faces the music.

Purgatory, Canto XXXI, Part 1: Heart Surgery

> *Directing her speech with the point towards me,*
>   *Which even with the edge had seemed sharp:*
>
> *"Say, say if this is true; to such accusation,*
>   *Thy confession must be joined."*
>
> *Confusion and fear together mingled*
>   *Drove forth from my mouth a 'Yea' such that*
>   *To understand it the eyes were needed.*
>
> *As a crossbow breaks, when shot*
>   *At too great tension, both its string and bow,*
>   *And with less force the bolt hits the mark,*
>
> *So burst I under this heavy charge,*
>   *Pouring forth a torrent of tears and sighs.*
>
> *So much remorse gnawed at my heart that*
>   *I fell vanquished.*

I find the final four cantos of the Purgatorio emotionally exhausting. As vivid as Dante's descriptions of the torments of the damned and the struggles of the penitents are, he truly hits his artistic stride here, and continues shining throughout the rest of the *Comedy's* final volume.

(Which is why it's so sad, by the way, that most readers—not to mention college courses—never make it past the Inferno.)

In Canto XXXI, Beatrice continues her rebuke of Dante, knowing as she does that the tears he's shed up to this point simply aren't sufficient. She has to move him away from feeling sorry for himself to genuine self-awareness and contrition. So she relentlessly hammers him about his substitution of lesser transient pleasures for

> *that Good*
> *beyond which there is nothing to aspire to.*

Shamed, humiliated, and shattered when he finally acknowledges that Beatrice speaks the truth, Dante emotionally snaps like an overstretched bow. The trauma of facing the ugly facts about himself is so overwhelming that he actually collapses. This "little death" is a turning point, a prolegomenon to his impending rebirth.

I'm struck by the emotional and spiritual violence of Dante the pilgrim's contrition. His move from self-pity to honest self-awareness isn't a gradual seepage. It's a tsunami that knocks him off his bearings. But then, that's what the very word "contrition" suggests, isn't it? Its Latin root means "to break" or "to grind away at." Genuine contrition breaks open the old self, grinds away at the defensive walls we erect to protect our egos, so that the Spirit can flood in and jump start our humanity. As God told the prophet Ezekiel, "I will give you a new heart and put a new spirit in you; I will remove from you your heart of stone and give you a heart of flesh" (36:26–27).

How could this kind of heart surgery not be brutal, especially for someone who, like Dante, is smugly confident that his or her sins have already been purged? And yet saying "yes" to the transplant, even if the "yes" is so faint and timid that "ears must have eyes" to discern it, is the first step toward health. We must endure the sword point/scalpel of truth if we wish to be whole.

Purgatory, Canto XXXI, Part 2: Blissful Forgetfulness

> *Then, when the heart restored to me the sense of outward things,*
> *The lady whom I had found alone I saw above me;*
> *And she said: "Hold me! Hold me!"*
>
> *She had drawn me into the river up to my neck.*
>
> *"Asperges me," so sweetly I heard,*
> *That I cannot remember it much less describe it.*

> *The fair lady opened her arms,*
> *Clasped my head, and dipped me where,*
> *I must needs swallow of the water;*

> *Then drew me forth.*

In one of his more insightful reflections, the philosopher Friedrich Nietzsche opined that one of the distinctive characteristics of humans is our ability to forget. Without it, we would be helplessly and hopelessly chained to the past.[15] So, at least in one manner of speaking, forgetfulness is an asset rather than a weakness.

In the second part of Canto XXXI, Dante the pilgrim, who was in a dead faint when we last saw him, awakens to discover that he's being pulled through water by a companion of Beatrice's. Her name, we'll discover in Canto XXXIII, is Matilda. At one point, while the Latin *Asperges me* (sprinkle me), Psalm 51's "Cleanse me of my sins," is being chanted in the background, she dips Dante's mouth in the water so that he swallows. Afterward, Dante is cleansed.

The water he drinks is from the River Lethe, a stream that hitherto separated Dante and Beatrice. It's one of two in the earthly paradise. The other, which appears in Canto XXXIII, is the Eunoë. The first Dante borrows from classical mythology. The second is his invention. (More on the Eunoë anon.)

To drink of the Lethe is to forget one's past. In the classical tradition, the forgetfulness was intended to make the shade's traumatic departure from life and loved ones easier to bear. Here, it's to make the redeemed soul forget his or her sins.

But we have to be careful. Dante the poet surely can't mean that the soul utterly forgets the past. As we'll see, souls in paradise apparently remember their lives on earth. What the waters must erase, then, is the burden of guilt and grief that the genuinely repentant soul experiences when contemplating his or her past transgressions. It probably also wipes away the final lingering residues of desire for them.

In this context, Nietzsche's observation about the benefit of forgetting seems spot on. For paradise to be blissful, it must be unblemished by the weight of recrimination and regret. The Lethe ensures that once past sins are acknowledged and repudiated, their burden is lifted. Forgetfulness, in this context, is a genuine blessing.

---

15. Nietzsche, *On the Advantage*.

I can't help but think that Dante was motivated to imagine Lethe in the earthly paradise at least in part because he recognized how very difficult it is for us humans to let go of our burdens of guilt and self-recrimination. Just as we ought never to whitewash our failings, so we oughtn't to believe that we're irredeemably sullied by them either.

Purgatory, Canto XXXII: From Koinonia to Empire

Ne'er did fire from dense cloud descend,
  With motion so swift,

As I saw Jove's bird swoop down.

And he smote the car with all his might; whereat it
  Reeled like a vessel in a storm, beaten by the waves,
  Now to starboard, now to larboard.

Then, from thence whence he first had come,
  I saw the eagle descend down into the body of the car,
  And leave it feathered with his plumage.

Could Christianity have become a world religion without its fourth-century adoption by the mighty Roman Empire?

From a purely historical perspective, I doubt it. The AD 313 Edict of Milan, which ended the persecution of Christians, and the AD 380 Edict of Thessalonica, which proclaimed Christianity the Roman state's official religion, steadily transformed the hitherto marginalized Christian community. In quick order, as the western empire began to disintegrate, the church commandeered its imperial trappings, bureaucratic structure, and aura of absolute authority. It became a state within the state. It became the new Caesar.

Back in Canto XXIX, we witnessed the first of two masques in the Purgatorio. A masque, recall, is a pageant that enacts, allegorically, tableaux drawn from classical mythology or the Bible.

The first masque recounted salvation history up to the incarnation.

In Canto XXXII, we see the second masque, a long sequence of scenes that present two primary tableaux: the wondrous restoration of fallen humanity by the cross and the tragic corruption of the church in the following centuries as it increasingly amassed wealth and geopolitical power.

The masque is quite detailed in its allegorical representations, making this canto, which clocks in at one hundred and sixty verses, the longest in the entire *Comedy*. I've chosen two scenes from it that I think are especially illustrative of the second tableau.

In the first scene, an eagle, a "bird of Jove," crashes into the procession's chariot or "car" (Dante's symbol for the church), nearly capsizing it. This represents the early Roman Empire's persecution of the primitive church in the first and second centuries. The eagle, of course, is a symbol of Roman imperialism.

But ironically, just a few years later, the very same imperial eagle swoops down again on the chariot, this time to insinuate itself into its framework and stamp it with a seal of ownership, its "plumage."

The early Christian community or *koinonia* of sisters and brothers who shared everything in common and thus posed a threat to the secular state has now become the church militant, a worldly empire whose corruption subverts the very message of love, peace, and reconciliation it pretends to endorse.

For Dante, the gap between what Christ proclaimed and what the institutional church has become is nearly unbridgeable. He remains loyal to the church as the mystical body of Christ. But his opinion of the worldly ecclesial body is a mixture of scorn and sorrow, so much so that at the end of the canto, he likens it to Revelation's whore of Babylon.

It's not surprising that Dante ran across so many princes of the church in the inferno. Nor is it surprising that the tension between Christ's message and institutionalized Christianity so spectacularly described in Canto XXXII still endures.

Purgatory, Canto XXXIII: Eternal Sunshine of the Spotless Mind?

> "But behold Eunoë, which there flows on;
> Lead him to it, and as thou art wont,
> Requicken his fainting virtue."
>
> I came back from the most holy waves,
> Born again, even as new trees
> Renewed with new foliage,
>
> Pure and ready to mount to the stars.

The philosopher John Locke argued that what gives each of us a sense of self or personal identity that endures over time is memory.[16] Kerry the septuagenarian remembers Kerry at sixty, forty-five, thirty-two, sixteen, ten, and so on. Granted, the clarity of remembered events tends to fade the further in time I move away from them, and it's certainly the case that my mind, like everyone's, is cluttered with false memories. But so long as I know that all the Kerrys of my past connect up with the present Kerry, my sense of self remains secure.

What happens, then, if my memory is interfered with? How does it affect my sense of personal identity if swaths of my memory are changed?

This is a question Dante unintentionally raised in Cantos XXVIII, XXXI, and here, in the conclusion of the Purgatorio.

In the two earlier cantos, we saw that the River Lethe ("forgetfulness") expunges from a repentant soul's memory shame and remorse over past misdeeds. Memory of the deeds endures, but the negative emotions coupled with them are exorcised. In Canto XXXIII, we see that the River Eunoë (Dante's neologism, meaning "good remembrance") enhances recollection and presumably enjoyment of past virtue or good behavior.

The twin baptism in these miraculous waters is obviously intended to create in the paradise-bound soul a spiritual tranquility that maximizes the ability to single-mindedly focus on the beatific vision.

But this raises the Lockean-inspired question of just who it is that enters paradise. If my memories of sinful actions have been whitewashed of negative emotions, or if my memory has been recalibrated to focus primarily on those times I exercised virtue in life, can I still be said to be me? So is it Kerry who enters paradise, or some other kind of identity—call it "Kerry 2.0"—who does?

To emotionally denude memories of bleak associations seems to make them oddly impersonal. They no longer feel like "my" memories so much as abstract scenarios banked in my head.

Similarly, to flood my consciousness with recollections of happy times at the expense of darker ones seems to excise whole chunks of my past from my memory attic. In either case, the chain of recollections that makes me Kerry seems hazarded.

All this reminds me of the 2004 film *Eternal Sunshine of the Spotless Mind*, the title of which is a quote from the poet Alexander Pope.[17] If it

16. Locke, *Essay*, 134–49.
17. Pope, "Eloisa to Abelard," 137–47.

were possible to expunge from me all my unpleasant memories, such that my mind becomes "spotless" and basked in "eternal sunshine," could I still be me?

Is Dante, "a tree renewed with new foliage, pure and ready," after drinking of the Eunoë, still Dante?

I honestly don't know. But Dante the pilgrim, undisturbed by my questions, continues his spiritual ascent. Just as the Inferno concluded with him looking at the stars, so now too his gaze is upward. And so begins the final third of his—and our—journey.

Paradiso

... in which Dante and we find what we're searching for ...

Paradise, Canto I, Part 1: Language Is the House of Being

> *In that heaven which most receiveth of his light,*
>   *Have I been; and have seen things which whoso descendeth*
> *from up there,*
>   *Hath not knowledge nor power to re-tell:*
>
> *Because, as it draweth near to its desire,*
>   *Our intellect sinketh so deep,*
>   *That memory cannot go back upon the track.*
>
> *O divine Virtue, dost so far lend thyself to me,*
>   *That I make manifest the shadow of the blessed realm*
>   *Imprinted on my brain.*

As a philosopher and author—in short, as someone who pays particular attention to language—I've always been struck at just how adroitly human experience eludes our efforts to speak it.

The philosopher Martin Heidegger famously said that "language is the house of being. In its home human beings dwell."[1] His point is that we must use language to explore reality. It's through our efforts, halting as they may be, to speak reality that it reveals itself to us.

But language is a clumsy suitor and reality is coy. We have difficulty enough speaking ordinary experiences. Can we really capture in words

---

1. Heidegger, "Letter on Humanism," 217.

the pain in our tooth, the texture of spaghetti, the sensation of water flowing over one's hand, or the sound a tin can makes when we kick it? I don't think so. How much more difficult it is, then, to speak chthonic experiences of the deep-down nature of things, the very heart of being itself. Words always fall short when we want them to express the fierceness of love, the tenderness of compassion, the *frisson* of beauty or terror, and the mysteriously dark radiance of God.

These kinds of experiences can only be gestured at in language that mirrors their very elusiveness and that generously allows for silent spaces between the words and perhaps even within the words themselves.

This means that poetry is perhaps the most appropriate way to express profound and essentially unspeakable experiences.

Dante is fully aware of both the limits of language and the unique ability of poetry to transgress, even if only minimally, those limits. So at the very beginning of the Paradiso he frankly acknowledges how difficult it will be to put words to the transcendent experience of God. I don't think this is false modesty on his part, nor do I believe that he's simply making an aesthetic judgment. His thirty-three Paradiso cantos surely suggest that Dante himself had a transformative but essentially inexpressible personal experience of reality's depth.

The Inferno and the Purgatorio were written in real time. Dante the pilgrim describes to us his experiences as he undergoes them. But the Paradiso is retrospective, a product of memory—

> "*In that heaven which most receiveth of his light,*
>   *Have I been*"

—an indication that the experience is simply too overwhelming to utter as it actually happens, and can only be clumsily expressed afterward. And yet language is the house of being. So we must do the best we can, even if only with "shadows."

Paradise, Canto 1, Part 2: The Truth Behind "You Shall Be Like Gods!"

Beatrice was standing.

Gazing on her such I became within,
   As was Glaucus, tasting of the grass that made him
   The sea-fellow of the other gods.

To pass beyond humanity may not be told in words,
   Wherefore let the example satisfy him
   For whom grace reserveth the experience.

Convincing lies gesture at but subtly distort truth. Such was the promise made by the tempter to the primordial couple when he seduced them into snatching fruit from the Tree of the Knowledge of Good and Evil. "Don't hesitate," he purred. "You've nothing to fear. Eating it, you'll grow into what you're destined to be. You shall be like gods!" (Gen 3:5).

The lie, of course, is that it's okay to claim as our own what's way outside our wheelhouse. It's not surprising that the lie was so compelling. Like all creatures, we have a deep-down longing, stamped into our DNA, to become the best we can be. That longing is what the tempter exploited.

Dante feels himself beginning to change simply by gazing upon Beatrice's beatitudinal face. He compares the experience to that of the mythical Glaucus.

A fisherman, Glaucus, ate a magical herb which transformed him into an immortal merman. In his *Metamorphosis*, Ovid has Glaucus tell us what happened:

> I casually plucked a couple of blades and stated to chew them.
> I'd barely swallowed the unfamiliar juices down,
> when I suddenly felt a powerful flutter inside my heart.
> The sea-gods received me and judged me worthy of joining
>   their number.[2]

Trashumanar is the Italian word Dante the pilgrim uses to describe the change he feels happening to him, rendered here as "to pass beyond humanity," as Glaucus did. But in the context of the Paradiso, I think this is misleading. Dante isn't experiencing a change that will take him

---

2. Ovid, *Metamorphosis*, 544.

beyond or away from humanness. On the contrary, it will propel him ever deeper into it.

In Christian theology, this is a process known as theosis or divinization: a transformation, effected by grace, that brings to fruition the God-like potential embedded in humans by virtue of the fact that we're created in God's own image. Each human is an *imago Dei*, the sort of creature who possesses God-like qualities. To embrace and live those qualities is to become fully human. It's the blessed state God intended for us in creating us. As St. Irenaeus famously said, the glory of God is a fully alive human,[3] and a fully alive human is one who glows with God-like qualities of love, compassion, wisdom, and patience.

Our primordial ancestors in Eden failed to appreciate this "original blessing." Generation after generation, we do likewise. In our fallen and confused arrogance, we strive to be gods, to usurp God's place, instead of embracing our God-likeness. That's a huge difference, isn't it? The former is a replication, manifesting in any number of pernicious ways, of the sin that closed the earthly paradise to us and drove us into exile in the first place. The latter is a grateful acceptance of our human destiny.

Dante the pilgrim feels the first stirrings of theosis. But it's faint, at this point merely an echo of the divine grace that dwells in and radiates from Beatrice. As she guides him closer and closer to God, the transformation will become more evident.

Paradiso, Canto I, Part 3: The Great Gravitation

Beatrice speaks:

> "Thou art not upon earth, as thou believest;
> But lightning, fleeing its proper site,
> Ne'er darted as dost thou who are returning thither.
>
> All things incline, by diverse lots,
> More near or less unto their principle;
>
> Wherefore they move to diverse ports
> O'er the great sea of being; and each one
> With instinct give it to bear it on.

---

3. Irenaeus, *Against Heresies*, 369. Irenaeus's Latin literally reads "the glory of God is a living man." But in context, "fully alive" is an appropriate (and standard) rendering.

> *And thither now, as to the appointed site,*
> *The power of the bowstring beareth us which directeth*
> *To a joyful mark whatso it doth discharge."*

The Middle Ages accepted a metaphysics often dubbed the "great chain of being." This model maintained that the universe is hierarchical (or chain-like) in structure, with God at the top of the chain and all created beings (or links) in descending order beneath Him.[4]

Each category of creature is positioned on the hierarchical chain in proportion to its resemblance to God. So, for example, angels are the descending link closest to God, followed by humans, then mammals, then reptiles, then invertebrates, then microcosms, then inanimate objects.

The chain ensures that creation remains orderly and hence stable. Every creature or link in the chain is connected to all the others and, ultimately, to God. Each is valuable in its own way. Each knows its designated place in the grand scheme of things.

The "great chain of being" model maintains stability, but at the expense of dynamism. It offers, after all, a rather static picture of reality which seems to deny the flow we sense all around us. So Dante the poet livens things up by replacing the chain metaphor with an alternative one borrowed from Aristotle.

Let's call it the "great gravitation" model.

Beatrice introduces the great gravitation model when Dante the pilgrim expresses perplexity at his experience of ascending from earth. (This is the beginning of his transhumanization discussed in the previous reflection.) Beatrice explains that all creatures, animate as well as inanimate, gravitate, by virtue of their natures, to their proper places or "ports" in reality. Stones fall downward, fire rises upward, and so on.

The appropriate port of call for humans, who alone of all creatures are made in God's image and who thereby possess God-like qualities of virtue and intellect, is paradise. This is the source of our specific gravitational pull, and this is why Dante the pilgrim, whose will and intellect have been purified, is ascending.

According to the great gravitation model, then, the universe is a kind of centripetal/centrifugal dynamism that holds all creatures in a vibrant equilibrium. This accounts for stability and orderliness without slipping into a "great chain of being" stasis, which freezes the universe and contradicts everyday experience.

---

4. See Lovejoy, *Great Chain*, chapter 2.

But if everything naturally gravitates to its appropriate port, Dante wonders, why do some humans seem heavily earthbound? Why do they not ascend to paradise? Beatrice and St. Augustine have a few things to say about this.

Paradise, Canto 1, Part 4: Spent Arrows, Cavitied Marble

> *True is it, that as the form often*
> *Accordeth not with the intention of the art,*
> *Because that the material is due to answer,*
>
> *So from this course sometimes departeth*
> *The creature that hath power, thus thrust,*
> *To swerve toward some other part,*
>
> *(Even as fire may be seen to dart*
> *From the cloud), if its first rush may*
> *Be wrenched aside to earth by false seeming pleasure.*

A foolish consistency, as Ralph Waldo Emerson wisely remarked, is the hobgoblin of little minds[5]—and, I might add, of narrow imaginations. Dante the poet's imagination is as expansive as the heavens, and he doesn't at all mind mixing his metaphors to get across a point.

In the previous reflection we heard him compare the ascent to God to the flight of a properly aimed arrow. He continues that image today in the middle tercet quoted above when he observes that arrows can also "swerve toward some other part."

But in the immediately preceding tercet, he uses a different metaphor. Sometimes what an artist intends to do ends up badly because the material she works with is unworthy. Even a Michelangelo can't sculpt a David if the chunk of marble he chisels is shot through with cavities and imperfections and "accordeth not" with the artist's intention or the form that lies within it.

With these two images, Beatrice answers the question Dante the pilgrim asked: If we humans have a natural gravitational pull toward God, why do some of us remain earthbound? It's because our wayward desires swerve us away from hitting the happy mark. It's because we've allowed

---

5. Emerson, "Self-Reliance," 263.

our original innocence to become so out of accord with righteousness that God the Sculptor—as that Renaissance gossip Vasari famously said, God is the first Artisan[6]—can't do anything with us.

Fire, because of its specific gravitational pull, should move physically upward. But occasionally it falls to earth in the form of lightning. Similarly, we creatures made in God's image should spiritually ascend toward our Source, the Original Archer, the Primal Artisan. But like spent arrows or inferior marble, we can, through our own faults, miss the mark or fall far short of the Artist's intention.

Paradise, Canto II, Part 1: Navigational Prelude

The water which I take was never coursed before;

Ye other few, who timely have lift up your necks
 For bread of angels whereby life is here sustained,
 But wherefrom none cometh away sated,

Ye may indeed commit your vessel to the deep
 Keeping my furrow.

In 1961, Russian cosmonaut Yuri Gagarin became the first person to launch into space in his own vessel. When he returned to earth, he's supposed to have remarked: "I looked, and looked, and looked, but I didn't see God."

There's some debate as to whether Gagarin actually said this or whether the officially atheist Soviet state put the words in his mouth. But the point either he or some apparatchik wanted to get across is obvious. The old way of thinking about God and paradise as "up there" is implausible to the modern mind. You won't find either by zooming up into the sky. To think otherwise is simply a throwback to pre-modern mythology.

If we adopt this (rather smugly superior) position, we might be tempted to dismiss the whole of Dante's *Paradiso* because, in keeping with both the theology and the cosmology of his day, he certainly does depict God and paradise as "up there." But I think this would be a sad mistake.

We oughtn't to let our disagreement with the "up there" architecture of Dante's heaven prevent us from appreciating the spiritual and moral

6 Vasari, *Lives*, 3–4.

insight—not to mention the sheer aesthetic beauty—of the Paradiso. So we would do well to allow our own vessels to sail the heavenly ocean in his wake.

It's helpful to have an orienting overview of the lay of his heavenly land. So, in quick order, here it is. Heaven is composed of nine concentric spheres, like transparent glass balls revolving inside one another. The first eight correspond to the sun, moon, and planets known during Dante's lifetime. (He often indiscriminately refers to all heavenly bodies as stars.) Each of these spheres has an "intelligence" or order of angels associated with it. Each of them also represents a virtue.

Above the revolving spheres lies the empyrean, the beyond-space-and-time realm of God. Godward-bound souls pass through all the spheres on their way to heaven.

Now, if this all seems quaintly arcane, let me assure you that Dante's description of a terraced heaven (a structure, by the way, that parallels the downward terracing of hell and the upward terracing of purgatory) offers a fascinating—and, to my mind, entirely plausible—explanation of the divine overflow that percolates throughout all of reality.

Paradise, Canto II, Part 2: God-Fountain, Divine Trickle-Down

> *The heaven, which so many lights make beautiful,*
> *From the deep mind which rolleth it,*
> *Taketh the image and thereof maketh the seal.*
>
> *And as the soul within your dust, through members*
> *Differing and conformed to divers powers*
> *Doth diffuse itself,*
>
> *So doth the Intelligence deploy its goodness,*
> *Multiplied through the stars,*
> *Revolving still on its unity.*

It's no secret that Aristotle, Thomas Aquinas, and Ptolemy are big players in Dante the poet's model of the universe. Their influence is everywhere in the Paradiso, which is one of the reasons it makes for such fascinating reading. But there's another key player too: the third-century pagan philosopher Plotinus, whom I've already mentioned.

We especially see his mark here, in Canto II.

Plotinus is famous for his claim that the "One"—the undefinable and essentially indescribable Source of everything that is—overflows Itself, much like a fountain sprays up and outward. In doing so, It gives rise to Intelligence or Nous, the principle of intelligibility, which in turn creates the multiplicity of objects and relations that comprise the universe.[7]

Think of a champagne fountain, in which the single topmost glass overflows to fill the multiple second tier, which in turn overflows to fill the even larger third tier, and so on.

What this means is that everything that exists carries within it traces of both the One and Intelligence. The originating power of the One animates all that is; the organizing power of Intelligence instills order and symmetry.

Now, in Canto II, Beatrice and Dante have zoomed up to the first heavenly sphere, the one that contains the moon. Dante is curious about why there are light and dark spots on the moon, and in the process of explaining the phenomenon, Beatrice offers an overflow model of creation that is very Plotinian indeed.

Her description of the ninth sphere, the one closest to the empyrean, is evocative of Plotinus's Intelligence. It takes its stamp, she says, from the "deep mind"—God (a.k.a. Plotinus's One)—which created it, and then "the Intelligence deploy[s] its goodness" throughout all the lower spheres and finally onto earth itself. This diffuse trickle-down of what we might call God-particles or sparks of divinity permeates all of reality, just as the soul permeates the "living dust" of the body.

There is, in other words, no place in creation where God is not present. The divine overflow is always and everywhere. And what that means is that there is no place, and no moment, and no experience that isn't extraordinary if seen in proper perspective.

Paradise, Canto III: Of Moons and Fingers

> *"I am Piccarda, who placed here with these*
> *Other blessed ones, am blessed*
> *In the sphere that moveth slowest.*

---

7. Plotinus, *Enneads*. The fifth and sixth Enneads are especially pertinent to Plotinus's understanding of the One.

> *Did we desire to be more aloft,*
> *Our longings were discordant from*
> *His will who here assorteth us.*
>
> *Nay, 'tis the essence of this blessed being*
> *To hold ourselves within the divine will, whereby*
> *Our own wills are themselves made one.*
>
> *And his will is our peace."*
>
> *Clear was it then to me how everywhere*
> *In heaven is Paradise.*

The fourteenth-century St. Catherine of Siena is famous for supposedly saying that "all the way to heaven is heaven."

Although one of the most influential women of her generation, Catherine was almost certainly illiterate. So she couldn't have read Dante's *Comedy* on her own. However, she must have been familiar with it—who wasn't in the generation following Dante's death!—probably having heard it read aloud, because her claim that all the way to heaven is heaven sounds a lot like Dante the poet's observation that the nine spheres of heaven are all paradise.

As we saw in the previous canto, he and Beatrice are in the innermost "moon" sphere in the concentric architecture of the heavens, closest to earth and farthest from the empyrean (and hence the "slowest" in its orbit). They encounter there souls that are so pale that at first Dante takes them for reflections. One of them is Piccarda, in life a nun who was forced to break her religious vows by marrying.

Through her, he discovers that in each of the spheres he'll encounter souls who have fallen short, in varying degrees, of achieving full rectitude. They're all blessed, but not equally so.

(In Canto IV we'll discover that things are much more complicated than this. But for now, let's follow Dante the poet's lead.)

Dante, a typical go-getting human who thinks it's only natural always to want more, asks Piccarda, "Are you desirous of a higher place?"

She replies, paraphrasing Ephesians 2:14, "His will is our peace."

What's the message here?

To be outside of paradise is to be alienated from God, and alienation is always a consequence of refusing to conform to God's will. The inferno is populated by souls who persisted in defiant nonconformity, and purgatory houses those who conformed eventually but still have a residue of alienation to work through.

In our day and age, "conformity" has a bad ring to it. We associate it with mindlessly following the crowd or servilely obeying orders: in either case, an abdication of personal responsibility and a foolish relinquishment of free will.

Now, in many cases, all of this is quite true. But conforming one's will to divine will isn't one of them. In fact, it's totally different. It brings a state of absolute freedom rather than bondage, because God always and everywhere lovingly wills for us what is in our genuine best interest.

To alienate ourselves from that will is to run in the opposite direction, into the darkness of self- and other-harm. To align oneself with divine will is to embrace the fullness God desires for us.

All souls in each of the heavenly spheres have aligned themselves with the Creator's loving will, and hence are perfectly satisfied (and rightly so) with where they are. Because they have conformed their will to God's, every sphere of heaven is for them paradise.

And this, I think, is what St. Catherine of Siena must have meant as well. We approach ever closer to God by progressively aligning our will to God's as we go through life. Such alignment or conformity is both the method and the goal. To invoke a Buddhist image, it's both the finger pointing at the moon and the moon at which the finger points.

Paradise, Canto IV, Part 1: This? Or That?

These spirits who but now appeared to thee

Have sweet life, with difference,
  By feeling more or less the eternal breath.

They have here revealed themselves, not that
  This sphere was given to them, but to make sign
  Of the celestial one that hath the least ascent.

Needs must such speech address your faculty,
  Which only from the sense-reported thing doth apprehend,
  What it then proceedeth to make fit matter for the intellect.

> *And therefore doth the Scripture condescend*
> *To your capacity, assigning foot and hand*
> *To God, with other meaning.*

> *And Holy Church doth represent to you with human*
> *Aspect Gabriel and Michael, and him too*
> *Who made Tobit sound again.*

When it comes to thinking and talking about God, we humans are stuck between a rock and a hard place.

Our knowledge in general originates with sense experience, and so our thoughts and language are most comfortable with concrete particulars. That's why we typically resort to symbols and metaphors in our God-talk. As Beatrice tells Dante the pilgrim, we ascribe hands and feet to God or human features (not to mention names!) to angels like Gabriel, Michael, and Raphael ("him who made Tobit sound again"). If we're not real careful, we fall into the error of taking these concrete descriptions literally.

That's the rock.

But if we try to avoid the rock by banishing all symbols and metaphors from our God-talk and God-thought, we run the risk of God becoming a distant, aloof, and unapproachable abstraction: the "God of the philosophers," as Pascal said after his mystical experience, not "the God of Abraham, Isaac, and Jacob."[8]

That's the hard place.

Beatrice gestures at the rock-and-hard-place conundrum in this canto when she explains that the souls in the moon sphere Dante the pilgrim sees are concessions to his mortal way of observing reality. They, like all other souls in paradise, dwell in the empyrean with God. But as a sign of the different degrees of blessedness among the souls in paradise, a sign that Dante is capable of absorbing, they appear to him scattered throughout the heavenly spheres.

It's not clear if the souls are bilocational (and why not, since they're spirit?) or if Dante is seeing simulacra. I suspect the former. But the takeaway here is that while we are mortal and have minds that apprehend primarily from sense perception, we will need to navigate between rocks and hard places when it comes to God.

---

8. Pascal, *Pensées*, 309.

Paradise, Canto IV, Part 2: Real-World Messiness

Beatrice speaks:

> *"If the will willeth not, it cannot be crushed.*
>
> *Should it bend itself, or much or little,*
>   *It doth abet the force.*
>
> *But such sound will is all too rare."*

If we're forced to do something against our will that we know to be wrong, how could anyone possibly hold us morally responsible? We had no choice, right?

This is the question at stake in the second half of Canto IV. It's sparked by the fact that two one-time nuns, Piccarda and Constance, although in paradise, are less than fully blessed because in life they allowed themselves to be forcibly removed from the cloister. But this sticks in Dante's craw. How is this their fault? Where's the divine justice in penalizing them?

I have to say that I find Beatrice's answer less than satisfying. She draws a distinction between absolute and conditional will. Absolute will is that innate impulse within us to act in conformity with God's will regardless of the circumstances. Conditional will is driven by circumstances.

When Piccarda and Constance allowed themselves to be removed from the cloister, their conditional will assented to avoid what they took to be a greater evil—perhaps bodily harm or even death—that might befall them if they resisted. But they could've chosen to follow absolute will by refusing to abandon their cloister regardless of the consequences of doing so. If will is firm or absolute, says Beatrice, it cannot be "crushed" by force or threat of force. Like fire, it will always rise.

Okay. In theory, I get what Beatrice is saying. Ideally, I agree with her. But surely, given the messiness of the real world, things are more complicated than this. Put yourself, for example, in the dilemma William Styron poses in his novel *Sophie's Choice*. If a wicked person forces you to choose which of your two children will live and which will die, how does holding fast to absolute will help? Absolute will, as Beatrice says, can never be forced to consent to wrong. But I don't even know what that means in a dreadful situation like this. Choosing one child over the other—conditional will—is both forced and horrible. Yet if I refuse to choose—if I hold firm to absolute will and refuse to do wrong—both children die.

How can sacrificing the good for the sake of the perfect, especially when the sacrifice is so unspeakable, really be what God wants from us?

So it seems rather harsh (to me, at any rate) that Piccarda and Constance are consigned to a lesser degree of blessedness in paradise because they weren't letter perfect when it comes to acts of will. Such resolve, as Beatrice admits, "is all too rare." And honestly, I think that's probably a good thing in some situations.

Paradise, Canto V: The Worst Kind of Promise-Breaking

Beatrice speaks:

> *"The greatest gift of God of his largess*
> *Made at the creation, and the most conform to*
> *His own excellence, and which he most prizeth,*
>
> *Was the will's liberty, wherewith creatures*
> *Intelligent, both all and only,*
> *Were and are endowed.*
>
> *Ye Christians, be more sedate in moving,*
> *Not unlike a feather unto every wind;*
> *Nor think that every water cleanseth you."*

Have you ever made a promise to God that you subsequently reneged on?

Often the promise is a conditional, a contractual quid pro quo sort of thing: "God, help me out in this scrape and I promise that I'll _____." But once the immediate crisis is over, thanks to God's quo, we tend to forget our quid, don't we? We assure ourselves that our super-generous God won't really hold us to our promise. After all, it was made under duress!

This is an egregious enough example of bad faith. Even worse is when we break a solemn vow made to God, one that isn't a garden variety quid pro quo promise. Think of priests who, after taking vows of chastity, are implicated in sexual scandals or chiefs of state who, after swearing an oath (on the Bible, no less!) to uphold the constitution, proceed to undermine it.

In Canto IV, we met the souls of two nuns, Piccarda and Constance, who broke their religious vows by agreeing to marry, even though they were coerced into doing so. As a consequence, they enjoy a state of lesser blessedness in paradise. Dante thinks this is a bit unjust, and wonders if their promise-breaking couldn't be washed clean in some way, perhaps by the doing of good deeds.

But here, in Canto V, Beatrice sets him straight. Whenever we make a promise to God, we vow to serve God: "I promise/vow, Lord, to do this for you." This is our sacrifice, our burnt offering, to Him. The nature of that sacrifice should be worthy of its recipient. To offer less is indecent.

Now, the greatest gift God bestows upon us, "the most conformed to his own excellence," is freedom of the will. So in making a promise or vow to God, we return to God this greatest of all gifts. We will that our will be in His service. As Beatrice says, our free will wills itself over to God.

If I say to God, "I promise that I'll spend an hour each day in prayer to you," the promised act (an hour of prayer) can be changed under certain conditions (for example, I might substitute two hours of service to the poor). But the solemn nature of the pact, my gifting God with my will, cannot be annulled, only fulfilled or not.

If we subsequently break that promise or vow, we transgress in at least two ways: first, by reneging on the promise (infidelity); second, by using our free will, which properly is no longer ours because we gifted it to God, to seize back the gift (theft). How can one possibly cover over this double offense with good deeds?

No wonder that Beatrice warns Dante, and us, to beware of rushing into vows. And yet, bizarrely, I suspect that the failure to take seriously our promises or vows to God, either those made on the spur of the moment (the quid pro quo types) or the ones that are formally solemnized (ordination, presidential oaths, and so on) is legion.

Paradise, Canto VI and Canto VII, Part 1: Both A and not-A Are True. Huh?!

> *It ran with Titus to wreak vengeance*
> *On the vengeance on the ancient sin.* (Canto VI)

> "*How vengeance justly was avenged,*
> *Hath set the pondering.*" (Canto VII)

How can vengeance ever be justified? Vengeance, as opposed to justice, is typically viewed as an extralegal, personal act of getting even—or, worse, responding to a perceived indignity with a disproportionately blitzkrieg-like response. So how can vengeance be just?

In Canto VI, a yawningly tedious discourse delivered by the soul of the Emperor Justinian on the history of the Roman Empire, we're told that one of his imperial predecessors, the third emperor, Titus, "wreak[ed] vengeance / On the vengeance on the ancient sin." The implication is that Justinian is referring to Titus's sacking of Jerusalem in AD 70.

Dante is clearly confused by this, but it's not until Canto VII that Beatrice explains.

Adam, the man who knew no birth, sinned, and in damning himself, damned all his progeny. God, moved by unselfish Love, joined Himself to human nature in the incarnation in order to infuse and rejuvenate humanity with its original innocence, thereby removing the stain of the ancient sin.

But for justice to be satisfied, a retribution—or what's translated here as "vengeance"—for Adam's/humanity's transgression was necessary. Therefore, the crucifixion of the New Adam, who represented humanity, was just.

But—and it's a big but—it was also unjust, because the man Jesus was innocent of sin, even though he took the retribution deserved by sin on his shoulders. (Not to mention that his execution was an unimaginable affront to his divine nature.) So Jesus's ignominious death was a crime that itself justly called for vengeance or retribution. Moreover, the Jewish collaborators with Rome who clamored for Jesus's execution had less than pure motives. Consequently, God used Titus's destruction of Jerusalem to exact just retribution or vengeance.

This is all rather Byzantine, isn't it? By invoking the penal substitution understanding of the atonement, Dante has no choice but to see the crucifixion as both just and unjust. Then, his hands tied by his own logic, he has to go the extra mile of claiming the destruction of Jerusalem as just retribution for the just/unjust crucifixion.

In Canto VI, in the midst of his long-winded discourse, Justinian remarks that all contradictions are both true and false. In simple Aristotelian logic, if someone asserts A and not-A, one assertion must be true and the other must be false. A and not-A cannot both be true. Clear enough. Beatrice's explanation of Titus's just vengeance against a just vengeance is more of a paradox than a contradiction, however, because both terms in the situation are simultaneously true: the crucifixion of Jesus was just and the crucifixion of Jesus was unjust. A and not-A are equally true.

It's the case that the penal substitution model of atonement is one accepted by many evangelical Christians today. But it's not the only game in town by any means. It's precisely because of the theological and moral knots it generates that many Christians, including myself, have trouble with it.

Although Dante the pilgrim accepts it, he's still a bit uneasy with it. So, he expresses his concern by asking Beatrice why the crucifixion was even necessary to begin with. Her response is what we'll look at next.

Paradise, Canto VII, Part 2: "Grace is everywhere"

Beatrice speaks:

> "All these points of vantage hath
>   The human creature, and should one fail,
>   Needs must it fall from its nobility.
>
> Sin only is the thing that doth disfranchise it,
>   And maketh it unlike to the highest good.
>
> Your nature when it sinned in its totality
>   In its first seed,
>
> Had not power, within its own boundaries,
>   Ever to render satisfaction.
>
> Wherefore needs must God with his own ways
>   Reinstate man in his unmaimed life.
>
> The divine Goodness which doth stamp the world,
>   Deigned to proceed on all his ways
>   To lift you up again."

At the end of his extraordinary novel *Diary of a Country Priest*, Georges Bernanos puts these words in the mouth of his dying priest protagonist: "Everywhere is grace."[9] This is a man who suffers mightily throughout the course of the novel, and thus has every reason to be embittered. Yet with

---

9. Bernanos, *Diary*, 298.

his last breath he affirms the vivifying presence of God in every aspect of life.

The point is that God's loving-kindness, what the Hebrew scriptures call *chesed*, saturates the cosmos. It's the atmosphere we breathe, the sacred water upon which we float.

Although earlier we saw Dante wrestling with the paradox that emerges if one accepts the penal substitution model of atonement—divine justice demands that somebody pay the piper for humanity's sinfulness, and an innocent Jesus is the guy, making his crucifixion both just and unjust—here his gentler awareness that grace is everywhere comes to the fore.

It's a story we all know but really ought to spend a lot more time thinking (and thanking!) about. Because of our own brokenness, we humans are unable to live up to our full potential as creatures made in God's likeness. We just can't muster the juice to bridge the gap between who we are and who we ought to be. Therefore God, who in His loving-kindness desires more than anything else to restore our wholeness, lovingly and willingly comes to us in the person of Jesus.

True, Dante still talks here about the need to make amends. But the emphasis is less on celestial courtroom proceedings and more on grace, the sacrificial self-emptying of God to infuse us with vitality, awaken submerged memories of our dignity, and bring us back to our senses. The love expressed in such an act goes way beyond the penal substitution's bookkeeping emphasis on settling accounts. It's a song of songs in which the divine Lover tenderly, patiently, and yearningly extends a hand to us.

Grace is everywhere indeed!

Paradise, Canto VIII: Memo to Parents

"Ever doth nature, if she find fortune
　　Unharmonious with herself, like any other seed
　　Out of its proper region, make an ill essay.

And if the world down there took heed
　　To the foundation nature layeth, and followed it,
　　It would have satisfaction in its folk.

> *But ye wrench to a religious order*
> *Him born to gird the sword, and make a king*
> *Of him who should be for discourse;*

> *Whereof your track runneth abroad the road."*

Parents can't always be held responsible if their grown-up kids turn out to be scoundrels. There are times when even a loving and wise upbringing can't overcome countervailing influences.

Dante agrees, as must anyone who has even the slightest lived acquaintance with the messiness of the real world. But it raises a difficulty for Dante: In a God-ordered universe, how could this happen? How could good give rise to bad?

In their ascent toward God, Dante and Beatrice have left Mercury, the second heavenly sphere, and zoomed with arrow-swiftness to Venus, the third. There, they encountered the blessed souls of those whose power-wielding on earth stained them without condemning them. Here, they meet the blessed souls whose intemperate amorousness did likewise. The Roman Emperor Justinian was Dante's interlocutor in the second sphere. Charles Martel, heir to the king of Naples, is his guide in this one.

Martel died young, so the throne he would've inherited went to his younger brother Robert. But Robert was an avaricious and reckless man, differing mightily in temperament from his and Martel's father Charles II. How, Dante wonders, is this possible?

Martel explains that divine providence decrees that there be a wide diversity of talents and aptitudes in humankind. One person is born a Solon, another a Xerxes, a third a Melchizedek. Otherwise, the collaboration and complementation necessary for social order would be impossible. So it's divine providence's plan that parents give rise to children possessed of a variety of characteristics, which adds diversity (to use a modern expression) to the gene pool. Were parents to have offspring identical to themselves, "slavish copies of the getters' line," diversity and social order would collapse.

That explains human diversity. But what of the original question about why good parents can have bad children? Dante's answer is that toxic social conditions can twist God-given talents and temperaments into caricatures of themselves, forcing kids into paths ill-suited to their natures. Thus natural-born warriors are forced into the cloister, and natural-born priests into positions of secular authority. The very fact that these sorts of uncongenial couplings occur speaks to the fallenness of humanity.

Paradise, Canto IX: Revolutionary Fire, Dogmatic Ice

> *The Gospel and great Doctors*
> *Are deserted, and only the Decretals are*
> *So studied, as may be seen upon their margins.*
>
> *Thereon the Pope and Cardinals are intent;*
> *Ne'er wend their thoughts to Nazareth,*
> *Where Gabriel spread his wings.*

The Soviet dissident Yevgeny Zamyatin has the honor of authoring the first book banned in the USSR: his 1921 dystopian novel *We*. Fleeing Russia to escape Stalin's wrath, he settled in Paris, where he died in poverty in 1937.

In his youth, Zamyatin had been a Bolshevik true believer. But the increasingly repressive ways in which the regime consolidated power convinced him that something had gone terribly wrong. *We* was his fictional attempt to express his worries. It was only later, in a provocative essay entitled "On Literature, Revolution, Entropy, and Other Matters," that he was able to articulate his thoughts more fully.

Zamyatin argues that there are two forces at work in the universe: the law of revolution and the law of entropy.

The first is explosively fecund. It shakes up the world, burning away the old and desiccated and clearing ground for fresh growth. As he says, "The law of revolution is red, fiery, deadly: but this death means the birth of new life, a new star."[10]

But new stars—revolutions—eventually cool. They, like that which they once supplanted, grow a hard and confining carapace. Creativity and novelty not only diminish but are actively discouraged, seen as threats to the established status quo. "The law of entropy is cold, icy blue, like the icy interplanetary infinities," says Zamyatin.

> Where the flaming, seething sphere (in science, religion, social life, art) cools, the fiery magma becomes coated with dogma— a rigid, ossified, motionless crust. Dogmatization in science, religion, social life, or art is the entropy of thought. What has

10. Zamyatin, "On Literature," 108.

become dogma no longer burns: it only gives off warmth—it is tepid, it is cool. Instead of the Sermon on the Mount, under the scorching sun, to upraised arms and sobbing people, there is drowsy prayer in a magnificent abbey.[11]

Dante the pilgrim, still in the sphere of Venus, is told by one of the blessed souls there that this collapse into entropy is exactly what's happened to the church. The revolutionary explosion of the annunciation, when Gabriel "spread his wings," has been tapped down under a frozen mountain of well-thumbed ("as may be seen upon their margins") volumes of doctrine, dogma, and canon law. Open-hearted and soul-enriching joy has been replaced by squint-eyed and judgmental institutionalism. Holy Scripture gives way to theological hair-splitting. Kneeling to lovingly wash the feet of Jesus mutates into a face-to-the-floor groveling before ecclesial authority. The fire of love cools to an elaborately Byzantine heap of tepid embers.

Yet both Dante and Zamyatin refuse to accept this death-dealing ossification as the final word. For Dante, the Holy Spirit will eventually blow new life into the church by reminding Christians that the institution is but a means, not the end. And for Zamyatin, no amount of entropy can ever completely destroy the possibility of a new revolutionary explosion. Eventually, "a new heresy explodes the crush of dogma and all the edifices of the most enduring stone which have been raised upon it."[12]

Paradise, Canto X, Part 1: Precision Means Plan, and Plan Means Planner

> *Then, reader, raise with me thy sight*
> *To the exalted wheels, directed to that part where*
> *The one movement smiteth on the other;*
>
> *See how thence offbrancheth the oblique circle*
> *That beareth the planets, to satisfy*
> *The world that calleth on them;*
>
> *And were their pathway not inclined,*
> *Much virtue in the heaven were in vain,*
> *And dead were almost every potency on earth;*

---

11. Zamyatin, "On Literature," 108.
12. Zamyatin, "On Literature," 108.

> *And if, from the straight course, or more or less*
> *Remote were the departure, much were lacking*
> *To the cosmic order below and eke above.*

Beatrice and Dante have left the three spheres (the moon, Mercury, and Venus) in earth's shadow and have now shot into the fourth sphere, the sun. In doing so, they've allegorically left the realm of the senses for the realm of the suprasensible, or mind. It's here they encounter the souls of twelve beautiful minds: philosophers and theologians, all lovers of wisdom.

It's appropriate that the canto opens with what's basically a version of the design argument for the existence of God, since the souls in this sphere were preoccupied in life with using reason and faith to demonstrate divine reality.

Dante the poet argues that the universe is so finely tuned that it simply must be the result of a plan, which of course implies the existence of a Planner.

For Dante and his contemporaries, the sensible heavens consist of two wheels, one solar and the other stellar. The first, upon which the sun rides, circles the earth (remember that Dante's cosmos is geocentric) once a day parallel to the equator. The second, on which the planets ride, circles yearly at an oblique angle. The two wheels, which move in opposite directions, intersect twice a year at the equinoxes.

Absent the two wheels' orbital difference, the seasons wouldn't exist. If the solar wheel wasn't oblique, most of earth would be cold, making life difficult if not impossible in vast regions of it. "Much would wanting be." Deviation of but one or two degrees would throw off the entire intricate machinery of the heavens and render "earth's potentialities stillborn."

That this precision should be a matter of chance is, for Dante the poet as well as the philosophers and theologians in the fourth sphere, inconceivable.

Paradise, Canto X, Part 2: Love's Knowledge

> *There, was the fourth household*
> *Of the exalted Father who ever satisfieth it,*
> *Showing how he doth breathe, and how beget.*

In the fourth sphere, the sphere of the illuminating sun, the souls of twelve philosophers and theologians who dwell there also strive to lighten the darkness of human ignorance.

They include those you'd expect to find there—Thomas Aquinas, Albertus Magnus, the Venerable Bede, Dionysius the Areopagite, and Richard of St. Victor—as well as a couple of surprises: King Solomon and, especially, Siger of Brabant, the thirteenth-century philosopher who raised questions about the soul's immortality. (As an undergraduate philosophy major, I was quite taken with this maverick.)

But for all their wisdom, there were some inquiries that defied these philosophers' reason. I'm speaking of the mysteries of faith, knowable through revelation but not understandable from a logical perspective. The chief of these mysteries is the Holy Trinity, which in its essence forever eludes human comprehension.

Or at least it does when we're alive. But Dante suggests that the mysterious Trinity has become transparent to the souls in the fourth sphere. They now know what they only believed when alive. As Dante says, the Father showed them "how he doth breathe" forth the Holy Spirit and "begets" the Son. In short, He shows them the Trinity. And this illumination forever sates them.

I find this fascinating. How is it that a divine mystery suddenly becomes transparent? Surely these twelve wise men haven't become gods themselves. How, then, can they possibly know that which is beyond mortal ken? And it won't do simply to say that God snapped His fingers and it was so. Abracadabra explanations are no explanations at all.

Two thoughts come to mind.

To begin with, the twelve are now pure intellect. This is indicated by the fact that they're in the fourth sphere, the one completely outside of earth's shadow. Earth represents the senses. Even though traces of the Trinity in the world are discernible through the senses, the senses ultimately get in the way of pure intellect. So that obstacle has been removed.

Second, the twelve's intellects have been illuminated by an unimaginable flood of divine love. This love is the ocean in which they swim (or, to follow Dante's description of them, in which they dance). Love provides us with insights that intellect (much less the senses) alone can't pick up. We may know through our intellects/reason *that* God is. But we know *what* God is through love. It's this combination of pure intellect and illuminating love that enables the souls in the fourth sphere finally to know the mystery of the Trinity.

What an exciting prospect!

Paradise, Canto XI, Part 1: Inside God's Head

> *"Even as I glow with its ray,*
> *So, gazing into the Eternal Light, I apprehend*
> *Whence thou dost take occasion for thy thoughts."*

Over and over again in the Paradiso, the souls of the blessed know Dante the pilgrim's thoughts before he utters them. It's as if they're able to read his mind, discerning with lightning-like speed what's in it before he has time to articulate.

The sense of immediacy these episodes convey is in keeping with the shimmering swiftness of paradise. Beatrice and Dante ascend through the heavenly spheres as instantly (to use Dante the poet's own images) as a shot arrow leaves the bow or the mind generates a thought. The souls in paradise dart hither and yon like sparks or gambol in scintillating circles around Beatrice and Dante. They are stunningly vital, alive, awake, alert.

So it's not surprising that Dante the pilgrim's unspoken thoughts and questions are instantaneously intuited by them. But what's the mechanism? How is the exchange possible?

Canto XI is devoted to St. Thomas Aquinas's praise of St. Francis of Assisi and his love affair with Lady Poverty. (More on this soon.) Near the beginning of the canto, however, Thomas "reads" a question in Dante's mind, just as other souls have in earlier Paradiso cantos. But this time, we're offered an explanation of how it's done.

Thomas suggests that he's not telepathically reading Dante's mind. Instead, he's hooked into the mind of God. "Looking into the Eternal Light," he tells Dante, he's able to grasp the pilgrim's thought.

This suggests that it's not simply Dante's thoughts that are in God's consciousness. Everything that happens in the universe, on both the macro and the micro scale, is contained in the "Eternal Light" of the divine mind. In a startling sense, you and I (not to mention the Milky Way, the second law of thermodynamics, Benedict XVI's death, and what a flock of Indiana sparrows ate for breakfast a year ago tomorrow) are ideas in the mind of God. The One contains the many—or, more accurately, the One contains the all.

This is what theologians call the divine attribute of omniscience.

The blessed in paradise are so attuned to God that they're able to "read" God's omniscient mind, or at least do so in part. Dante wisely reminds us just three tercets later that

> "The providence which governeth the world,
>   With counsel wherein every creature's gaze must stay,
>   Defeated, e'er it reach the bottom."

So actually, then, neither Thomas nor any of the other blessed are plugging directly into Dante's mind. Reflecting as they do the radiant beams of the Divine, they intuit Dante's thoughts because they're contained in the all-knowing God with whom they commune.

To experience through the mind of God, with the proviso that we'll never "reach the bottom": how utterly extraordinary!

Paradise, Canto XI, Part 2: Lady Poverty

> *She, reft of her first husband, a thousand and*
>   *A hundred years and more, despised, obscure,*
>   *Even till him stood without invitation*
>
> *And nought availed her the report that she was found*
>   *Unterrified together with Amyclas, when sounded that*
>   *Man's voice, who struck all the world with terror;*
>
> *And nought availed her to have been so constant and*
>   *Undaunted, that she, when Mary stayed below,*
>   *Mounted the cross with Christ.*

I think these three tercets are some of the most exquisite Dante the poet gives us in the entire *Comedy*.

St. Thomas Aquinas delivers them. His subject is how St. Francis of Assisi, *el Poverello*, embraced "Lady Poverty" as an essential aspect of the spirituality he practiced and taught. When Francis wed himself to Lady Poverty, he resolutely stripped away ego and human desire, striving for utter interior emptiness to make room for God. The broken-down abandoned church he rebuilt was, actually, himself.

On the surface, Francis's radical asceticism might come across as harshly world-despising. But it isn't. Anyone who could take such delight in nature and its creatures, a delight he immortalized in his Canticle of the Sun, is seriously in love with God and God's creation.

The quest for absolute receptivity to God via rigorous spiritual and material poverty is too daunting for most of us. We prefer less extreme measures, thank you very much. That's why Lady Poverty, says

St. Thomas, has been "alone" since she joined her first Lover on the cross until her marriage to St. Francis. The use of words like "reft" and "nought" is haunting, isn't it? In using them to describe both Lady Poverty and Mary at the foot of the cross, Dante really does get across a forlorn sense of abandonment.

The one interlude during those eleven centuries in which Lady Poverty had companionship was with the Roman fisherman Amyclas, a character in Lucan's *Pharsalia*. Amyclas lives in contented poverty by the Adriatic:

> "O! happy life
> That poverty affords! great gift of heaven
> Too little understood!"[13]

During the bloody feud between Pompey and Julius Caesar, the latter, whose "voice had the power to terrify the world," shows up at the door of Amyclas's humble hut demanding to be rowed across the straits. He promises Amyclas all kinds of riches as payment. But Amyclas is totally unimpressed. His love of Lady Poverty is too enduring for him to be tempted by wealth or cowed by power.

(By the way, Dante's chronology is obviously off here, since the Pompey/Caesar conflict occurred before the birth of Christ. But let's not quibble. Dante is a poet, and as such has license the historian doesn't.)

Paradise, Canto XII: We Rise and We Fall—and We Rise Again

> *Christ's army, which it cost so dear to re-equip,*
> *Was following the standard,*
> *Laggard, fearsome and thin-ranked;*
>
> *When the Emperor who ever reigneth*
>
> *Came to the succor of his spouse*
> *With two companions, at whose doing, at whose saying,*
> *The straggling squadron gathered itself again.*

I'm not fond of martial imagery when it's applied to Christ and Christ's church. God knows that Christians too often have played the *Gott mit uns*

---

13. Lucan, *Pharsalia*, 143.

card to justify violence. I suppose that, at best, such imagery is invoked as an alternative to death-dealing armies. God's "army," as opposed to those bristling with life-destroying missiles, single-mindedly wields the more powerful life-giving "weapons" of love and compassion. But I'm still uncomfortable with such language.

Dante apparently isn't. In Canto XII he uses military images to describe the influence of the two most important European Christians of the twelfth century: Saints Francis and Dominic. The mendicant orders they founded helped reform the sadly corrupted church, the divine Emperor's "spouse," by reuniting the scattered and tardy company of Christ-followers. Between them, these two saints ignited one of those fiery revolutions that the Russian author Yevgeny Zamyatin insisted were essential to breathing new life into moribundly worn-out institutions. (See my reflection on Paradise IX.)

In a clever twist, Dante the poet has the Dominican St. Thomas Aquinas describe St. Francis and the movement he launched (Canto XI) and now, in Canto XII, has the Franciscan St. Bonaventure do the same for St. Dominic.

The scene is spectacular: two shimmering, gamboling concentric rings of saints surround Beatrice and Dante the pilgrim. The inner ring is made up of the souls of learned teachers; it represents knowledge. In the outer ring dance the souls known for their great love. The symbolism suggests that for Dante the poet, knowledge precedes love. We can love only that which we first know to be lovable.

But back to Zamyatin. He warned, you'll remember, that all institutions born of fiery revolution are threatened by the icy spread of spiritual entropy. The two twelfth-century mendicant orders that infused spiritual vitality back into the church are no exceptions. In Cantos X and XI, St. Thomas Aquinas blasts his fellow Dominicans for losing their way. The flock, he says, has grown greedy and fat.

For his part, Bonaventure is equally harsh in Canto XII with his fellow Franciscans, who have fallen away from the teachings of their order's founder. They are, he laments, walking backward instead of forward.

Entropy is, of course, something to be feared. But it never has the final word. Zamyatin holds out the possibility that new fires will come along to reignite what's grown hard and cold. Richard Rohr, himself a Franciscan, agrees. But he uses a specifically Christian image to make his point: what he calls "the great parabola," a rising-and-falling-and-rising again pattern that's woven into the very fabric of God's creation (it reminds me a bit of Laozi's Tao) and is most dramatically expressed in the death and resurrection of Christ.

This up-and-down-and-up, death-and-rebirth, fire-and-ice-and-fire oscillation is the way things are until the endtime and a reminder that in a God-ordered universe, no fall is ever final. No matter now deeply entropy paralyzes religious orders, churchy institutions, governments and societies, or you and me, *everything rises*. Everything, like the phoenix, is reborn in the purifying flame of the Holy Spirit.

Paradise, Canto XIII: Two Perfect Beings

Were the wax exactly molded, and were
  The heaven in its supremist virtue, the light
  Of the signet would be all apparent;

But nature ever furnisheth it faulty,
  Doing as doth the artist who hath
  The knack of the art and a trembling hand.

Wherefore if the warm Love, if the clear Vision,
  Of the primal Power dispose and stamp,
  Entire perfection is acquired there.

Thus was the clay made worthy
  Once of the full animal perfection;
  And thus the Virgin was impregnated.

Imagine a row of mirrors ranged from highest to lowest in their reflective ability. A brilliant, almost blinding light shines on the first, which in turn reflects it onto the second, the second onto the third, and so on. With each reflection, given the progressively inferior quality of the mirrors, the light's brilliance diminishes. But it never totally disappears, even in the very last mirror in the row.

In Canto XIII, Dante the pilgrim invites us to think of creation in a similar way. God the Father's Absolute Being is reflected in progressively diminishing ways through the nine heavenly spheres and, finally, onto *terra firma*, the final mirror of the analogy. The greater the distance from the Source, the more attenuated the traces of the Source are in the raw material or "wax" that receives it. Nature, as Dante says, is incapable of absorbing the Source's plenitude. Otherwise, all of creation would be identical to the Source. There would be nothing but God.

We saw an earlier version of this metaphysical trickle-down theory of creation in Paradise Canto II. It's one of Dante's fundamental convictions.

So everything created by God is necessarily good, because it originates from a supreme Good, but also imperfect, with two exceptions: the first man, Adam, created from the earth's clay and Jesus, the child conceived by the Holy Spirit and born of the Virgin. In both cases, God infused His light directly without any intermediary or diminution. Thus both Adam and Jesus were creations stamped with perfection in all ways.

They were, in other words, absolutely perfect human beings.

I know that this invites the question of how a perfect human, Adam, could've fallen from perfection. The presumption is that built into perfection is a failsafe that prevents the loss of perfection. Otherwise, it wouldn't really be perfection.

But intriguing as this puzzle is—and it allows for no simplistic solution such as the old standby appeal to free will—Dante's more important point is that both the prelapsarian Adam and Jesus the man serve as role models for the rest of us because they are humanity brought to perfection. Each shows us what it means to be fully human, creatures endowed with reason and imagination and capable of the godlike qualities of love, compassion, and mercy.

Paradise, Canto XIV, Part 1: A Brilliance for Which We Yearn

> *Whenas the garment of the glorified and sainted*
> *Flesh shall be resumed, our person shall be*
> *More acceptable by being all complete.*
>
> *So shall this glow which doth already swathe us,*
> *Be conquered in appearance by the flesh which*
> *Yet and yet the earth o'ercovereth;*
>
> *Nor shall such light have power to baffle us,*
> *For the organs of the body shall be strong*
> *To all that may delight us.*

If Dante's intuition about the endtime is correct, medieval, Renaissance, and modern artistic depictions of Adam have been inaccurate.

But wait: What's the connection between the firsttime and the endtime?!

In Canto XIV, the question on the table is whether disembodied souls who scintillate with the brilliant light of love will be able to endure one another's mega-watt illumination when they are enfleshed again on the day of judgment. How can mortal eyes tolerate such light?

On the surface, the response to the question may seem a bit lame: "the organs of the bodies shall be strong." But I think there's more to it than meets the eye.

According to Christian belief, the souls of the blessed will be reunited with their bodies at the endtime. But they won't be exactly the same bodies; they'll be perfected to match the perfection of the souls that will inhabit them. So it stands to reason that the new eyes will have no trouble taking in the souls' brilliance.

Now, in Canto XIII, we saw that only two perfect humans ever existed: Adam and Jesus. Adam splintered the perfection of humanity through his waywardness, and Jesus restored the possibility of reattaining it through his deep obedience. Consequently, at the endtime, all righteous embodied souls will enjoy the same perfection given to prelapsarian Adam. They'll be what God intended them to be.

They'll glow, Dante tells us, because they'll be saturated in divine love, unblemished by any sin. That brilliance is the sign of human perfection.

It follows that the original Adam, likewise unblemished, must've glowed, a characteristic missed in artistic portraits of him. The firsttime perfect human anticipates endtime perfect humans.

Now, before you harrumph with twenty-first-century derision at what you take to be nothing more than a made-up story, just spare a thought for the deep longing that motivates it.

Whether we're God-believers or not, all of us can sense a fundamental fact about our existence: for all our occasional grandeur, there's something broken in human beings that longs to be whole. We intuit an incompleteness in ourselves, an I-know-not-what something we lack that, once found, would complete us. The firsttime and endtime stories are archetypes of that longing, and Dante's insistence that rejuvenated and perfected humans will radiate brilliance is his way of expressing the state of wholeness for which our hearts pine.

Paradise, Canto XIV, Part 2: "There's many a slip..."

With all my heart, and in that tongue
Which is one unto all, to God I made burnt sacrifice
Such as befitted this new-given grace.

We've all heard the proverbial warning "there's many a slip twixt cup and lip." Dante seems to be gesturing here at the equally evident truth that there's many a slip twixt mind and lip.

Dante and Beatrice find themselves shooting up to the next heavenly sphere, the realm of the planet Mars. When he senses the ascendency, a prayer of thanksgiving in "the tongue which is one unto all" wells up in him.

What is this common vernacular?

To begin exploring that, let me pose a few more questions.

Has a doctor ever asked you to verbalize your pain on a scale of one to ten? Have you ever tried to express in words the sensation of wet water, the taste of a banana, or the sound of an empty tin can being kicked on pavement? Does the simple phrase "I love you" come close to capturing your feelings for the beloved? Can you satisfyingly speak the experiences of intense fear, or orgasm, or profound gratitude, or religious exultation?

These are rhetorical questions, because I think you'll agree with me that the answer to them all is "no." Words are paltry things indeed when it comes to expressing inner states. So we flounder around, doing the best we can by assigning numerical equivalents to pain or using strings of metaphors to express love, emotions, or physical sensations. Yet for all our efforts, we know—don't we?—that our words just don't adequately express what's going on inside us.

There's many a slip twixt mind and lip.

The language common to all that Dante mentions is precisely the spontaneous inner experiences of pain, joy, anxiety, gratitude, fear, dismay, revulsion, attraction, and even (to a certain extent) ideas that are immediately self-evident but lose something in translation when we try to utter them. They shed their vitality and clarity, frequently forcing us to confess, "I know what I feel/think but I just can't put it into words."

After a lifetime of writing, I've come to the conclusion that this "common language" of inner states is never communicable in straightforward description. But I'm okay with that for two reasons. First, because we all have a pretty good idea of the common-language experiences of pain, joy, gratitude, and the wetness of water, and so we can speak meaningfully about them to one another. Second, the very struggle to capture the vitality of inner states generates some of the most exquisite metaphors and similes we humans are capable of. Think, for example, of poet Robbie Burns's "O my luve is like a red red rose." Any of us who've experienced romantic love can appreciate just how much truth is packed into that simple comparison.

So Dante doesn't need to verbalize his inmost prayerful offering. Simply telling us that he experienced it strikes a chord in us because we speak the same inner language.

Paradise, Canto XIV, Part 3: A Misinterpreted Sign?

> *Thus did those rays, star-decked, make*
> *In the depth of Mars the venerable sign which*
> *Crossing quadrant lines make in a circle.*
>
> *From horn to horn, from summit unto base,*
> *Were moving lights that sparkled mightily*
> *In meeting one another and in passing.*
>
> *There came to me, "Rise thou up and conquer!"*

Tradition has it that in AD 312, before the Battle of the Milvian Bridge, which consolidated Constantine's grip on the Roman Empire, a giant cross appeared in the sky as a voice intoned in Latin *in hoc signo vinces*, "in this sign conquer." (The fourth-century historian Eusebius writes that the heavenly voice actually spoke in Greek, but never mind. The point's the same.)

Constantine had banners bearing the sign of the cross, marched into battle with them flying, and defeated his foe Maxentius. This was the beginning both of his conversion and eventual designation of Christianity as the official state religion.

I think the apparition at the Milvian Bridge must be the inspiration for the dramatic scene in Canto XIV in which Dante the pilgrim sees a giant cross in the heavens with souls dancing around it like dust motes in sunlight chanting "Arise" and "Conquer."

Dante and Beatrice are in the fifth sphere of heaven, the sphere of Mars. Mars, of course, is the Roman god of war. So in this sphere, Dante will encounter the souls of holy warriors. His homage to the *in hoc signo vinces* legend is an appropriate prelude.

Whether "holy warrior" is an oxymoron can be legitimately debated. So can whether the Emperor Constantine's official recognition and endorsement of Christianity in the AD 313 Edict of Milan was a good or bad thing.

On the one hand, it had the effect of spreading the faith throughout the Roman Empire. On the other, it stamped the church with both a cumbersome bureaucratic structure and an imperial tone strikingly out of step with the spirit of Jesus. On the most charitable reading, the heavenly assurance of *in hoc signo vinces* was meant to convey that the hearts of humanity could be "conquered" with love. Unfortunately, as we'll see in Canto XV, it's too often been interpreted as a justification for "holy warriors" taking up arms and going into physical combat with the battle cry *Deus vult!*—"God wills it."

Paradise, Canto XV: Narcissus's Folly

> *The benign will, wherein distilleth*
> *Ever the love that hath the right perfume,*
> *As doth, in the grudging will, cupidity.*
>
> *Right is it he should grieve without a limit,*
> *Who, for the love of what endureth not,*
> *Eternally doth strip him of this love.*

When I was a youngster, I was astonished at the frequency with which the Hebrew prophets accused their people of adultery. How randy these ancient folks must have been, I marveled, to earn this constant rebuke!

It was only later that I cottoned on to the fact that adultery in the Hebrew scriptures almost always means idolatry. Idol worship was considered a form of adultery because it's a betrayal of the marriage covenant, the covenant of love, between Yahweh and the Hebrews. To worship an idol is to spurn the true Lover, and to add insult to injury by taking a baser one. It's to abandon a long-term and fulfilling relationship for a glitzy one night stand.

In Canto XV, Dante gestures at the consequences of this betrayal. He says that it substitutes self-seeking love for the open-heartedness characteristic of genuine love. It replaces eternal love for a love that can't endure.

The one-night stand may be exciting while it lasts, but the next morning you wake up hating yourself for what you've foolishly thrown away.

There are plenty of idolatrous candidates—wealth, fame, power, sex, and so on—to whom we pledge an unholy troth. But the Ur-idol, the foundational seducer, is our ego. When we fall into a me-centric way of responding to reality, we worship ourselves. We become our own god.

But I promise you: our egos just don't have enough oomph to substitute for God. So to fall in love with ourselves is to collapse in on ourselves because there's no substance there to uphold us. The possibility of magnanimity, which means "great souled," flies out the window. Because we're already small in comparison to the real God, we become truly desiccated when we betray God for a new lover: ourselves. We become mean souled, grubby, frayed, and whiny, instead of great souled.

Think of the Greek story about Narcissus, the unfortunate youth who so worshiped the reflection of his own image that, unable to tear himself away from it, he starved to death. Think on his fate, and smash the idol of self.

Paradise, Canto XVI: Neither Moth nor Rust

Ah puny blood-nobility of ours!

Verily thou art a mantle that soon shrinketh,
  So that, if day by day there be nought added,
  Time goeth round with the shears!

Your affairs all have their death,
  Even as have ye; but in such an one as long endureth,
  It escapeth note because your lives are short.

We don't know much about Dante the poet's family. Apparently, neither did he, if the scanty remarks about his ancestry he makes in the *Comedy* are any indication. But in the middle cantos of the Paradiso, XV, XVI, and XVII, the central figure is Cacciaguida, Dante's great-great-grandfather, a holy warrior who perished around 1148 in the Second Crusade.

Dante clearly venerates him, and even addresses him with an honorific second-person pronoun typically reserved for the Roman Caesars. For his part, Cacciaguida launches into a recital of once noble but now forgotten Florentine families as well as more recent ignoble ones whose perfidy has ruined the once great city. It makes for tedious reading, even after one realizes that this is Dante the exile's way of giving tongue to his anger and sorrow.

What intrigues me here is Dante the pilgrim's ambivalence both about his pride in his ancestor Cacciaguida and his obsession with the noble lineage. We know from cantos in the Inferno and Purgatorio that Dante considers pride to be his chief sin, and at the beginning of this canto he warns readers that pride in one's bloodline is a risky thing: "time goeth round with the shears" on one's family's reputation. Moreover, even noble families, just like individuals and cities, eventually fade from memory.

But at the same time, he can't help basking in the reflective glory of having Cacciaguida as one of his forebears. His guide Beatrice, who knows him better than he knows himself, gently smiles at his inconsistency. It's as if she has in mind that wonderful passage from Matthew's Gospel about what's truly valuable and what's not:

> Lay not up for yourselves treasures upon earth, where moth and rust doth corrupt, and where thieves break through and steal: But lay up for yourselves treasures in heaven, where neither moth nor rust doth corrupt, and where thieves do not break through nor steal. (6:19–20)

I actually find Dante's inconsistency rather endearing. He's a pilgrim who longs to be a good man, and his long journey has always had as its one goal the beatific vision and personal purity. But he is, after all, but human—remember, Dante the pilgrim is still very much wrapped in the coil of mortal flesh—and so aspects of his old nemesis, pride, peek through even here, in the fifth heavenly sphere. There will come a point in his journey, however, when he fully embraces that which neither moth nor rust, time's shears, doth corrupt. So let's allow him his little inconsistency here, smiling as patiently as Beatrice does.

Paradise, Canto XVII: The Horrible Void of Loneliness

> *Thou shalt abandon everything beloved*
> *Most dearly; this is the arrow which*
> *The bow of exile shall first shoot.*

> *Thou shalt make trial of how salt doth taste*
> *Another's bread, and how hard the path*
> *To descend and mount upon another's stair.*
>
> *And that which most shall weigh thy shoulders down,*
> *Shall be the vicious and ill company with which*
> *Thou shalt fall down into this vale,*
>
> *For all ungrateful, all mad and impious*
> *Shall they become against thee.*

In 1301, midway through his journey of life, Dante was exiled from his beloved Florence. In the two decades remaining to him, he wandered hither and yon, seeking a place to settle, even if only temporarily, relying on the kindness of friends and the forbearance of strangers: "descend[ing] and mount[ing] upon another's stairs." He was heartsick, having lost everything dear to him—family, wealth, reputation—simply because of a shift in the political wind.

These were horribly lonely years, a loneliness that sunk down bone-deep in him. In the middle tercets of this middle canto in Paradiso, quoted above, Dante expresses his loneliness in what I think are some of the most poignant lines in the entire *Comedy*.

Loneliness isn't the same thing as solitude. As the Italian Renaissance humanist Petrarch famously wrote in the mid-fourteenth century, solitude allows us the peacefully serene space to mindfully "delight and sweeten" the soul.[14] Loneliness, however, is a void, a sere and unwelcoming landscape whose emptiness swallows the soul. Every manifestation of loneliness is, in its own way, a forced exile that separates us from what gives our lives meaning and fulfillment.

When I'm surrounded by people on a crowded sidewalk or in a store, I often wonder how many of them in fact are far, far away in the void of loneliness, one-dimensional shadows hollowed out by their bleak alone-ness, flitting through a three-dimensional space.

There are any number of ways to experience the void of loneliness. One that we don't attend to as we should is the loneliness of chronically or terminally ill persons. In his short story "The Death of Ivan Ilych," Tolstoy suggests that these folks are exiled to a land that healthy friends

---

14. Petrarch, *Life of Solitude*, 140.

and family can neither fathom nor follow. They, unlike the rest of us, have been forced to leave behind those things they love most dearly.[15]

The interests and preoccupations of those who still reside in the land of the living—rooting for a favorite sports team, filling the bird feeder, following the latest celebrity gossip, or making sure that socks match—are increasingly unimportant to those exiled to the land of the dying. Everyday chatter to them about such things, well-intended as it is to "take their minds off" their situation, often serves only to make them feel even more isolated and lonely—even more exiled.

And yet they have to bear our company in that sad vale where they now find themselves.

The painful void of loneliness captured in both Tolstoy's story and Dante's tercets is heartbreaking. No wonder Dante the poet has his great-great-grandfather Cacciaguida assure him that his words, "once well digested," will become "a vital nutriment" for future generations. The loneliness of his exile was unfixable during his lifetime. His hope, both pitiful and noble, was that the beauty of his verse would at least offer him fellowship with future generations.

And it has.

Paradise, Canto XVIII, Part 1: Breathed On and Through

> *O goddess Pegasaean, who givest glory unto genius,*
> *And renderest it long life,*
> *As with thy aid doth it to cities and to realms,*
>
> *Make me bright with thyself, that I may throw into relief*
> *Their figures as I have them in conception!*

In the Platonic dialogue *Ion*, Socrates describes poetic inspiration like this: "The poet is a light and winged and holy thing, and there is no invention in him until he has been inspired and is out of his senses, and the mind is no longer in him."[16]

Artistic creativity in general and poetry in particular are instances of what the Greeks called *theia mania* or "divine madness" and the Romans *furor poeticus* or "poetic frenzy." To be inspired—literally, to breathe in

---

15. Tolstoy, *Death of Ivan Ilych*.
16. Plato, *Ion*, 223–24.

(Latin = *inspirare*)—is to be filled by and speak forth the voice of the gods. Cicero, who frequently used the verb *afflatus*, "to blow upon," to describe inspiration, was fond of comparing poets to Aeolian harps.

I love that.

Throughout the entire *Comedy*, Dante has called upon the Muses, the goddesses of creativity who drink from a spring created by the winged horse Pegasus's hoof, for inspiration. That the poet solicits their aid instead of the Holy Spirit's, God's *pneuma* or breath, gestures at both his love of the classical tradition and his commitment to his poetic vocation. In his appeal to the Muse quoted here, he uses the metaphor of light/enlightenment instead of breath. But the general point that inspiration is insight gifted to the poet remains: "let your power show through these few lines of mine!"

The creative process is such a strange and beautiful thing, isn't it? No one doubts that creativity demands a staggering amount of self-discipline, concentration, and hard work on the part of the artist. But artists testify that there comes a point when what they're working on takes on a life of its own. The painting itself guides the hand of the painter. The characters in a novel seize the pen of the author. The slab of marble reveals to the sculptor what's hidden inside it.

It's at those moments that the artist experiences *theia mania* or *furor poeticus*. It's then that Cicero's *afflatus* blows through the studio or onto the keyboard.

I think that all of us are Aeolian harps, creatures initially tuned so expertly and lovingly that we give rise to harmonious and haunting music when the winds of inspiration blow through us. Our music—our poetry—expresses itself in any number of ways, depending on context and temperament. Not all of us can write novels or paint portraits. But all of us can make our lives beautiful works of art.

Still, it can happen that the exigencies of life throw our attunement off kilter, and the divine breath that ceaselessly blows through us gets distorted into discordant sounds. Thankfully, the words of a Dante, the music of a Bach, the painting of a van Gogh, or the sculpture of a Michelangelo can retune the Aeolian harps we are back to perfect pitch. As Dante says, the divine wind that blows through these artistic geniuses is passed on by them to us. The Muses kiss them, and they in turn kiss and awaken us.

Paradise, Canto XVIII, Part 2: Loving Righteousness

> *Diligite justitiam,* were the
> First verb and substantive of all the picturing;
> *Qui judicates terram* were the last.

"Love righteousness, you who judge the earth." This is the opening sentence (1:1) in the apocryphal (and lovely) book of Wisdom, traditionally attributed to King Solomon but actually written a mere generation before the birth of Jesus.

It's also the keynote of the sixth heavenly sphere, associated with the planet Jupiter, to which Dante and Beatrice have ascended. In it, the spark-like souls of the just pirouette to spell out in bold neon letters Wisdom's counsel to rulers. It's a totally cinematic scene. You can see with your mind's eye the fabulous light show Dante describes.

Dante highly regards Solomon. Along with the prophet Nathan, he was the only non-Christian sage Dante the pilgrim met in the fourth heavenly sphere of sunlit wisdom. So it's appropriate that David's successor, the wisest king who ever lived, should offer advice on righteous leadership.

It's interesting. We normally expect political leaders to respect and uphold the laws of the land, but at the same time we tend to be cynical to one degree or another about their honesty and motives. We tolerate a bit of moral slipperiness on their part so long as they get the job done. I've heard many people say, especially in a couple of recent national elections, "I'm voting for a president, not a saint."

But Dante, a man who suffered greatly at the hands of unscrupulous political power holders, is having none of it. He insists that political rulers properly are called to do more than respect the law. They must *love* righteousness. In both their public and private lives, they should disdain to do anything that violates the good. Saintly leadership, to his mind, is a good thing.

We often hear that politics is the art of compromise. That would make sense to Dante up to a certain point. At its best, a willingness to compromise encourages civility, attentive listening to opposing perspectives, humility and generosity, and open dialogue. These, after all, are the qualities of a wise person. But to compromise righteousness—by, for example, trying to justify wicked means by appealing to good ends—is unacceptable. Doing so is a betrayal of righteousness, and true lovers don't betray that which they love.

A final word. The book of Wisdom was originally written in Greek, not Hebrew. The word translated as "righteousness" is *dikaiosuné*. In the Jewish and Christian traditions, *dikaiosuné* always suggests a divine origin. The standards of righteousness or justice are grounded in God. So to love righteousness is to love God, the Author of righteousness. And this in turn means that righteousness, whether exercised by ordinary folks like you and me or powerful leaders of nations, is heavy on love, compassion, patience, mercy, and privileging the oppressed and light on fire-and-brimstone speech, strong-arm tactics, and a moral compass whose true north is expediency.

Paradise, Canto XIX, Part 1: Job Redivivus

> *Thou didst say: "A man is born upon the bank*
> *Of Indus, and there is none to tell of Christ,*
> *Nor none to read, nor none to write;*
>
> *And all his volitions and his deeds*
> *Are good so far as human reason seeth,*
> *Sinless in life or in discourse.*
>
> *He dieth unbaptized and without faith;*
> *Where is that justice which condemneth him?*
> *Where is his fault, in that he not believes?"*
>
> *Now who art thou, who wouldst sit upon the seat*
> *To judge at a thousand miles away with*
> *The short sight that carries but a span?*

The book of Job is one of the most poignant documents in world literature. Through the calamitous misfortunes of its central character, it takes on the unsettling perplexity of innocent suffering. But it offers no real answer to the question of why people suffer through no fault of their own. Instead, the divine "voice from the whirlwind" tells Job that his question is presumptuous, and that neither he nor any human would be able to comprehend the answer anyway.

> Where were you when I laid the earth's foundation?
> Tell me, if you understand.

> Who marked off its dimensions? Surely you know!
> Who stretched a measuring line across it?
> On what were its footings set,
> or who laid its cornerstone—
> while the morning stars sang together
> and all the angels shouted for joy? (Job 38:4–7)

In Canto XIX, Dante raises the specter of Job by questioning God's justice himself. Why, he asks, must virtuous pagans be condemned who, through no fault of their own, have never heard of Christ? This seems blatantly unfair.

This is a question that haunts Dante the poet, steeped as he is in classical literature. Recall that throughout the Inferno and the Purgatorio, his beloved guide is the pagan Virgil who, like so many other non-Christian poets and sages admired by Dante, is stuck in Limbo. He just can't bring himself to imagine them in hell, even though they aren't Christians. Instead, he puts them in a place where they dwell "with desire but no hope"—which, to my mind, may be even worse than the torments of hell.

Justin Martyr, the second-century apologist, could've given Dante a way out, because Justin argued that any virtuous pagan who honored logos, or reason, were "partakers" of Christ, Logos Itself, "even though they may have been thought atheists."[17] Granted, it's not at all clear how far Justin was willing to take this, but he at least implicitly tries to do something about the apparent unfairness of damning people ignorant of Christ.

But Dante refuses to seize the Justinian lifeline. Instead, he adopts a Job-like conclusion (albeit, I think, reluctantly). The ways of Divine Justice are unfathomable to puny human intellects. If sacred scripture and inspired tradition state that there's no way to heaven except through the faith, that's that. End of story. Dante the poet even has Divine Justice rebuke Dante the pilgrim's presumption for worrying about such things. The truth, "hidden by the depth" of existence, is unknowable to humans.

I know. This voice-from-the-whirlwind-toned non-answer is hardly satisfying, and does nothing at all to assuage our nagging suspicion that it's worse than unjust to condemn people who've never even heard of Christianity. What decent person, much less a loving God, would do such a thing? So Divine Justice rather impatiently throws us a bone: since God

---

17. Justin Martyr, *Apologies*, 55.

is "the Good Supreme," anything coming from God is necessarily good, including the dictum that the only way to heaven is through Christ.

Is this a bit of sophistry, or should we take it seriously?

Paradise, Canto XIX, Part 2: Common Decency

> *O animals of earth, minds gross!*
> *The primal Will, good in itself, never departed*
> *From its own self which is the highest good.*

The spark-like souls of the just who inhabit the sixth heavenly sphere have coalesced to shape the form of an eagle, a symbol of Divine Justice. They respond as one to Dante's question: How is it just that those who never heard of Christ should be condemned for not believing in him?

It's a genuine perplexity. The condemnation is troubling from both a logical perspective (how can one be responsible for not believing in something one has no familiarity with?) and a moral one (how is it fair or decent to penalize someone in this situation?).

It reminds me of those once ubiquitous mini comic books written by fundamentalist Jack Chick that spelled out in lurid panel after panel the fate of sinners who failed to accept Christ. True, the victims in these wretched stories weren't ignorant of Christianity. But their condemnation always struck me as wildly disproportionate to anything they may have done or failed to do while alive, just as the fate of Dante's pagans does.

Theologians have long debated something that's traditionally called the Euthyphro dilemma, so named because it was introduced in an eponymous Platonic dialogue. Here it is: Is something good because God says it is, or does God say something is good because it is? If we go with the first option, then it's logically possible that God could one day decide that genocide or betrayal or rape is good and ... Presto! The moral landscape horrifyingly shifts. But if we go with the second option, we must posit that goodness exists independently of God, which suggests that God is subservient to it. This saves the moral landscape but at the cost of making God seem less than God.[18]

---

18. Plato, *Euthyphro*.

My guess is that Dante wanted to avoid getting gored on either horn of this dilemma. So he insisted that whatever God wills is supremely good (and not whimsically unpredictable) because God *is* the Supreme Good.

I can go along with this. But I'd insist on this qualification: Whatever runs counter to our deepest intuitions about common decency can't be willed by God. If we are indeed created in the likeness of God, then surely, deep within our very being, is some implanted awareness of divine will when it comes to the good. If an act immediately strikes us as unfair, it may well be because of that hardwiring, and we should take heed. As Cardinal Newman famously said, conscience is God's voice. It is "the echo of a voice, imperative and constraining, like no other dictate in the whole of our experience."[19]

Of course there's always the possibility that we're allowing self-interest, cultural mores, religious intractability, or psychological hang-ups to cloud our moral sensibilities, and so we should always reflect on our first intuitions to make sure they're reliable. Sometimes coming up with good arguments to bolster our moral intuitions might be difficult. But in some cases, what's decent is glaringly self-evident. The postmortem fate of folks ignorant of the Christian story is one of them.

Paradise, Canto XX: A Riddle Inside a Mystery Wrapped in an Enigma

> *The kingdom of heaven suffereth violence*
> *From warm love and living hope*
> *Which conquereth the divine will;*

> *Not in fashion wherein man subdueth man, but*
> *Conquereth it because it willeth to be conquered, and,*
> *Conquered, with its own benignity doth conquer.*

Dante the poet's dark conclusion in Canto XIX was that pre-Christian pagans ignorant of the faith are out of luck, no matter how virtuous they may have been in life. The best postmortem existence they can expect is in Limbo, an eternal state of desire without hope.

To his credit, Dante's clearly uneasy with this. Why else would he initiate a discussion of it in the sixth heavenly sphere, the one devoted

---

19. Newman, *Grammar of Assent*, 107.

to divine justice? The implication, as we've seen, is that most people have the fundamental intuition that condemnation of pre-Christians is unjust.

Dante the poet tried to navigate his way through these troubled waters by telling us that no act of the divine will can be unjust because God is supremely good. But apparently even he isn't satisfied with that, because he continues to chew on the bone in Canto XX.

Dante the pilgrim sees six of the spark-light souls coalescing to form the eye and eyebrow of the eagle, the emblem of divine justice. Two of the souls belong to Jewish rulers, two to Christians, and—*mirabile dictu!*—two to pagans, one of whom lived before Christ (the Trojan Ripheus) and the other after Christ (the Roman emperor Trajan).

If your reaction to this, especially after Canto XIX, is "What the hell?!" join the crowd. It's also mine. And Dante the pilgrim's as well.

The explanation given him and us is a riddle inside a mystery wrapped in an enigma. God allows the walls of the heavenly kingdom, to be breached by "warm love" and "living hope." (He has in the back of his mind here an equally mysterious saying from Jesus in Matthew 11:12: "From the days of John the Baptist until now the kingdom of heaven has suffered violence, and men of violence take it by force.") But—and it's a crucial qualification—God initiates and allows the conquest. It is God's will that wills its own defeat out of an abundance of love and mercy. So it's not that a mortal's warm love and living hope beat down God's resistance. Rather, God infuses warm love and living hope in humans and then allows Himself to be conquered by them.

This is what happened when it comes to Ripheus and Trajan.

Okay. Good enough. This is a roundabout way of essentially saying that God is willing to break His own rule about the fate of pre-Christian pagans, and that He twists himself in acrobatic knots—*My divine will is that you love Me enough for Me to allow Myself to be conquered by your will!*—to bring this about.

But here's the obvious question: Why doesn't God play this game with all pre-Christian pagans, or post-Christian ones, like Trajan? Why is the rule bent for some but not for others? Why weren't Virgil and his Limbo compatriots included?

Not even the souls of the just can solve this puzzle, for they confess to Dante the pilgrim that

> "Ourselves, who look on God,
> We do not know as yet all the elect."

I suppose, on the one hand, that this canto ought to assure us that God's mercy and love are inexhaustible and, being inexhaustible, can be surprisingly and even shockingly revealed. But on the other hand, the torturous twisting in Cantos XIX and XX to defend a particular understanding of divine justice suggests, to me at least, that the whole thing could use some rethinking.

Paradise, Canto XXI: A Deep, Dazzling Darkness

> *"The divine light doth focus it on me,*
>   *Piercing into that wherein I am embowelled;*
>
> *Uplifting me above myself so far that I perceive*
>   *The supreme essence whence it is milked.*
>
> *But that soul in heaven which is most illuminated,*
>   *That Seraph who hath his eye most fixed on God,*
>   *Hath given no satisfaction to thy question;*
>
> *Because so far within the abyss*
>   *Of the eternal stature lieth the thing thou askest,*
>   *That from all created vision it is cut off."*

You can't help but be struck at how increasingly luminous everything becomes as Dante and Beatrice ascend the heavenly spheres. The souls they've encountered along the way are like fiery sparks dancing about in the wind, and Beatrice's face becomes progressively brighter, so much so that in the seventh sphere of Saturn, where the two have now landed, she tones down her radiance. "Were it not tempered," she tells Dante, he would "be like foliage that the thunder shattereth."

In short, the closer Beatrice and Dante come to the Godhead, the brighter the light.

This makes sense. Light is a symbol for love, truth, and goodness, and God is all three of these. It's not that God possesses them as attributes or qualities. No, they constitute the very essence of God. God as Love opens our hearts, dispelling the darkness of self-centeredness. God as Truth illuminates the darkness of deception and falsehood. God as Goodness radiates grace to replace wickedness with righteousness. So God is Eternal Light, and we are illuminated in proportion to our proximity to God.

And yet, as the soul of Peter Damian tells Dante in this canto, there's something about God that remains forever dark and unknowable, even to the highest rank of angels. The twentieth-century philosopher Alfred North Whitehead called this unfathomable aspect God's "primordial nature."[20] Christian mystics as well as astute theologians beginning with St. Paul acknowledge that God's inner nature is ultimately incomprehensible, and that it's folly, if not perfectly Babelesque, to presume otherwise.

Still, there's something about the divine darkness, in the words of the seventeenth-century poet Henry Vaughan, that is "deep and dazzling."[21] When we catch glimpses of it, much less during those rare moments when we can enter into and be absorbed by it, we emerge with a deeper relationship into the Divine Mystery.

It is a darkness that, paradoxically, enlightens.

The Cloud of Unknowing, that gem of fourteenth-century English mysticism, tells us that there's always a darkness separating us from God.[22] I take this darkness to be the divine unfathomability. But occasionally the darkness is flash-illuminated by grace, just as a bolt of lightning momentarily flashes in the night sky. I used to think that the book's author meant us to focus our attention and efforts on catching the moments of illumination when they occur. But now I believe that we're also meant to appreciate the value of the surrounding darkness, and that the seconds of illumination granted us over a lifetime draw us ever more deeply into the dark but dazzling heart of God.

As Vaughan beautifully puts it in the final stanza of his poem "The Night,"

> There is in God (some say)
> A deep, but dazzling darkness; As men here
> Say it is late and dusky, because they
> See not all clear;
> O for that night ! where I in him
> Might live invisible and dim.[23]

---

20. Whitehead, *Process and Reality*, 343–51.
21. Vaughan, "Night," 199.
22. Anonymous, *Cloud of Unknowing*.
23. Vaughan, "Night," 199.

Paradise, Canto XXII: The Vastness of It All

> With my sight I turned back through all and every of
> The seven spheres, and saw this globe
> Such that I smiled at its sorry semblance;
>
> And that counsel I approve as best
> Which holdeth it for least; and he whose thoughts
> Are turned elsewhere may be called truly upright.

Dante isn't just a spectator in his journey through the three realms of the afterlife. He's a participant who's transformed in and by the journey. In the Inferno, he comes face to face with all the dark recesses in his soul. In the Purgatorio, he's cleansed, terrace by terrace, as he ascends the mount to the earthly paradise. And in the Paradiso, he's imbued with at least a bit of the purity he encounters in the heavenly spheres.

In Canto XXI and most of Canto XXII, he and Beatrice are in the seventh sphere, where the souls of contemplatives like St. Benedict greet him. His proximity to them opens his inner eye so that when at the end of Canto XXII he and Beatrice zoom, swifter than a finger is snatched from a flame, to the eighth sphere, the Realm of the Fixed Stars, he's able to contemplate the vast stretch of creation.

It's a dramatic scene. From his high point, Dante looks down upon the preceding seven spheres, and when he sees his mortal home, the earth, he smiles at what he takes to be its paltriness. This might give the impression that Dante is indulging in the original sin of Christian asceticism, a nay-saying condemnation of the material world that operates as if love of God and love of God's creation is in a zero-sum competition.

But I think something entirely else is going on.

What Dante the pilgrim is experiencing isn't disdain for the earth but awe at the sheer vastness, intricate complexity, and breathtaking beauty of creation. Now that he has a galaxy-eye view of things, he recognizes how telescoped his vision was when, in bygone days, he thought the earth—and not the whole earth, even, but only his tiny portion of it—the end all and be all. This wider appreciation of cosmic splendor doesn't rob earth of its beauty and value. It puts it in perspective.

I think that Dante is experiencing here the contemplative mood of ecstasy or rapture (no, not the rapture made famous by those wretched *Left Behind* novels). Ekstasis (from the Greek *ek* = "out" and *histanai* = "to place") is a state of being removed from the concrete here-and-now context that normally defines who one is so that one's spiritual and moral vision becomes more acute.

We've all experienced this, although perhaps not in the dramatic way described in Canto XXII. A sunset, a storm coming in on the horizon, a piece of music or a bit of verse, a lover's embrace: all of these moments can be ecstatic for us, clueing us in to the wondrous fact that reality is deeper and broader and richer than we normally take it to be. All of them can snatch us out of our tiny worlds by giving us a glimpse of the breathtaking vastness of it all.

Paradise, Canto XXIII, Part 1: Christ-Koan

> *I saw, thousands of lamps surmounting,*
> *One sun which all and each enkindled,*
> *As doth our own the things we see above;*
>
> *And through the living light outglowed*
> *The shining substance so bright upon*
> *My vision that it endured it not.*
>
> *Even as fire is unbarred from the cloud,*
> *Because it so dilateth that it hath not space within,*
> *And counter to its nature dasheth down to earth,*
>
> *So my mind, grown greater 'mid these feasts,*
> *Forth issued from itself, and what it then became*
> *Knoweth not to recall.*

If there's one thing everyone knows about the Zen Buddhist tradition, it's the koan, a riddle that a master will pose to a student stuck on her way to enlightenment or no-mind or satori. You're all familiar with the one most frequently cited: "What's the sound of one hand clapping?"

The distinctive feature of a koan is that it's absolutely unanswerable in rational terms. Clever responses such as slapping a hand against one's chest and triumphantly proclaiming, "There! That's the sound of one hand clapping!" are reason's ham-fisted attempts to make sense of the riddle. But they always fall short, and inevitably frustration and confusion set in. After a while, the student's reason, stymied in every direction by the koan, begins to short-circuit, so to speak.

When this happens, when reason runs up against the limits of its mandate, a moment of no-mind, of absolute receptivity, stripped of calculation and interpretation, can occur.

Satori.

Dante the pilgrim encounters the supreme koan—Christ—in Canto XXIII, and his reason breaks its bounds, flying away so abruptly that he doesn't know what became of it. The vision of Christ Triumphant he experiences fries his cerebral circuits and jams his cognitive radar. He becomes what the Zen masters call an "empty mirror," unimpededly absorbing and reflecting the glory of Christ without trying to analyze, classify, or explain it. He's taken out of himself, becoming less so that Christ can become more.

Satori!

Christ is a paradox, a koan, an uncrackable riddle. What possible rational sense can we make of an entity who is both fully human and fully divine? Centuries of torturous credal and theological debates have piled up mountains of jargon and logical knot-tying in an attempt to rationally domesticate Christ, to fast-freeze this cosmic nova in sayable, understandable, and manageable terms. But to no avail. As John honestly (albeit in an extraordinarily low key tone) confesses at the end of his Gospel, there aren't enough books in the world to tell the whole story of who and what Christ is.

The point of a koan isn't to explain, but to create an experience. The same thing goes for the Christ-koan, as Dante the pilgrim learns here. This doesn't mean that we should slip into a lazy anti-intellectualism when it comes to the faith. But it does suggest that ultimately we need to let the "translucent substance, bright, so bright" of the Christ-event flood us with the flash of insight that only an encounter with Mystery can bring.

Then: satori.

Paradise, Canto XXIII, Part 2: Music of the Spheres

> *Whatever melody soundeth sweetest*
> *Here below, and most doth draw the soul unto itself,*
> *Would seem a rent cloud thundering,*
>
> *Compared unto the sound of that lyre*
> *Whereby was crowned the beauteous sapphire,*
> *By which the brightest heaven is ensapphired.*

If you were a student in the Middle Ages, your course of instruction would include the quadrivium: arithmetic, geometry, astronomy, and music. Music may seem like the odd-one-out here. The first three parts of the quadrivium focus on number and mathematics. What does music have to do with that?

Everything, said all thinkers right up to the Renaissance. In the sixth century BC, Pythagoras discovered that music is all about numerical proportionality: a musical note's pitch is inversely proportionate to the length of string that produces it. This led him to conclude that the universe, whose deep structure is best described mathematically, must emit a celestial music.

When the Greek astronomer Ptolemy concluded eight centuries later that the heavens were a series of concentric spheres rotating, one within the other, in nonsynchronous but mathematically coordinated ways, Pythagoras's earlier theory about heavenly music seemed even more plausible. Surely the mobile relationship between the spheres, just like plucked strings on a lyre, creates musical notes, even if the human ear can't pick up on them.

So Pythagoras's celestial music became the "music of the spheres."

Dante bought into this notion entirely, most probably getting it from the sixth chapter of Cicero's *Scipio's Dream* (a rigorous deflation, by the way, of human pretension still well worth reading).[24] That's why music plays such a large role in his *Comedy*, as in Paradiso XXIII, when the appearance of the Virgin Mary is heralded with tones more "melodious" than the "sweetest sounding notes enrapturing a man's soul here below."

Dante refers to music no less than 146 times throughout the *Comedy*. In the Inferno, the sounds produced are musically cacophonous, in keeping with the absence of harmonious proportionality there. So, for example, back in Inferno XXI, each soldier demon salutes his devilish captain by making a raspberry sound with his tongue and lips and the captain returns the salute by passing gas.

In the Purgatorio, music, generally a psalm ("*In exitu Israel de Aegypto*," Canto II, or "*Miserere*," Canto V), is sung by penitents on each of the seven terraces. The purpose of this music is simultaneously to remind them of their sins on earth and to aid them in their quest for expiation and purity.

---

24. Cicero, *On Friendship*.

In the Paradiso, each of the heavenly spheres through which Dante and Beatrice pass likewise has its own music, so indescribably beautiful and true that Dante the poet/pilgrim simply can't find words to adequately describe it. Here, finally, we arrive at that music of the spheres that no mortal ear (except Dante the pilgrim's) can hear more than a faint echo of. The exquisite music goes hand in hand with the scintillating and increasingly brilliant light of heavenly truth, beauty, and goodness encountered in the ascendency to God.

Please don't dismiss music of the spheres as another one of those "silly things" our ancestors accepted. If we accept that there's an underlying mathematical harmony to reality—a harmony, by the way, that underpins and makes possible the natural sciences—there's nothing at all outlandish about supposing that the vast system of numerical proportionalities is translatable into music. And if one believes in God, neither is there anything at all extraordinary about the claim that the superstructure of the universe can be thought of as a gorgeous harmony. The cosmos, to use Dante's invented and glorious verb, is "ensapphired" (*s'inzaffira*) by celestial music.

Paradise, Canto XXIV: First Principle

> *"Faith is the substance of the things hoped for,*
> *And argument of things which are not seen;*
> *And this I take to be its quiddity.*
>
> *The deep things*
> *Which grant me here the largess to appear before me,*
> *Are from the eyes of those below so hidden*
>
> *That their existence is there only in belief,*
> *Whereon is built the lofty hope; and so*
> *Of substance it embraceth the intention;*
>
> *And from this belief needs must we syllogize*
> *Without further sight; there it includes*
> *The intention of argument."*

In this and the next two cantos, Dante the pilgrim is quizzed on the three theological virtues of faith, hope, and love by, respectively, the apostles Peter, James, and John. In each case, the format is in the style of a medieval classroom *disputatio*, in which the master poses a series of questions to which the student responds.

In this *disputatio*, Dante offers a conventional definition of faith taken verbatim from Hebrews 11:1: "Faith is the substance of those hoped-for things and argument for things we have not seen."

This, he says, is the heart of the matter, its "quiddity" or substance.

"Substance" here should be read in its original Latin sense as "that which stands under" or "upholds." So the foundation of our hopes, that upon which they firmly rest, is faith. Like the other two theological virtues, faith is an infused (to use the technical term) grace-gift. We can't think or argue our way into it, although we can make ourselves receptive to its bestowal.

It's only after we possess the foundation that we can then proceed to build arguments on and from it. As Anselm famously said a couple of centuries before Dante, *credo ut intelligam*: "I believe in order to understand."[25]

Skeptics often point out that any argument based on Anselm's dictum is immediately suspect, because faith is an assumption, not the conclusion of an inferential chain of reasoning. But I don't find this terribly compelling. All arguments, when traced back as far as we can take them, have axiomatic foundations or first principles, which can't be proven but must be accepted as self-evident. We believe them in order to understand. These foundational beliefs serve as our conceptual and practical compasses.

Descartes, for example, took his "I think, therefore I am" as the self-evident first principle on which he proceeded to build an entire philosophy. When he was a schoolboy intoxicated with geometry, Bertrand Russell said he balked at accepting Euclid's axioms until his brother told him that he couldn't progress without them.[26] You and I base our ordinary daily routines on certain axiomatic assumptions about reality that we confidently accept but can't prove. There's simply no getting around the fact that *all* of us subscribe to Anselm's *credo ut intelligam*.

So there's nothing outlandish about the claim that faith is the axiomatic substratum of all our subsequent reasoning about God. Think of it as a basic attitude about existence that assumes as its foundational or

---

25. Anselm, *Proslogion*, 87.
26. Russell, *Autobiography*, 38.

first principle the claim that the universe is benevolent and purposeful because created by an all-good and loving God.

Paradise, Canto XXV, Part 1: Hope, Beer, and the Eternal Now

Should it e'er come to pass that the sacred poem
  To which both heaven and earth so have set hand,
  That it hath made me lean through many a year,

Should overcome the cruelty which doth bar me
  Forth from the fair sheepfold wherein I used to sleep,
  A lamb, foe to the wolves which war upon it;

With changed voice now, and with changed fleece
  Shall I return, a poet.

Hope is a certain expectation
  Of future glory, the product of divine grace
  And precedent merit.

The apostle James arrives on the scene to quiz Dante the pilgrim about the second theological virtue, hope. Dante gives a lackluster and canned answer—hope is "the certain expectation of future glory"—cribbed directly from the eleventh-century anthologizer Peter Lombard, whose immensely popular *Four Books of Sentences* was a compilation of quotations from scripture and church fathers.

I don't find Dante the catechist rotely reciting his lessons very interesting. But Dante the poet, who expresses an intensely personal hope in the opening tercets of this canto, is an entirely different matter. There's no formal, canned response here. Dante's expression of hope comes straight from his heart and, accordingly, speaks to ours.

Dante was exiled in 1302 from Florence. His property was seized, his reputation was sullied, and he was warned, on pain of death, never to return to the city he so loved. Heartbreakingly, he never did. But his hope of the "future glory" of a homecoming remained always with him. For the nearly twenty years left to him after his exile, he dreamt of the day when he, recognized and revered as the *Comedy's* author, would return, wiser and older, with deepened voice and white fleece/hair.

Whatever else hope is, it's an imaginative projection of ourselves into the future. It seems to be an essential characteristic of humans that we rarely stay in the present. We're haunted by the past's what's-been and beckoned to by the future's what's-yet-to-come. At times we anticipate the future with hope or wishful thinking (not that the two are at all the same), at other times with anxiety or dread, and at still other times with goal-oriented single-mindedness. But regardless of our motives, we move beyond the here and now to project ourselves into the not-yet.

Not always, though. All of us have experienced those moments in which the past drops away, the future recedes beyond the horizon, and we find ourselves in a timeless now. These departures from temporality often arrive unannounced and unanticipated in the most mundane of circumstances: washing dishes, strolling down a sidewalk, or simply sitting on the porch. But they can also come to us when we experience beauty or are overwhelmed by goodness and truth.

And of course these timeless moments are also the occasions when mystics encounter the eternal Godhead. That's why even though the apostle James quizzes Dante the pilgrim about hope, there's no hope in paradise (nor faith, for that matter), because paradise is where the future becomes an eternal now.

Hope is the grace-gift that gets us through our days and nights, reassuring us in our brokenness, pain, and disappointment of eventual fulfillment. But one day there will be no more days and nights, only an ever-lasting now, and hence no more need of the gift. The old song has it that "in heaven there is no beer; that's why we drink it here." In heaven there is no hope; but we desperately need it here to cope.

Paradise, Canto XXV, Part 2: Why Is Dante Darkened?

> *Ah, how was I stirred in my mind,*
> *Turning to look on Beatrice,*
> *For that I might not see her, albeit I was*
>
> *Nigh to her and in the world of bliss!*

I find Dante the pilgrim's blindness at the end of Canto XXV, a condition that continues through the first twenty-three tercets of Canto XXVI, the single most baffling episode in the *Paradiso*, and perhaps even the entire *Comedy*.

Why, so close to his God-goal, is he struck blind? And not just blind but also deaf, because we're also told that the celestial music he's been hearing likewise suddenly ceases.

Dante himself describes this experience of sudden sensory deprivation as an unsettlingly uncanny feeling running through his mind.

I honestly don't quite know what to make of it.

It coincides with the appearance of the apostle John, who will shortly quiz Dante on the third theological virtue of love. There's some suggestion that Dante goes blind because he's been staring too directly at the brilliant light that John is. But how, on this account, to understand the sudden cessation of music? And why didn't the brilliance of Peter and James, the first two apostles he encountered, similarly affect him?

Some commentators suggest that the blindness is symbolic of the nature of love. Faith and hope, they argue, are products of the intellect, traditionally associated with vision. Love, on the other hand, is willed activity. So to highlight that love is an act of the will rather than the intellect, Dante the poet has Dante the pilgrim go blind.

But I find this absurd. Faith serves as the axiomatic first principle upon which the intellect can work, but it surely isn't a product of intellect itself. We can think ourselves into the conviction *that* God exists, but not *what* God is. That's the point when faith needs to kick in. Moreover, inferring from the past and present to the future is absolutely an act of the intellect. But it's odd to say that Christian hope is nothing more than an inductive inference. Otherwise, why would it be an infused theological virtue—that is, a capacity God infuses in us rather than one we singlehandedly cultivate.

Or perhaps this is a case of darkness before the dawn, a dark night of the soul in which everything that offers spiritual comfort to Dante is taken away from him as a preparation for the upcoming beatific vision. But why would such a stripping down be necessary at this point in his spiritual journey? He's already been thoroughly vetted by his terrace-by-terrace climb up Mount Purgatory.

So why the swift loss of sight and hearing?

I think I may have an explanation.

The blindness and deafness—the darkness—happens when John, the author of the Fourth Gospel, appears. In the famous Prologue (1:5) to his gospel, John writes of the Word,

> the light shines in the darkness,
> and the darkness has not overcome it.

Could it be that the sensory darkness that overcomes Dante is intended as a poetic homage to both John and this passage from his Prologue? Could it be a prelude to the ensuing discussion of love, the divine force that the darkness can't overcome, as symbolized by the restoration of Dante's senses? Could it be that this episode of soul-darkness and subsequent soul-awakening is an allegory for the entire economy of salvation encapsulated in the Prologue?

Paradise, Canto XXVI, Part 1: Loving What's Good

> *Good, as good, so far as understood,*
> *Kindleth love.*
>
> *Then to that Essence which hath such privilege*
> *That whatsoever good he found outside of it*
> *Is nought else save a light of its own ray,*
>
> *More than to any other must the mind needs move,*
> *In love.*
>
> *Of thy loves keep for God the sovereign one.*

A school of philosophical thought emerged in the eighteenth century that came to be called "Scottish common sense." Don't read "common sense" as synonymous with knowing how to put together an IKEA table or wearing a mask during a pandemic. Instead, think of "common sense" as a human capacity for picking up information. Our commonly shared five physical senses enable us, for example, to acquire knowledge visually, tactilely, and so on.

One of this school's leading lights, a Presbyterian minister named Francis Hutcheson, argued that we have a "common" moral sense analogous to the five physical ones. When someone holds a stick up before our eyes, our visual sense tells us immediately what it is. We don't need to go through a long chain of reasoning to identify it. Similarly, when we witness a good or evil act, our commonly held moral sense tells us immediately what's going on. We don't need to be familiar with centuries of moral philosophy or go through an elaborate ethical analysis to discern good from evil.

Moreover, argued Hutcheson, we're naturally drawn to those acts that our moral sense tells us are good, and naturally repelled by their opposites. If you doubt that, he says, ask yourself how you'd respond to someone motivated by benevolence to lend you a hand as opposed to being motivated by self-interest. We immediately applaud the first but feel (at best!) ambivalent about the second.[27]

Granted, some people may have impaired moral senses, just as others can have impaired eyesight. But this no more casts doubt upon the reality of the moral sense than myopia calls into question vision.

In Canto XXVI, the apostle John puts Dante through the final part of his disputatio quiz, this time asking him to talk about love, the third theological virtue. Unlike his treatment of faith and hope, Dante doesn't actually offer a definition of love. Instead, he says that good perceived as good enkindles love, and since God is the Supreme Good, we just naturally should love God above all else.

I find this simplicity every bit as refreshing as Hutcheson's argument for the moral sense. I worry that sometimes we wind up needlessly over-complicating and hence obfuscating what should be pretty obvious moral appraisals. Perhaps part of the explanation is that we moderns feel awkward about designating actions as good, much less evil, because we've bitten so deeply into the relativistic apple that we think all moral judgments are necessarily subjective.

But neither Dante nor Hutcheson are inhibited in this way. Both believe that we're perfectly capable of discerning goodness, first because it's objectively real and second because we have an innate common moral sense that enables us to pick up on it. And to discern goodness is to be attracted to it—or, as Dante says, to love it and, ultimately, to love its Source.

Paradise, Canto XXVI, Part 2: "Whát I dó is me!"

> *The leaves wherewith all the garden*
> *Of the Eternal Gardener is leafed, I love in measure*
> *Of the good that hath been proffered to them from him.*

27. Hutcheson, *Essay*.

That most tragic and beautiful of poets, the Victorian Jesuit Gerard Manley Hopkins, coined a couple of terms, "inscape" and "instress," which have intrigued and sometimes befuddled all of us who love his verse.

In his journals and letters, Hopkins offers a variety of thoughts about these two words, not all of them consistent. But at the end of the day, inscape seems to be his term for the irreducible unique pattern or form of each thing that exists. Instress plays double duty by designating both the inner dynamism that holds the pattern together and our intuitive apprehension of it.[28]

Hopkins, a keen observer of nature, was especially fascinated by the delicate inscape of leaves. Each, like everything else—snowflakes, clouds, and rocky formations—proclaims its uniqueness. As he writes in "As Kingfishers Catch Fire,"

> Each mortal thing does one thing and the same:
> . . . myself it speaks and spells,
> Crying Whát I dó is me: for that I came.[29]

But for Hopkins, the irreducible uniqueness of everything that is points beyond itself to the Creator. Somehow, Christ is present in, and hence discernible in, the leaf, snowflake, or cloud, and in fact is what stamps the individual thing with its own peculiarity. So in intuiting uniqueness, we also intuit the divine presence responsible for it. In the same "Kingfishers" poem, Hopkins goes on to say,

> Christ plays in ten thousand places,
> Lovely in limbs, and lovely in eyes not his.[30]

Similarly, in his exquisite "Pied Beauty," Hopkins praises the diversity of "dappled things" such as brinded cows, rose-colored trout, finches' wings—inscapes all—before declaring them to be "Father-forthed" and, presumably, reflective of Christ:

> All things counter, original, spare, strange;
> Whatever is fickle, freckled (who knows how?)
> With swift, slow; sweet, sour; adazzle, dim;
> He fathers-forth whose beauty is past change:
> Praise him.[31]

28. Hopkins, *Poems and Prose*, 105–35.
29. Hopkins, *Poems and Prose*, 51.
30. Hopkins, *Prose and Poems*, 51.
31. Hopkins, *Poems and Prose*, 31.

So inscape holds in tension both uniqueness (the brinded cow, the rose-hued trout) and universality (Christ) without in any way watering down either. Think of it as a kind of taxonomy. We can locate all cats in the carnivorous family of Felidae, while at the same time recognizing that each cat uniquely "speaks and spells" itself, "Crying Whát I dó is me: for that I came." In celebrating his love of "the leaves wherewith all the garden / of the Eternal Gardener is leafed" Dante anticipates what Hopkins says about inscape and instress six centuries later.

Dante intuits each leaf's unique pattern—or, closer to Dante's own time, what the theologian Duns Scotus called its "*haecceity*"—but he additionally intuits, riding on its particularity, the stamp or enleafment of the Eternal Gardener. For Dante and for Hopkins, Christ does indeed play in ten thousand places.

Or, put another way, the deep-down presence of God is discernible everywhere. And that makes the universe in which we dwell, whose pied beauty and majesty we too often take for granted, a wondrous place indeed.

Paradise, Canto XXVI, Part 3: The God Who Won't Be Named or Tamed

> *Never yet did product of the reason*
> *Maintain itself for ever.*
>
> *Ere I descended to the infernal anguish,*
>   *"El" was the name on earth of that supreme good*
>   *Whence cometh the gladness that doth swathe me;*
>
> *"Eli" was he called hereafter;*
>   *And this is fitting, for the use of mortals is as the leaf*
>   *Upon the branch which goeth and another followeth.*

I believe it was Martin Buber who once said that whenever we think about the divine Name we should tremblingly fall to our knees. That's how powerful it is. Its very sound thunders through the heavens, capable of disintegrating anyone who hears it.

That's why observant Jews to this day refuse to speak the Tetragrammaton, the four-letter name God discloses to Moses at the burning bush.

That name, YHWH, is too sacred to be uttered. So synonyms like Adonai, Elohim, or (my favorite) HaShem ("The Name") are substituted.

But observant Jews aren't the only people who substitute synonyms for the divine Name. We all do, don't we? Father, Jesus, Allah, Krishna, the Unmoved Mover, Odin, Vishnu: generation after generation has struggled to find a word capable of expressing who and what God is. These designators have come and gone in past centuries, and quite probably will continue to morph in future ones.

In Canto XXVI, Dante gestures at this fluidity when he says that at one time God's name was "El" but later became "Eli," because no "product of the reason"—including what we choose to call God—can last. Instead, one generation's way of thinking falls like leaves in autumn only to be replaced by the next generation's.

So there are at least two reasons why it's foolish to try to name God. The first, as Dante suggests, is that we simply don't have the smarts to do so. Names are identifiers—"Kerry Walters" refers to me and me alone—that tell us something about that to which they refer—"Kerry possesses this particular set of qualities." But my name identifies me only because I'm temporal and finite (frighteningly so, in fact), and hence information about me is graspable by other humans. God, on the other hand, is eternal and infinite, completely beyond our comprehension. God's response to Moses' request for God's Name is "I AM." This I AM is the Tetragrammaton, YHWH, derived from the verb "to be." How can our finite intellects possibly soak up the meaning of The Act of Being Itself?

This brings us to the second reason why naming God is a mug's game. It's an arrogant punch way beyond our weight. Why? Because to know the name of anything is to exert some kind of control over that which it designates. Psychoanalysts tell us that to name our repressions and anxieties is to exert power over them, thereby breaking their hold on us. In Genesis, God gives Adam license to name every creature he encounters, thereby establishing the power to categorize them. But hang-ups and taxonomies are one thing, God another. Why would we think we could possibly exert power over God?

Yet this immediately raises a second question: If knowing a name means exerting power over its referent, why in the world would God tell Moses His Name?!

We could spend years meditating on this marvelous and bewildering puzzle. But in brief, I think that God's revelation of the Tetragrammaton is at one and the same time both a supreme gesture of vulnerability and a declaration of untameability. God willingly speaks His own Name in order to show a willingness to enter into covenant with humans, a willingness that runs through the entire Bible. This self-identification at the burning bush is, if you will, an act of kenosis. But the very nature of the Name God offers—YHWH, The Great I AM, the Ground of All Being, The Supreme Foundation—more than suggests that this Being Who makes Himself vulnerable is totally beyond human ken and can't be neatly encapsulated, much less controlled, by the fragile leaves of language.

Paradise, Canto XXVII, Part 1: When the Universe Smiles

> *All paradise took up the strain,*
>   *"To the Father, to the Son, to the Holy Spirit, glory!"*
>   *So that the sweet song intoxicated me.*
>
> *Meseemed I was beholding a smile*
>   *Of the universe; wherefor my intoxication*
>   *Entered both by hearing and by sight.*
>
> *O joy! O gladness unspeakable!*
>   *O life compact of love and peace!*
>   *O wealth secure that hath no longing!*

When I was a graduate student at Marquette University, I was so poor that I routinely, under the darkness of night, fished pennies, nickels, and dimes out of the small fountain in front of the school's Joan of Arc chapel. (God knows why tourists and visiting parents tossed them in, but I was glad they did.) I lived in a rented room in a broken-down house (hotplate for a kitchen, shared bathroom down a grimy hallway) whose windows frosted over on the inside during Milwaukee winters. I had a part-time job as a janitor at an equally rundown Lutheran church that sometimes had trouble paying me on time.

On top of everything else, I was desperately lonely.

In short, it was a hard and sometimes bitter time in my life.

And yet one day the most wonderful thing happened. I was walking to the university. The sidewalk and street were crowded and noisy. I don't recall having anything in particular on my mind. Suddenly, like Dante in Canto XXVII, I was overwhelmed with the sense that the universe was smiling, and a surge of unalloyed joy tsunamied through me. In that moment, I intuited with rock-hard certainty that all of reality was shot through with beneficence and goodness, and that pain and wickedness and loneliness, although real enough in their own way, were contrary to the genuine nature of things.

I realized, as Dame Julian of Norwich was assured in the fourteenth century, that "all shall be well, and all shall be well, and all manner of things shall be well."[32] After that, no matter how occasionally dark life became, the memory of the smile sustained me.

Since that day nearly fifty years ago, I've had three or four identical but completely unanticipated experiences of the universe's eternal smile, and each of them filled me with "gladness unspeakable!"

Clearly this is what's going on with Dante when he experiences souls in paradise singing the Gloria. His joy is such that he feels inebriated, zoomed to an entirely new level of awareness, taken out of himself. He senses, with his entire being, the universe's beneficent smile.

For him, the experience of cosmic beneficence occurred in an explicitly Christian setting. But the universe's smile is broad enough to accommodate any number of contexts. For some people, it's intuited in nature; for others, in art; for still others, in the caress of a lover or the laughter of a child. Sometimes it's overtly religious, at other times not.

How different both individual lives and social interactions would be if we took these ecstatic experiences seriously (instead of dismissing them as pathetic defense mechanisms or wishful thinking) and opened ourselves up to them. Although they come as gifts, often when we least expect them, spiritual traditions the world over affirm their reality and insist that we can discipline ourselves to become more receptive to their possibility.

Clearly this is what Dante has done in his journey through hell and purgatory. Had he been swept straight away from the dark wood in which he was lost to the eighth heavenly sphere, I doubt he would've had the capacity to sense the universe's smile. Had my cocky-youngster-studying-at-an-elite-Jesuit-university egoism not been fragmented by poverty and loneliness, I doubt I would've either.

---

32. Julian of Norwich, *Revelations*, 56.

Paradise, Canto XXVII, Part 2: Love Fuels the Cosmic Machine

> *The nature of the universe, which stilleth*
> *The center and moveth all the rest around,*
> *Hence doth begin as from its starting point.*
>
> *And this heaven hath no other where*
> *Than the divine mind which is kindled in love*
> *Which rolleth it and the power it sheddeth.*
>
> *Light and love grasp it in one circle*
> *As doth it the other, and in this engirdment*
> *He only who doth gird it understandeth.*
>
> *Its movement is by no other marked out;*
> *But by it all the rest are measured.*

In the eighteenth-century Enlightenment, philosophers pretty much abandoned traditional Christianity, dismissing it as nonsensical superstition. Instead, they preferred the "rational religion" of deism that posited the existence of a divine First Cause, which set in motion the clockwork-like universe and then discretely stepped off stage to let the celestial machine run itself.

There was one problem, though: What was the force or power that fueled the grinding of the gears? What was the impetus that kept natural laws in good working order? If God was out of the picture, did that make the universe a perpetual-motion machine, fueled by its own internal mechanisms? For the most part, Enlightenment thinkers never really addressed these sorts of questions. It was enough for them that their universe was orderly, predictable, and manipulable.

This absence of explanation wouldn't have satisfied Dante or the generations that preceded him. They acknowledged that the physical universe was analogous to a finely tuned machine. But they dismissed as an absurdity the idea of a machine that perpetually generated its own fuel.

Enter the primum mobile, the "first movable," which in Dante's *Comedy* is the ninth heavenly sphere. He and Beatrice have now moved into it.

Dante's universe, like that of the deists', is perfectly ordered. But it's Ptolemaic, which means two things. First, it's geocentric; the fixed core, the "center still," is earth. Second, the other heavenly bodies, the planets (which include the sun and moon) and the stars, revolve around earth on nestled spheres whose circumferences enlarge in proportion to their distance from earth. Each sphere revolves at a different velocity and slightly different angle to create the complex movement of constellations and the "rising" and "setting" of sun and moon observable from earth.

Now, the outermost sphere, which moves more swiftly than any of the eight it encircles, is the primum mobile. It's the master gear that turns all the others. It is the universe's outermost physical limit. Nothing bounds it except the light and love that radiate from the mind of God. And the source of its energy, which moves all else around it, is precisely the love "kindled" in God's mind.

If this sounds quaint to you, it may be that you're reducing love to a mere emotion. Think of it instead as a force that encourages stability and relationality, both of which seem to be on display in the physical universe.

It's worth pondering the possibility, as Dante suggests, that we live in a reality created, generated, and sustained by the dynamic-yet-stable power of love. And because the ultimate source of that love is God, it's an ever-renewable energy. If love is what animates everything, our attitude to the physical world, which since the Enlightenment has been one of slash, burn, and exploit, is tragically off kilter.

Paradise, Canto XXVII, Part 3: Original Sin or Original Blessing?

'Tis true the will in men hath vigor yet;
But the continuous drench turneth true plum fruits
into cankered tubers.

Faith and innocence are found
Only in little children; then each of them
Fleeth away before the cheeks are covered.

John Calvin's 1563 *Institutes of the Christian Religion* has spawned a lot of mischief, but perhaps none more damaging than his insistence that the biblical Adam "ruined his posterity by his defection, which has perverted the whole order of nature in heaven and earth" such that all of us are "corrupted by a natural depravity" and suffering from a "death of the soul."[33]

---

33. Calvin, *Institutes*, 225, 231.

This relentless doctrine of original sin and total depravity, which I'd argue locks humans inside prisons of self-loathing—one only has to read the tortured private diaries of colonial Puritans to appreciate how psychologically and spiritually corrosive it can be—has a long pedigree, going all the way back to the fifth-century Augustine. In his decades-long feud with Pelagius, who had argued that every new infant is as free from sin as Adam was at the moment of his creation, Augustine insisted that we're all born necessarily tainted by Adam's fall.

I bow to no one in my admiration of Augustine's mind. But it must be said that his insistence on congenital human depravity is hurtful nonsense.

The Augustine-Pelagius debate over human nature being either innately wicked or innately good has been rehashed any number of times since (by, for example, John Calvin, as we've just seen). Perhaps the best known revival of it is the Hobbes-Rousseau kerfuffle. In his 1651 book *Leviathan*, Thomas Hobbes argues in a neo-Augustinian vein that humans are by nature so vicious that our lives would be "solitary, poor, nasty, brutish, and short" without the strong arm of external authority to keep us in line.[34] By contrast, Jean-Jacques Rousseau defends the neo-Pelagian position in his 1755 *The Social Contract*'s claim that "man is born free but is everywhere in chains."[35] His point is that the upside-down values of supposedly civilized culture inevitably corrupt and enslave us.

To his great credit (or at least so I think), Dante is more Pelagian than Augustinian when it comes to human nature. In Canto XXVII, he has Beatrice proclaim that the blossom of human will is always good. That's why children are so touchingly innocent. It's only as they become acculturated to corrupt society that their "true plum fruits" rot "before the[ir] cheeks are covered."

I believe that Dante found himself unable to embrace Augustine's bleak view of humanity because he was so in love with the beauty, aesthetic, intellectual, spiritual, and moral, that we're capable of birthing. How could an innately and totally depraved humanity produce a Virgil or any of the other great poets of antiquity? How, for that matter, produce a Dante (although he was too modest to ask that)? There's no reason to be naively Pollyanish about humans; we indeed are capable of committing horrible acts of wickedness. But for Dante, and for me, the wickedness

---

34. Hobbes, *Leviathan*, 76.
35. Rousseau, *Social Contract*, 3.

isn't ingrained. It's acquired as we endure the drenching of society's incessant rain.

And yet, because we aren't totally depraved, because we carry with us an original blessing stronger than any original sin, we remain capable of genuine goodness, beauty, and truth.

Paradise, Canto XXVIII: Big Bang(ish)

> *A point I saw which rayed forth*
> *Light so keen, needs must the vision that it flameth on*
> *Be closed because of its strong poignancy;*
>
> *At such interval around the point there whirled*
> *A circle of fire so rapidly it had surpassed*
> *The motion which doth swiftest gird the universe.*
>
> *My Lady said: "From that point*
> *Doth hang heaven and all nature."*

In 1931, a Belgian priest and cosmologist named Georges Lemaitre published a paper that speculated about the origin of the physical universe. He argued that it was birthed by the explosion of a single particle which created shock waves still hurtling away from the explosion's epicenter.

Imagine a single point of light in the blackness of space that suddenly goes brilliantly nova—BOOM! The nova's detritus became the universe in which we dwell.

This, of course, is the Big Bang theory.

In Canto XXVIII, you can't help but be struck by the way Dante's description of God and angels resembles the broad contours of Big Bang.

Still in the primum mobile, Dante sees a point of light so tiny that physical stars would dwarf it, but also so intensely brilliant that it hurts the eyes. Around the point are nine vibrantly whirling concentric rings of fire from which thousands—no, millions!—of sparks fly.

The point is the light of God shooting down from the empyrean, the rings of fire represent the nine orders of angels associated with each of the nine heavenly spheres, and the millions of sparks are the individual angels who belong to each of the orders.

On the one hand, this all sounds quaintly medieval, doesn't it? But at the same time, two rather astonishing Big Bang(ish) similarities in it stand out for me.

The first, as Beatrice tells Dante, is that all nature and all the heavens emerge from the point of light. Divinely explosive love shoots detritus across the firmament, creating both the physical universe and its inhabitants as well as the heavenly spheres and their angelic guardians. Love is the explosion that created everything that is. I often think that what God really said at the beginning wasn't so much "Let there be light, earth, sky, animals" and so on, so much as "Let there be love" and—BANG!—the universe came into being.

The second is the incredibly explosive vitality or energy associated with divine love that expansively radiates throughout and enlivens the entire universe. Each order of angels in each of the heavenly spheres experiences the explosion's force in varying degrees depending on its proximity to the Point. (So, to invoke Dante's angelic hierarchy model, the seraphim, the highest order of angels and the ones closest to the Point, whirl swiftest.) The shock waves of creative love radiate outward to the farthermost limits, quickening the earth and, indeed, each person's heart.

The upshot is that we live in a vibrant universe, animated by the Big Bang of divine love. Although our senses tell us that the world is made up of solidly concrete objects—the "hard" desk on which I write this, my enfleshed fingers tapping on the keyboard, the inert books surrounding me, and so on—we know that at the subatomic level things are anything but "solid." Instead, what our senses perceive as objects are in fact tightly compressed bundles of energy or quanta. We, and everything else that exists, quiver at our deepest core with the shock waves of love shot out by the divine Big Bang.

Paradise, Canto XXIX: Separate Substances?!?

> *These substances, since first they gathered joy*
> *From the face of God, have never turned their vision*
> *From it wherefrom nought is concealed;*
>
> *This nature ranketh so high in number*
> *That ne'er was speech nor thought*
> *Of mortal that advanced so far:*

The primal light which doth o'erray it all,
Is received by it in so many ways as are
The splendors wherewithal it paireth.

As a first-year graduate student in philosophy at a Jesuit university, I signed up for a required seminar in Thomas Aquinas. I wasn't happy about it. Somewhere between my admission application and my actual matriculation, the faith that motivated me to want to attend a Jesuit institution in the first place had dimmed. So in my newly discovered (and, in hindsight, insufferably cocky) apostasy, I disdainfully pooh-poohed Thomas and everything he stood for.

The seminar had only one written requirement: a major term paper, on a subject assigned by the professor, due at semester's end. I'll never know why Professor Ed Rousseau handed me the topic he did, but on first receiving it I was mystified. I was to write on "separate substances," and strongly urged to read Thomas's treatise *De Substantiis Separatis*.

Huh?!

I had no idea what a "separate substance" was. But a tiny bit of legwork revealed, horrifyingly, that it was one of the terms Thomas used to refer to angels. Rousseau had assigned me, quite possibly in mischievous response to my showy contempt for Thomas, the topic of angelology.

What the hell!

I huffed and sulked my way through the seminar and somehow managed to produce an utterly uninspired fifty+ page essay on separate substances. I remember thinking that writing the damn thing was a colossal waste of time, and to this day I don't remember a single thing I said in it.

It took me years to mature into an appreciation of the sheer brilliance of Thomas's mind, regardless of whether or not I agree with him. Dante, on the other hand, was a fan from the get-go, and his description of angelic beings in Canto XXIX comes straight out of *De Substantiis Separatis*.

According to Thomas and Dante, angels are spiritual beings who, being pure act (an Aristotelian expression denoting an absence of potentiality or changeability; calling them "separate substances" is just another way of saying the same thing) are pinnacles of creation. In the hierarchy of being, they're right below God.

It's stupid to think of angels as chubby, winged androgynes. Dante always depicts them as sparkling flashes of vitality. This is because they're plugged into the Divine Life, reading reality by gazing upon the omniscient mind of God—they "never turn their eyes away" from "God's face"—and thus absorbing the dynamism of divine love and wisdom. No wonder Isaiah has the angelic host ceaselessly singing, "Holy, holy, holy is the LORD of hosts; The whole earth is full of His glory!" (6:2–3).

And since Dante, in agreement with Thomas, claims that "no scale of mortal numbers" is high enough to count the tens of bazillions of angels in existence, it stands to reason that their endless chanting of praises harmonizes with the music of the spheres.

Is all this made-up nonsense, as the youthful Kerry once believed? Who can tell? If there is a God, why must we conclude that the only kind of conscious creatures He brought into being are the ones striding, flying, swimming, or crawling on *terra firma*? How could it be that the fecund plenitude of the great I AM is expressed in only the material universe? Given the vastness of reality and the mystery of existence, an open mind when it comes to such things isn't necessarily abject credulity.

Paradise, Canto XXX, Part 1: Through the Empyrean Looking Glass

> *As the brightest handmaid of the sun advanceth,*
> *So doth the heaven close up sight after sight*
> *Till the most fair.*
>
> *Not otherwise the triumph which ever sporteth*
> *Round the point which vanquished me,*
> *Seeming embraced by that which it embraceth,*
>
> *Little by little quenched itself from my sight.*

What would it be like to enter into a dimension for which our five senses, our conceptual framework, and our basic intuitions leave us totally unprepared?

Our senses accustom us to a certain kind of proportionality: near and far, up and down, left and right, and so on. But what happens when these reference points disappear? Our conceptual frameworks rest on a handful of fundamental rational principles, such as the laws of identity and noncontradiction (something is what it is and not what it is not). When those no longer apply, how do we orient ourselves? And our basic instincts, the most primordial of which are our internal compass points of space and time: without them, where and when are we? Without them, does that kind of question even make any sense?

To be abruptly cast into such an utterly foreign through-the-looking-glass world would be, I think, so utterly discombobulating that it would wreck us. A sudden transition to it would launch us into a genuine hell, infinitely more shattering than the most dreadful scenarios in the Inferno.

I believe that's why Dante the pilgrim's transition in Canto XXX from the primum mobile, the ninth and last of the physical heavenly spheres, to the nonphysical empyrean, the Godhead's realm, is slow. Recall that his movement from one physical sphere to the next has been lightning quick: faster, he tells us, than the flight of an arrow or the emergence of a thought.

That mega-velocity was safe in those contexts. Head-spinning as Dante's experiences of ascending to the various spheres were, they weren't crushingly uncanny. That's because they were transitions from one physical realm to another. So Dante's senses, conceptual framework, and basic instincts had no trouble "reading" them. He was filled with wonder, not shattered by the utterly unfamiliar.

But in entering the empyrean, Dante's usual ways of orienting himself are no use to him. As we'll see, three-dimensional perspectives fly out the window, fundamental logical laws are transcended, and basic instincts of space and time fall flat because the empyrean is beyond space and time.

So Dante's entry into the empyrean has to be just as slow and steady as the rising sun gradually lightens the darkness of early morning. In the still physical primum mobile, Dante saw the point of God's light surrounded by nine fiery rings, representing the nine angelic ranks (seraphim, cherubim, thrones, and so on). Although the angels seemed to contain the point, the point of course contained them. But as Beatrice and Dante enter the non-physical empyrean, this vision "little by little," slowly, gradually, faded away. Dante's acclimation to his new surroundings will take time.

Having said that, though, it should be clear that we've reached the outer limits of language. We still use words like "enter," "slowly," and "take time," but they fall short when trying to speak about the empyrean. Dante, the consummate wordsmith, is all too painfully aware that once we pass through the empyrean looking glass, language would do well to mute itself. And yet he must struggle to find words that at least gesture, howsoever inadequately, at this new dimension into which he's taken us.

Paradise, Canto XXX, Part 2: Speaking the Unspeakable

> *At this pass I yield me vanquished more than e'er*
> *Yet was overborne by his theme's thrust*
> *Comic or tragic poet.*

While serving in the Great War, an eccentric young man from a wealthy and talented (but also heartbreakingly tragic) Austrian family spent his time in the trenches of No Man's Land writing what became a classic of twentieth-century philosophy. His name was Ludwig Wittgenstein, and the book, the only one he published in his lifetime, was the *Tractatus Logico-Philosophicus*. You may remember I mentioned him in passing back in the Purgatorio, Canto III.

The title is every bit as austere as its contents. Riding on a wave of rebellion against nineteenth-century metaphysical speculation that, according to critics, made a hash out of knowledge by stretching language beyond its proper limits, Wittgenstein sought to declutter speech by reducing it to a precisely unambiguous "picture" of facts. This meant tossing the gobbledygook of metaphysical and religious chatter into the trash bin—after all, they referred to no observable facts in the world—but also, for the same reason, the boggy discourse of morality and aesthetics.

Wittgenstein didn't exactly deny the reality of God, value, or beauty. He just insisted that our language couldn't say anything meaningful about such things. So if we wish to exorcise ambiguity and unclarity from discourse, we need to recognize the limits of words and keep doggedly to them. That's why he closed his *Tractatus* with this famous line: "Whereof one cannot speak, thereof one must be silent."[36]

Wittgenstein later repudiated this early work (a remarkable and rare thing for a philosopher to do!). But the *Tractatus* remains important for two reasons. First, contrary to what Wittgenstein hoped to achieve, it jolts us into the recognition that language has a hard time pinning down even the most ordinary of human experiences, much less transcendent ones. Ineffability always haunts our speech. Second, it raises a fundamental

---

36. Wittgenstein, *Tractatus*, 108.

question: Given this, why do we struggle so mightily to capture our experiences, especially transcendent ones, in words?

If you doubt me when I say that we're not very good at speaking even our most ordinary experiences, consider this. As I write this, a fierce wind is blowing outside, raising cascades of notes from the back porch chimes. What words could I possibly find that would adequately describe their sound to someone who's never heard wind chimes, much less to a deaf person who's never heard anything? Or what about this: How could I describe the color orange to a colorblind person such that she'd genuinely grasp what I'm talking about? How could my words stretch that far?

Transcendent experiences that go beyond the here and now—my experience of a divine presence, my intuition of goodness, my sense that beauty is whispering something fundamental to my well-being—are even more inexpressible in straightforward language. We use metaphors, similes, and images to convey them. But their ineffability is such that we can never find words to address them head-on. Trying to do so merely distorts them, taking us further and further away from them. (This, by the way, is why poetry is the best medium for them.)

In Canto XXX, Dante recognizes this. In struggling to find words to describe the shimmering beauty of Beatrice's face as well as his experience of the beyond-space-and-time empyrean, he acknowledges defeat. His theme has "overborne" him.

If so, why does he continue? Or for that matter, why do you and I persevere in trying to put our own experiences of love, beauty, goodness, God, and so on into words? It seems a fool's game, doesn't it? Surely whereof we cannot speak, we ought to remain silent.

But here's the thing: our experiences of the ineffable suffuse us with a sense of love and wonderment. They enspark us with a connection to the glorious richness of creation. They expand our horizons, allowing us to glimpse vistas that we may not have the language to describe but that awe us by their depth and imprint us with their beauty, truth, and goodness. These sorts of experiences beg to be shared with others.

How many times have you and I tried to describe for others our breathtaking experiences of a gorgeous sunset or the sweetness of a tender caress, even when we knew that our words could never capture them? How often, after being touched in our deepest places by an experience of the universe's beneficence, have we struggled to convey to others what was revealed to us, knowing the whole time that we can't adequately speak it to ourselves, much less to others?

Experiences like these are generous gifts to us, and in receiving them, they awaken in us a similar generosity. Love and wonderment are always profligate, and hence always overflow.

In writing his *Comedy*, Dante lives and conveys one of the greatest (and yet, paradoxically) commonest mysteries of human existence: we experience more than we can speak, and yet what we experience awakens in us the urge to speak it. This mystery is hardwired in us, I believe, because we're made in the likeness of a God who, we're told, spoke creation into existence. God is able, through words/Word, to perfectly express what's in the divine mind. We mere mortals are unable to stretch that far. But to speak, and in speaking to creatively express, howsoever inadequately, is our inheritance. And, my oh my, what a wonderful thing it is!

Paradise, Canto XXX, Part 3: Secondhand Vision, Third-Eye Vision

> *Kindled with such new-given sight that*
> *There is no brightness unalloyed that mine eyes*
> *Might not behold their own with it,*
>
> *I saw*
> *Both of the two Courts of Heaven manifested.*

"Sight is the sense that especially produces cognition within us and reveals many distinguishing features of things."[37] So wrote Aristotle in his *Metaphysics*. Before him, Plato drew a distinction between physical and spiritual vision. Our physical eyes see material objects in the world. The eyes of the soul discern spiritual truths.

Hindu and Buddhist traditions call the organ responsible for spiritual vision the Third Eye, the Mind's Eye, or the Inner Eye, and traditionally represent it as located in the forehead's middle.

In Canto XXX, Dante the pilgrim's spiritual vision has achieved clarity. His Third Eye has been awakened, first through the careful tutelage of Beatrice as they ascended through the heavens, but finally by bathing his eyes, and thus symbolically clarifying his vision, in a flowing stream representing the flow of divine grace:

---

37. Aristotle, *Metaphysics*, 4.

> *"Then did I, to make yet better mirrors*
> *Of mine eyes, down bending to the wave*
> *which floweth that we may better us."*

After that washing, he saw the "two Courts of Heaven" in all their glory.

Up until that moment, Dante's vision of the empyrean was secondhand. He'd literally been seeing everything as it was reflected, dimly, as all reflections are, in Beatrice's eyes. In other words, his vision was physical. His spiritual vision was as yet too weak for a direct perception of divine brilliance. But the holy lathing scrubbed the sleep out of his Third Eye, enabling him to tolerate the Light of God.

I think this is one of the most powerful parables in the entire *Comedy*.

For many of us (and I don't exclude myself from this) our relationship with God is secondhand, isn't it? Our vision, for the most part, remains physical. We "see" dim reflections of God in the "eyes" of theologians, preachers, philosophers, novelists, poets, artists, scriptures, parents, Sunday school teachers, and so on. This means that for the most part, we focus on representations of God rather than directly "seeing" God. Like Dante prior to his head-dunk in the flowing stream, our Third Eyes are heavy with sleep.

We see through a glass darkly. Our eyes are not, as Dante's become, "mirrors." I'm not saying that we're bad or somehow inauthentic if we haven't had a naked Third-Eye experience of God. It's probably the case that very few of us ever will this side of paradise. That kind of clarity may be reserved for those mystics among us who practice ascetic disciplines that awaken spiritual vision. But what I *am* saying is that it's important to acknowledge that what we typically "see" when it comes to God are secondhand representations. They can offer us glimpses, hints, tantalizing-because-ephemeral flashes. But they should never be mistaken for the Real Thing, because doing so breeds complacency and, even worse, intolerance.

Paradise, Canto XXX, Part 4: Addio, Beatrice! E Grazie!

> *Within the yellow of the eternal rose,*
> *Which doth expand, rank upon rank, and reeketh*
> *Perfume of praise unto the Sun that maketh spring for ever,*
>
> *Me, as one who doth hold his peace yet fain would speak,*
> *Beatrice drew, and said: "Behold*
> *How great the white-robed concourse!"*

I'll soon have a lot more to say about the "eternal rose" of paradise filled, row upon row, with the "white robed concourse" of souls. It's one of the most magnificent poetic images ever written. But more immediately, it's time to say farewell to Beatrice. Although she'll make a couple of cameo appearances in the *Comedy*'s concluding cantos, she speaks for the last time in this one and shortly afterward relinquishes her role as Dante's guide.

It's fitting that she disappear, just as it was appropriate for Virgil to step away after steering Dante through hell and purgatory. Beatrice's task, like the Latin poet's, is completed. Both she and Virgil were essential guides in Dante's voyage of self-discovery. No one else could've done for him what they did. The very fact that they eventually step away from him signals that they succeeded in their commission.

The pagan Virgil guided Dante through a scouring of his reason and his will. Beatrice then took the next step by midwifing Dante's growth in wisdom.

Because at the end of the day, I think that Beatrice is a personification of Lady Wisdom or Sapientia. She seems to have a fluid identity, sometimes displaying as the soul of the earthly woman whom Dante loved from afar and sometimes as the Virgin Mary or even Christ. But I think her primary persona is Sapientia, the overflow of divine Wisdom, present from the birth of time, that percolates through and animates all of reality.

Sapientia or Lady Wisdom speaks in several biblical books—the Wisdom of Solomon, Ben Sirach, and Baruch—accepted by the Catholic and Orthodox traditions but rejected as apocryphal by Protestants. But she also makes a strong appearance in the canonical book of Proverbs, telling us that her creation was "the first of the LORD's acts of old. Ages ago I was set up, at the first, before the beginning of the earth" (8:22–23).

When God marked out the foundations of the earth, "I was constantly at His side, like a master crafter; and I was daily His delight" (8:29–30).

So there's a primordial, chthonic, and creative depth to Lady Wisdom. She knows the ways of God; in fact, she's a collaborator in them. Her task is to inspire us as we make our way through life, gently nudging us, as our boon companion, back home to the divine Source whence we came. As she tells us (8:32–36),

> Now then, my children, listen to me;
>   blessed are those who keep my ways.
> Listen to my instruction and be wise;
>   do not disregard it.
> Blessed are those who listen to me,
>   watching daily at my doors,
>   waiting at my doorway.
> For those who find me find life
>   and receive favor from the Lord.
> But those who fail to find me harm themselves;
>   all who hate me love death.

Beatrice's very name suggests that she's the personification of Lady Wisdom in the *Comedy*. It's a combination of *viatrix*, the feminine noun for "voyager," and *beatus*, "blessed." Beatrice, a spirit clearly favored by the Divine, journeys with Dante, lovingly guiding and occasionally gently chiding him, until he stands before the eternal rose of paradise, spiritually mature enough to look directly at God's light, no longer needing to observe its secondhand reflection in her eyes. Wisdom has brought him home, just as she will us if we listen, watch, and wait for her.

Paradise, Canto XXXI, Part 1: God-Pollen, Divine Eros

> *In form, then, of a white rose,*
>   *Displayed itself to me that sacred soldiery which*
>   *In his blood Christ made his spouse;*
>
> *But the other, which as it flieth seeth and doth*
>   *Sing his glory who enamoreth it, and*
>   *The excellence which hath made it what it is,*

Like to a swarm of bees which doth
  One while plunge into the flowers and another while
  Wend back to where its toil is turned to sweetness,

Ever descended into the great flower adored
  With so many leaves, and reascended thence
  To where its love doth ceaseless make sojourn.

When they descended into the flower, from rank to rank
  They proffered of the peace and of the ardor
  Which they acquired as they fanned their sides.

In religious, literary, and artistic traditions across the globe, the rose is a symbol of love. Sometimes it's a sign of passionate eros. Think of the medieval poem *Romance of the Rose* or, closer to our own time, Georgia O'Keeffe's vulva-like paintings of roses. Sometimes it's a token of chaste, courtly love. And in the Christian tradition, it's variously a symbol of the purity of the Virgin Mary, the holiness of Christ, and the sanctity of the church, all birthed from divine love.

But no lover, poet, mystic, or painter offers a more breathtaking image of the rose of love than Dante.

What he gives us in Cantos XXX and XXXI is a rose-shaped vision of paradise. He sees an immense white rose with a thousand tiers of ascending layers of petals. Seated on each of the tiers are the souls of the blessed, heaven's sacred host saved by the blood of Christ.

The rose's golden core, that which holds the paradisial rose together, is the light of God's glory. I find this immensely significant. The center of a flower is the pistil, its female reproductive part. It's as if Dante is clueing us into the wondrous fecundity of divine love, divine eros. The fourteenth-century English mystic Dame Julian of Norwich had the same intuition, so much so that she gladly described God as a maternal S/he. As she writes in her *Revelations*, "Jesus Christ that doeth good against evil is our Very Mother: we have our Being of Him, where the Ground of Motherhood beginneth, with all the sweet Keeping of Love that endlessly followeth."[38]

In keeping with the rose imagery, Dante tells us that the other host, the angels, are like bees who murmurate from the divine Source to the souls of the blessed on the flowers and then just as gracefully fly back to the Source. This happens again and again, without cease. And each time

---

38. Julian of Norwich, *Revelations*, 147.

the angelic bees swarm to the rose, they spread the "peace and ardor" of God's love that they gathered on their wings.

What an incredible image this is! Bees pollinate flowers, carrying on their wings, bodies, and legs fecund dust that keeps the earth covered in colorful beauty and succulent fruit. In paradise, angels continuously fructify the souls of the blessed with God-pollen, ensuring that they enter into the fullest state of joy love can offer. Note that the angelic pollination's insemination now ascribes male reproductive imagery to God that complements the earlier female imagery. Astounding!

Dante's depiction of paradise as a rose is organic, alive, aquiver with a highly erotic vitality. So much for the excruciatingly monotonous images of a static heaven in which souls do nothing more than stare in a frozen, zombie-like way at the celestial throne. There's nothing immobile or freeze-framed about the eternal white rose. It pulses with energy and ecstasy. Dante, who celebrated romantic love in his earlier work *La Vita Nuova*, remains an essentially erotic poet. If we forget that, or worse, if we mistakenly assume that eros has nothing to do with our yearning for God, we miss the richness of the *Comedy's* climactic final cantos.

In fact, I think that O'Keeffe's sexy rose is a perfect visual image of them. And that's why Bernard of Clairvaux is a fitting guide for the culmination of Dante's journey. But more on that later.

Paradise XXXI, Part 2: "O that thou wouldst kiss me with the kisses of thy mouth..."

> "She, the Queen of Heaven, for whom I am all
> Burning with love, will grant us every grace,
> Because I am her faithful Bernard."

I was SOOOOO bored in Sunday School when I was a kid. The well-intentioned but saccharine sermonettes by pious blue-haired ladies, the cheesy exercise books which invited us to color cartoonish sketches of Jesus, Moses, and John the Baptist, the rote memorization of Bible verses for which we were rewarded with little stickers that proclaimed us members of the "Jesus pack": ye gods! It was perfectly awful.

Even today a tiny shudder runs through me when I recall those dismal Sunday mornings. It didn't take too many of them to convince me that this church stuff was for the birds.

But in eighth grade, I experienced a revival of sorts. One of my pals, a good Baptist boy named Darryl, breathlessly whispered to me in algebra class that he'd discovered a "hot" part of the Bible called the Song of Solomon. So when I got home I went straight to the largely unused family Bible, flipped to the Song, and read the opening line: "O that thou wouldst kiss me with the kisses of thy mouth; for thy love is sweeter than wine."

I was puzzled. How else could you kiss than with your mouth? As I read on, there were lots of other allusions that, in my adolescent innocence, I didn't quite get. But I understood enough to see that Darryl was right: this *was* hot. Perplexity danced with a hormonal rush, and I exulted in the sensation. It didn't exactly make me a true believer, but it did show me that the Bible was an infinitely more complex document than Sunday School made it out to be.

The Song of Solomon is one of the most exquisite love poems in world literature. It's a highly charged paean to the erotic longing we feel for one another and for God. The sometimes shyly coy and sometimes unabashedly lusty interplay of the poem's lover and beloved apply equally well to both human–human and human–God intimacy.

Bernard of Clairvaux, the twelfth-century Cistercian monk, was so struck by the Song that he wrote no fewer than forty-three long sermons on it, easily filling up four good-sized volumes. Of all the thousands of commentaries on the Song, his is the most insightful. It makes for good reading even today.

In the final three cantos of the *Comedy*, Bernard replaces Beatrice as Dante's guide. This makes perfect sense. As I've already suggested, Dante's vision of paradise is thoroughly erotic in the fullest sense of the word. "Erotic," mind you, isn't synonymous with "sexual," although we usually conflate the two in ordinary language. Instead, it's a yearning for the beloved with everything we are, body, soul, and mind. This certainly includes but is not exclusively defined by physical desire.

The essential eros of paradise is symbolized by its rose shape, described in Cantos XXX and XXXI. Roses are traditionally symbols of both romantic, courtly love (red) and spiritual love (white).

So Bernard, the medieval celebrant of love par excellence, becomes Dante's final guide. Dante, the poet of love, surely would've known and admired Bernard's commentary on the Bible's most passionate praise of love. It's totally fitting, then, that he has the honor of leading Dante through his final paces in the *Comedy*.

But Bernard's also present because he constantly burns with fire's love for the Virgin Mary, Queen of Heaven. We'll explore the significance of that next.

Paradise, Canto XXXI, Part 3: Remembering What We've Forgotten

Bernard speaks:

> *"But look*
> > *Until thou seest enthroned the Queen*
> > *To whom this realm is subject and devoted."*
>
> *I lifted up mine eyes, and as at morn*
> > *The oriental regions of the horizon*
> > *Overcome that where the sun declineth,*
>
> *So was that pacific oriflamme*
> > *Quickened in the midst, on either side*
> > *In equal measure tempering its flame.*

When you and I forget the deep meaning of everyday words, our horizons shrink.

Our ancestors were wiser than we are. They knew that the commonest words carry locked within them great mysteries. So, for example, the ancient Greeks understood that the word "truth" (*aletheia*) refers to an "unforgetting" of that which it's crucial to remember, or that "conversion" (*metanoia*) is a literal "going beyond one's mind," one's conventional ways of thinking, to envision new possibilities.

How much richer these are than our parochial understanding of truth as "just the facts ma'am" or conversion as an emotional come-to-Jesus experience.

"Peace" is another of those words whose deep meaning for the most part has been lost. We tend to think of peace as simply the absence of conflict. But the Hebrews and Greeks knew better.

The Hebrew word for peace, *shalom*, certainly can mean an absence of conflict, but more fundamentally it signifies a state of wholeness, fulfillment, completeness. So a broken pot, for example, loses its shalom. A person who commits a sin likewise is no longer in a state of shalom. She's performed a deed which dis-integrates her character.

The Greek word for peace, *eirene*, comes from the name of Eirene, the goddess of peace. In paintings and sculptures she's typically shown holding a cornucopia, a torch of some kind, and a scepter-like emblem of authority. Peace brings plenty, its light purifies that which was ominously dark, and it ought to govern our behavior. Like shalom, peace brings plenitude, wholeness. In its absence, there is want, brokenness, and pain.

St. Bernard of Clairvaux, Dante's guide in the final three cantos, tells him to raise his eyes and gaze upon Mary, the Queen of Heaven. She sits atop the pinnacle of the eternal rose, aglow with God's love, illuminating the entire rose just like the light of dawn brightens the eastern horizon. She is, says a bedazzled Dante, the "pacific oriflamme."

And here we once more encounter the too often forgotten deep meaning of words. "Oriflamme" is derived from the Latin *aurea flamma* or "flame of gold." It signifies the presence of the divine; think of the burning bush in Genesis, the pillar of fire in Exodus, or the Pentecostal flames that descended on the apostles' heads in Acts. Wherever God is present, fullness, wholeness, and plenitude—peace—abound. Mary isn't the source of the *aurea flamma*, but she, above all other humans, is its best reflection.

Dante wants to remind his contemporaries and us of the deep meaning of oriflamme, because by his time the word had come to signify something else indeed. It's what the battle flag of the French kings was called. The flag was long, narrow, and tapered to aggressively jagged points. Typically flown from the end of a lance or spear, it depicted a yellow flame on a red background. As long as it remained raised during battle, it signified that no mercy was to be offered to the enemy. Prisoners weren't to be taken. Everyone was to be slaughtered.

Thus what is actually a profound symbol of peace, as it is in the Paradiso, became a symbol of war. Peace, proclaimed the banner, the mere absence of conflict, was the fruit of mayhem and death. The oriflamme signaled the presence of a warrior God pleased by the brokenness that comes from bloodthirsty hacking and hewing. *Deus vult!*—God wills it! Never mind that nothing is more dis-integrating, more darkly destructive, than warfare. It's the only way to achieve the absence of conflict. Simply destroy those with whom you disagree, and you have peace.

However, the Queen of Heaven hasn't forgotten what peace really means, nor has Dante. How different our lives would be if we too could remember.

Paradise, Canto XXXII, Part 1: When Heaven Freezes Over

Bernard speaks:

> *"Mayst thou see from rank to rank*
> *Descending even as I, naming their proper names,*
> *Go down the rose petal by petal."*

I first struggled my way through all the *Comedy*, as opposed to earlier fitful starts and stops, sometime in my mid-thirties (the same age, by the way, in which Dante found himself lost in the dark wood). Since then I've returned to it again and again, and each time I've discovered treasures that previously eluded me.

There's one exception: this, the penultimate canto. It puzzles and disturbs me a bit more each time I re-read it. Let me explain.

Dante's journey through the heavenly spheres has progressively revealed that paradise and all that dwells therein swim in an ocean of divine eros. Throughout the Paradiso, and particularly in Canto XXXI, Dante the poet goes to great pains to create for the reader an experience that cinematically shimmers with vitality: angels are sparks cascading and gamboling hither and yon, or tricolored bees murmurating between God and the souls of the blessed; music accompanied by strobe-like flashes fills the heavens; and Dante's ascent to and from each heavenly sphere is vibrantly swifter than a shot arrow or a spontaneous thought.

All this brilliantly conveys a sense of dynamic, fluid aliveness. The revivifying energy of divine eros quickens all creation, and we don't just read about it. Dante's poetry actually makes us feel it.

But in Canto XXXII, this cinematic vitality freezes into an immobile snapshot that's anything but alive. In it, St. Bernard offers Dante and us a rather uninspired seating chart/roll call of saints and souls seated on the eternal rose's multiple tiers.

The chart is nothing if not orderly, with Hebrew saints on one side paralleled by Christian ones on the other. It's also hierarchical, with Mary atop one vertical axis, John the Baptist atop the opposing one, and Hebrew and Christian saints ranked under each of them in order of their importance.

Given that Dante's culminating beatific vision is just around the corner, it's reasonable to expect that the vitality of the earlier cantos would be ratcheted up even more here. But it isn't. Instead, we're given an anti-climactic, deflationary, one-dimensional seating chart. The only action is the monotonous drone of Bernard's rather pedantic roll call.

So help me God, Canto XXXII's description of the rose is so paralytically frozen that I can't help thinking of that lowest depth of the Inferno where damned souls are forever ice-locked in an utterly still wasteland.

How to account for this abrupt move from the cinematic to the snapshot?

I think there are at least three possibilities.

The first is that Dante is trying to cram in what he thinks needs to be said before he reaches the end of his poem. This is a breathless strategy, reminiscent of how an abruptly canceled Netflix series whirlwinds in its final episode to say everything in an hour that the writers had planned to convey in an entire second season. Dante is constrained by his self-imposed rule of one hundred cantos. He needs to save the final one for the beatific vision. So, realizing that he's up against the end of the season, he tries to shove as much as he can in Canto 99, and the effect (for me, at any rate) is woodenly artificial.

The second possibility is that Dante the poet deliberately hits the pause button on his magnificent paradisial video to give us a long look at the eternal rose's details. This is a move that makes sense, but the timing seems off. From a stylistic perspective, it's deeply dissatisfying to freeze-frame in the middle of an action scene. It induces a kind of aesthetic coitus interruptus which collapses the momentum and excitement that's been building up.

But there's a third possibility, which doesn't, by the way, negate elements of the first two. Perhaps Dante knows exactly what he's doing. He deliberately mutes the vitality of divine eros in the *Comedy's* penultimate canto to make the beatific vision in the final one all the more explosive. We move from an uninspiringly tedious description to a moment of sheer energy that takes us by surprise and blows us sky-high. The contrast effect drives home the sheer explosiveness of an up-close-and-personal encounter with Eros Itself.

Paradise, Canto XXXII, Part 2: The Unbearable Weight of Pre-Programmed Salvation

Within this kingdom's amplitude
 No chance point may have place,
 No more than sadness may, nor thirst, nor hunger,

Because established by eternal law
 Is whatsoe'er thou seest, so that the
 Correspondence is exact between the ring and finger.

The King,

As he createth all minds in his own glad sight,
 Doth at his pleasure with grace endow
 Them differently.

A way of thinking about God traditionally known as classical theism has it that God possesses "omni-attributes": God is all-knowing (omniscient), all-powerful (omnipotent), and all-loving (omnibenevolent). Moreover, God possesses impassability and aseity, absolute independence from any other being.

This understanding of the Divine has deep philosophical roots, going all the way back to Plato. It's certainly how Thomas Aquinas thought about God. And, at least in the *Comedy's* penultimate canto, so did Dante.

The virtue of classical theism is that it tries to honor our human intuition that if God exists, God must be that than which nothing greater can be conceived. But the downside is that classical theism's description of God spawns some pretty hefty problems.

Take, for example, the claim that God is absolutely independent of any other being. What, then, is the point of prayer or, for that matter, any kind of ritualistic worship? If we're unable to influence God, even in the slightest way, what possibility is there of establishing any kind of human–divine relationship?

Or take the omni-attributes. They too generate vexing perplexities. What exactly does it mean to be all-powerful? Can God square the circle? Magically upend moral codes? Destroy Himself? Or what about omnibenevolence? Why would an all-loving God allow innocent beings to suffer? For that matter, how is impassability compatible with omnibenevolence? To love surely is to be affected by the joys and pains of the beloved. Finally, if God is omniscient, knowing all that was, is, and will be, doesn't that suggest that the future has been predetermined? And if that's so, doesn't God predestine, long before we're born, those of us who will be saved and those who won't?

This final possibility is especially disturbing. It seems to stress omnipotence and omniscience at the expense of omnibenevolence, makes divine providence seem arbitrary and even whimsical, and only underscores the futility of prayer (not to mention good works).

Yet Dante, in meditating on the eternal rose in Canto XXXII, seems unbothered by these objections. He tells us that God distributes grace according to a preset plan and "at his pleasure." Every soul in paradise is predestined to be there. Chance, by which I take Dante to mean a genuinely real (not illusory) range of possibilities, cannot exist in a universe ruled by an omni-attributed deity. There are no loose ends, no open doors, no flexibility built into reality. Everything is divinely ordained with the absolute precision of a perfectly fitting finger ring.

I don't know about you, but this kind of a universe, this kind of a God, and this kind of a frozen paradise leave me feeling as if I'm simply a pawn in a celestial board game or a pre-programmed cog in the cosmic machine. I may feel as if I'm free, but in fact my future has already been laid out for me.

This makes me feel suffocated by the weight of a preset destiny and utterly, utterly alone in an indifferent universe. And it makes me dread the prospect that I may be one of the "lucky" ones for whom a seat on one of the eternal rose's tiers has been ordained.

Happily, Dante's basic intuition, that eros is both the essential nature of God and the life breath of reality, is woven throughout the entire *Comedy* until he gets to Canto XXXII. Divine eros, which leaves plenty of open-ended room for chance—exploration, individuality, freedom, creativity, moral responsibility, and discovery—just doesn't fit well with the God of classical theism, and I for one would be happy to drop talk about omni-attributes and divine aseity as being contrary both to human experience and the biblical record.

I think Dante slightly loses his way in Canto XXXII. Fortunately, though, as we'll see, he returns to his senses toward its end when he's reminded by St. Bernard, the singer of divine love, that there's more to heaven and earth than is dreamt of by classical theism.

Paradise, Canto XXXII, Part 3: Taking the Plunge

Here let us make a stop,

And let us turn our eyes to the Primal Love,
So that gazing toward him thou mayest pierce
As far as may be into his shining.

For centuries, saints and mystics have noted a bizarre phenomenon: oftentimes, the closer we draw to God, the more beset by distractions we are. Earlier generations said this is because the Evil One doubles down at such times in an all-out effort to snatch souls away from God. In fact, in our own day, this is a theme that runs through C. S. Lewis's mordantly wise *Screwtape Letters*.

While I have no problem with that explanation, I'd offer an additional one: Rudolf Otto's insight that God, the Holy, is *mysterium tremendum et fascinans*.[39] This means that we are at one and the same time attracted to (*fascinans*) and fearful of (*tremendum*) the Divine Mystery. We sense that God is the Absolute Plenitude, the great I AM, for which we crave. But we also sense that the I AM is a mystery beyond our comprehension, and getting too close to it overwhelms us with fear and trembling.

This is a perfectly biblical understanding of God. Think, for example, of Moses' ambivalent response to the burning bush, or the prophets' initially hesitant reactions when called by God. Think of the Pharisees' obsessive and fearful hostility to Jesus.

I think this may account for the flatly frozen bulk of Canto XXXII. Dante the poet and the pilgrim is on the threshold of encountering the *mysterium tremendum et fascinans*, the intensely vital Love that creates and sustains the cosmos, and he's temporarily overwhelmed by craving/dread. So he retreats into a tedious but safe rollcall of the saints perched on the eternal rose. It's as if he needs a preparatory time-out to muster the courage to "pierce" the "radiance of Primal Love."

(Note, by the way, the erotic flavor of the language. Dante is getting his groove back.)

Eventually he's ready to take the plunge. That's when his spiritual guide, St. Bernard, tells him that it's time to cease the rollcall, open wide his arms, and simply fall forward into the Mystery.

---

39. Otto, *Idea of the Holy*.

Look. As a philosopher and theologian, I spend most of my time in my head, analyzing ideas and constructing conceptual models. That's just how I'm built. But I have enough self-insight to recognize that my habitual thinking about God throws up a protective buffer between me and a red hot, living experience of God. I insulate myself with abstractions so as not to get scorched by the burning bush.

So I totally get Dante's retreat strategy in most of Canto XXXII.

One day perhaps I, like Dante, will find the courage to cease my own delaying tactics, take off my philosophical and theological safety vest, and plunge into Primal Love. Dante the pilgrim's journey through hell, purgatory, and paradise takes place in the space of but a single week. My own pilgrimage, spanning more than three score and ten years at this point, is still very much a work in progress.

Paradise, Canto XXXIII, Prelude: To See the Stars

> ... the Love which moves the sun and the other stars.
> (... l'amor che move il sole e l'altre stelle.)

There are lots of ways to read Dante's *Comedy*. The historian ferrets out what the poem suggests about political and cultural events contemporaneous with the poet. A psychologist looks out for what the cantos reveal about the poet's inner life. The theologian and the philosopher are intrigued by the *Comedy's* metaphysics and the literary critic by its style.

Each of these approaches, in its own way, is proper and good.

But that's not how I read the *Comedy*. For me, to read Dante's journey through hell, purgatory, and paradise is to travel with him, not as a spectator but as a participant who experiences shock and horror in the infernal regions, contrition and healing on the purgatorial terraces, and transformative insight in paradise.

The first leg of the journey forces a painful soul-searching in which I come face to face with the nest of scorpions swirling and stinging within me. I awaken to the ugly fact that I contain each and every one of hell's tiers. The second leg offers me counsel on how to climb out from under the messes I've made of my life. It makes me want to be a better human being, and assures me that I can be. Both of these are necessary preparations for the journey's final stretch: the lived, felt, experienced recognition, not a merely abstract acknowledgment, that the Divine Mystery is richer and deeper and truer than I can ever possibly imagine. In coming a bit closer to it, I grow more human. In touching it, even if only slightly, I glimpse the face I had before I was born.

So, as we saw in the introduction, the entire trajectory of the *Comedy* aims at personal transformation. Dante invites us to move beyond the quotidian, instead fixing our gaze on the depths and heights of reality. I think that's why each of the poem's three books ends with an evocation of stars:

> Inferno: "... we came out once more to see the stars."
> Purgatorio: "... eager to rise, now ready for the stars."
> Paradiso: "... the Love that moves the sun and the other stars."

Now that I've arrived at its final, one hundredth canto, I unexpectedly find myself reluctant to write about it. It feels as if doing so is spiritually immodest or somehow inappropriate, as if the transformative journey Dante's taken us on should properly culminate in silent wonder-filled gratitude. Words, as Dante himself confesses, reveal their paltriness when tasked with describing such things.

But words are all we have. So I'll struggle to shape them in such a way as to convey, howsoever clumsily, what Dante has done: opened our eyes so that we better see the stars and what lies beyond them.

Paradise, Canto XXXIII, Part 1: Into the Wild

> *Thou Virgin Mother, daughter of thy Son!*

Christians have a tendency to domesticate God.

Sometimes we neuter God in thought, word, and deed because we simply can't bear to open ourselves to the Divine's explosive presence. Who can see the face of God and live?! How could we not be reduced to ashes in God's presence? Far better to keep one's distance.

But most often, I suspect, it's complacency or indifference that domesticates God. The busyness of life, the tedious routine of the quotidian, the eye-glazing predictability of formal worship, liturgical readings, and rotely mouthed dogmatic formulae: all these can gradually enshroud God in a thick, non-threatening fog. God becomes just another safe and not terribly interesting object in our landscape: a declawed pussycat instead of the Lion of Judah or a stupidly blinking parakeet instead of the Paraclete.

Transcendence, numinosity, edginess, unfathomability: Poof! Gone! Nothing to see here. Move along.

Although we go through periods in which strident atheists capture the public imagination—witness the meteoric rise and short-lived notoriety twenty years ago of the so-called New Atheism movement—infidelity has never been the most worrisome threat to Christianity in particular and religion in general. Domestication is. The dangerous inflection point is when Christians themselves lose a sense of God's untameability, a divine wildness that defies language and logic.

In the final canto of his *Comedy*, Dante wants to reawaken those of us who complacently genuflect before a caged parakeet instead of falling, Paraclete-stricken, to the ground before the Living God.

So the very first line of the canto hits us right between the eyes with a double dose of rattlingly paradoxical language: "Virgin Mother" and "daughter of thy Son."

We've become so familiar with "Virgin Mother" that it's hard to appreciate just how utterly uncanny the expression is. "Virgin Mother" is equivalent to a logical contradiction: "A = not-A." It's a reminder that in the wild terrain of Godland, anything is possible.

But anticipating that our familiarity with the expression might've blunted our appreciation of its bizarreness, Dante weds it to "daughter of your Son." What?! How can someone be daughter to her own son?! This description is just as uncanny as "Virgin Mother," but because we've never heard it before, it raises our eyebrows and perks up our ears. It's not been domesticated through constant use.

Now it's quite possible to don an academic robe and launch into a calm lecture about Dante's clever use of metaphorical imagery or the theological point that all humanity, including Mary, has been born anew by the incarnation. But we ought to stick with the immediate psychic and spiritual shock effect of "daughter of your Son." It shakes us, discombobulates our comfortable complacency, and slaps us into a recognition of the equally strange ascription of motherhood to a virgin.

This is the frame of mind and state of soul, one radically open to the futility (and foolishness!) of trying to tame the Divine, that prepares us to join Dante as he stands before the wildly roaring Lion of Judah.

Paradise, Canto XXXIII, Part 2: The Grace-Favored Vessel

Virgin Mother,

Thou art she who didst human nature
So ennoble that its own Maker
Scorned not to become its making.

In thee is united
Whatever in created being is of excellence.

Athena may have sprung fully mature and armored from Zeus's forehead, but Christian doctrine didn't and doesn't leap fully developed from the pages of sacred scripture.

This is just another way of saying that the Bible isn't (thank God!) a persnickety recipe book or a catechism that exhaustively dots all the i's and crosses all the t's.

Christians believe that the Bible contains "all that's necessary for salvation." But in the mid-nineteenth century, John Henry Newman, one of the wisest Christians of the modern era, argued that this doesn't mean every Christian doctrine is fully elaborated in it. Instead, scripture offers a host of inspired hints, insinuations, and gestures that point to doctrine but that require centuries of prayer, reflection, and *sensus fidelium* for their full expression.[40]

In other words, the Christian community's awareness of doctrine develops over time, just as an individual Christian's appreciation of his or her faith does. Spiritual phylogeny and ontogeny mirror one another.

To a skeptic, what Christians call development of doctrine may come across as a spurious revisionism that pretends to excavate hidden treasure from barren soil in order to justify nonscriptural beliefs. But viewed through the eyes of faith, the assumption of doctrinal development is a humble acknowledgment that it takes a long time for humans to assimilate the providential pattern that, once recognized, connects dots that earlier seemed disjointed.

One of those doctrines whose awareness develops over time is the immaculate conception of Mary, the Mother of God. Although not officially promulgated as a dogma until 1854, hints of it stretch all the way

---

40. Newman, *Development of Christian Doctrine.*

back to Justin Martyr in the second century. It's just that it took nearly two millennia for all the pieces to finally come together.

The Christian story is this. After who knows how many efforts—covenants, miracles and disasters, prophetic proclamations—to recall humanity to its true nobility, God decides it's time to personally step in. So in the incarnation's self-emptying, God becomes human to show us, firsthand, what it means to be perfect.

Now, the only way to be human is to be born of a human woman. But women, no less than men, are broken. How, therefore, can any son or daughter born of woman be immune from that brokenness? How can God incarnate as a perfect human, the New Adam, from a flawed vessel? And if God incarnates as a broken human, the game is up. Nothing's been accomplished.

That's the conundrum. The only way to salvage the story is to infer that when Gabriel tells Mary she is favored by God (Luke 1:28) he means that she was "immaculately conceived" and hence is exempt from human brokenness. Therefore the fruit of her womb will be, as Elizabeth proclaimed, "blessed" (Luke 1:42) with human perfection.

This isn't some kind of disingenuous back-filling. It's a reasonable inference that fills a gap in an otherwise coherent story. It's a perfect example of Newman's insight about the development of doctrine.

In the poem to Mary that opens Canto XXXIII, St. Bernard clearly has an intuition of this yet-to-be formalized doctrine when he says that Mary's merit was such that the Creator didn't disdain to incarnate in her womb. She was so pure that all that creation knows of excellence found a home within her. She was the necessary, although not sufficient, condition for the success of God's plan to salvage humankind.

Doctrinal development is still going on. We'd be foolish to think that we've exhausted the depths of inspired scripture in the short span of two thousand years. New insights into the ways of God await us if we keep our inner vision clear and our hearts open.

Paradise, Canto XXXIII, Part 3: Like Calls to Like

> *And I, who to the goal of all my longing*
> *Was drawing nigh, even as was meet the*
> *Ardor of the yearning quenched within me.*

> *Bernard gave me the sign and smiled to me*
> *That I should look on high, but I already*
> *Of myself was such as he would have me.*

I think humans have a connatural desire for God that is, as Dante the pilgrim says here, "the goal of all [our] yearning." It springs from the affinity between humans and God.

We may be made, as cosmologists tell us, of stardust. But we're more fundamentally made of Godstuff, stamped through and through with divine DNA, bearing the imprint of our Maker, our Godparent. Like calls to like. In a pre-reflective and even pre-conscious way, we feel an affinity with our Source that's more primal than a womb-child's syncopation with its mother's heartbeat. The Source, in turn, feels just as connected to us. We are God's beloved womb-children.

That iconic image in Michelangelo's creation of God and Adam straining to touch one another's fingertips: a perfect representation of the mutual yearning born of connatural affinity.

Dante is about to touch God's fingertip. Bernard, who replaced Beatrice as his mentor on this final leg of his journey, suggests with a gesture that his ward raise his eyes to God. But there's no need for such a prompting because Dante's connatural desire has already instinctively directed his attention to where it needs to be. Bernard's guidance is no longer needed.

Our connatural desire for God is innate. But for any number of reasons that desire can be misdirected toward objects that will never fulfill us. In Dante's Inferno, each and every one of its inhabitants are there because of disordered desire. They perverted their inborn yearning for God into ravenous appetites for substitutes—power, lust, wealth, and so on—fast foods all, that may assuage hunger for a brief moment but fail to ultimately satisfy, much less nourish.

What they failed to do is to strain upward. Because just as like calls to like, only like can satisfy like.

Still, no matter how far we stray from the Divine object of our connatural yearning, our affinity to It remains deeply a part of us. And precisely because like calls to like, we can't help being pulled in the right direction, even though it may take centuries and centuries for us to consciously recognize and embrace the genuine object of our spiritual instinctive craving. In the fullness of time, the Inferno, even its lowest depth, will be empty.

Paradise, Canto XXXIII, Part 4: Shhh!

> *As he who is dreaming seeth,*
>   *And when the dream is gone the passion stamped*
>   *Remaineth, and nought else cometh to the mind again;*
>
> *Even such as I; for almost wholly*
>   *Faileth me my vision, yet doth the sweetness*
>   *That was born of it still drop within my heart.*
>
> *So doth the snow unstamp it to the sun,*
>   *So to the wind on the light leaves*
>   *Was lost the Sybil's wisdom.*

Although it may sound a bit fishy coming from a person whose entire adult life has been devoted to speaking and writing, I think we humans talk too much.

Don't get me wrong. Speech, our ability to translate ideas and sensory perceptions and emotions and fears and joys into words goes way beyond extraordinary. It's a phenomenon that will astound and humble me as long as I have breath left.

But we nonetheless talk too much.

What I mean by this is that we persist in trying to speak that which either can't be spoken or shouldn't be spoken.

Sometimes we have experiences that so break through our ordinary conceptual frameworks that language simply can't cope with them. They make deep and lasting impressions on us—we can feel, as Dante says of his experience of the Divine, that we're distilling them in our hearts, the very deepest parts of ourselves—but they remain beyond the reach of accurate description. We struggle to put them into words, but the harder we try, the more we risk dispersing their effect.

These sorts of fundamental experiences are generally called "ineffable," unable to be uttered. It's paradoxical, isn't it? They reveal so much to us, yet we can't hold on to them. Dante's likening them to fleeting memories of dreams, melting snow, and windblown leaves is so on target.

Consequently, after we gesture toward them with a few inadequate but hopefully evocative metaphors and similes, it's best to lock them away in our hearts and keep still, treasuring and appreciating them without trying to seize and control them with words.

There's a second meaning to the word "ineffable," one that seems to arise in the late sixteenth century: that which shouldn't be uttered. Some experiences are so holy that it's impertinent at best and downright sacrilegious at worst to try to peg them down with mortal speech. It's not only that we should remove our shoes when we stand on holy ground. We should also silence our tongues and allow the Presence before Whom we kneel to overpower us with its Plenitude.

Let's face it: Our mouths should catch fire every time we venture to speak the word "God."

Dante is fully aware of this. His journey through the three realms has impressed this truth upon him in an unforgettable way. So although his explosive poetic imagination and religious zeal compel him to speak, he's scrupulous about trying not to overstep the limits of language. And this brings us to a second paradox: to discern the boundary of speech is already to go beyond it. Otherwise, how would we know it's the boundary? So our recognition that our experiences of the Holy are ultimately unspeakable actually—and wonderfully!—leads us, even if only a step or two, across the frontier to that place where speech is beside the point.

Paradise, Canto XXXIII, Part 5: Scattered Leaves, Divine Book

> *O grace abounding, wherein I presumed*
> *To fix my look on the eternal light*
> *So long that I consumed my sight thereon!*
>
> *Within its depths I saw ingathered,*
> *Bound by love in one volume,*
> *The scattered leaves of all the universe.*
>
> *The universal form of this complex*
> *I think that I beheld, because more largely,*
> *As I say this, I feel that I rejoice.*

Every so often this happens. In the middle of reading a book, I discover that the volume was screwed up in production, and that a number of pages are missing. There's a gap in the novel's storyline or in the essay's argument. Sometimes the discontinuity isn't fatal. Although irritating, the empty space can be leapt over with relative ease and the journey continued. But occasionally the gap is a chasm there's no getting across.

The last time this happened to me was in a volume of Anglican philosopher Austin Farrar's essays. Farrar is an extremely logical thinker. To miss a single step in his tight reasoning, much less a page or two, is to lose the entire thread.

A missing page or two is a frustration for anyone wanting to read an entire bound volume. But now imagine that you're walking along one day and suddenly a breeze scoots a printed sheet along the ground in front of you. You pick it up, see that it's page forty-nine from some book or other, and are intrigued by what's written on it. You look around for other loose pages, and eventually find a dozen or so.

Each of them offers you fascinating snippets. But the pages aren't in consecutive order and the volume they belong to remains missing. You get a few vague and fragmentary ideas from them about the possible plot or thesis of the book, but the big picture eludes you. You're alternately intrigued and frustrated.

This image of discovering and deciphering scattered pages is a parable about how we humans read the Book of Nature. Our intellects, although capable of real greatness, are nonetheless limited. So are our senses. We simply can't hold in our minds or imaginations the cosmic book's entire storyline. We're not bad at honing in on particular episodes in it and drawing provisional connections between them. But the Big Picture eludes us.

Whereas you and I see only scattered leaves, God sees the entire cosmos bound by love into a single book. Or perhaps "sees" isn't quite the right word here. God contains the book. Within God is the "universal form" and the "fusion of all things." In God are the laws of physics that infuse orderliness and symmetry into the created universe and the psychological patterns that regulate human behavior. In God are the prototypes of every genus and species of animate and inanimate things. In God is every particular creature: not a sparrow falls; not a hair goes uncounted. The entire volume of past, present, and future, in all its manifold complexity and underlying simplicity, is within God.

Which, I suppose, is a way of proclaiming God's eternal and infinite nature. But Dante's poetic expression of this rather unnourishing abstraction makes it stick to one's ribs.

In his vision of God, Dante the pilgrim is vouchsafed an awareness of the fusion of all things in God. It's not clear if he actually discerns the

Big Picture in all its details or simply (as if this would be "simply"!) sees that the Big Picture is contained in and sustained by God. We do know from earlier cantos that the souls of the blessed see what's in God's mind. They view the universe through God's eyes. But remember that Dante is a mortal sojourner in paradise, and still has a mortal's mind.

Just spare a thought, though, about what it would be to catch even a split-second glimpse of cosmic unity, a unity that simultaneously reveals the majesty of the unifying Creator. After that, our gathering up of the Book of Nature's "scattered leaves" would take on a whole new feel, wouldn't it? We'd be better able to intuit the golden thread that binds them together. And the frustration over missing pages we once felt would give way to an overflowing sense of joy and gratitude. Being mortal, we'll never in this life be able to read the whole book. But our split-second vision of God assures us that it exists.

Paradise Canto XXXIII, Part 6: The Time I Met God

Thus all suspended did my mind
Gaze fixed, immovable, intent,
Ever enkindled by its gazing.

Such at that light doth man become
That to turn thence to any other sight
Could not by possibility be ever yielded.

For the good, which is the object of the will,
Is therein wholly gathered, and outside it
That same thing is defective which therein is perfect.

When Dante the pilgrim writes of staring full throttle into the Divine Light, so entranced that it's impossible for him even to think of turning away, I wince a little. His word-picture of that brilliance makes me involuntarily shut my eyelids.

But even though my reaction is an unintended homage to his poetic genius, it's also a bit absurd, isn't it? Dante's quite clear that the light he's writing about isn't the physical phenomenon that hurts my eyes and makes me squint. He sees it with his mind, he's attracted to it by his will, and he's transformed by and within it.

He's not referring to garden variety light. He's talking about *Light*.

I have some idea of what Dante means because of an extraordinary thing that happened to me forty years ago. Despite all the time that's passed, my memory of it is fresh and clear.

I was in my second year as a philosophy professor at a rural liberal arts college. On a perfect late autumn afternoon, one with a breathtakingly beautiful azure sky, I took a bike ride after my final class of the day. A half hour or so in I paused on the road to take a swig of water. To my right was a soybean field. The soy leaves had turned that deep, rich gold they do in the fall, and a gentle breeze was rippling them in what looked like the soft susurration of low tide.

So there I was, one foot on the macadam road, one foot on a bike pedal, water bottle raised to my mouth, eyes fixed on the soybean field. I remember thinking "that looks just like a golden sea." And then suddenly WHOOSH!—I was gone. There was no longer an "I" there, no longer a Kerry on a bike. Nor was there a beanfield, or a deep blue sky, or a soft breeze. Time and space vanished. There was nothing but liquid gold, golden motion, golden brilliance, without horizon or boundary or time. It wasn't that I was gazing at it, because I was no longer there. I'd been absorbed by the liquid gold. I was in it—and yet "I" wasn't, because I no longer was.

I was transformed within that Light, as Dante would say.

I've no idea how long the experience lasted. But just as suddenly as I'd disappeared, WHOOSH!—I was back, water bottle raised in mid-air, feet on macadam and pedal, soybean field to my right, azure sky above, breeze rippling the leaves. Everything was as it had been before the experience—and yet everything was completely different. For a few seconds—for an eternity?—I'd been absorbed by the Transcendent.

And immediately following the experience, I was suffused with the conviction that what had happened to me was supremely good, that everything I'd ever desired or ever would desire would fall short of the goodness of that golden sea, that

> *Outside it that same thing is defective*
> *Which therein is perfect.*

I wouldn't call this a conversion experience, if by that one means a sudden transformation. No, the effects over the past four decades of my experience in the golden Light have been more subtle, more organic than that. But I do know that what happened to me was so significant that the time frame of my life can be divided into pre–golden-sea and post–golden-sea periods.

And I can't help but think that Dante, whose words so accurately describe the time the Transcendent scooped me up, must have had his own golden-sea moment too.

Paradise, Canto XXXIII, Part 7: Rainbows, Fire, Kisses, Breath

> *In the profound and shining being*
> *Of the deep light appeared to me*
> *Three circles, of three colors and one magnitude;*
>
> *One by the second as Iris by Iris*
> *Seemed reflected, and the third seemed a fire*
> *Breathed equally from one and from the other.*
>
> *O Light Eternal who only in thyself abides,*
> *Only thyself dost understand, and to thyself*
> *Self-understood self-understanding, turnest love and smiling!*

The first Sunday after the Christian Feast of Pentecost strikes fear or at least anxiety in the hearts of priests and pastors. That's because it's Trinity Sunday, the one day in the liturgical year clergy are expected to preach on the Trinitarian God whom Christians at least claim to believe in. For my money, I suspect that theologian Karl Rahner was more right than not when he suggested that many Christians are probably secret unitarians.[41]

If Rahner's correct, it's undoubtedly because God as Trinity is so difficult to wrap one's mind around. For twenty-one centuries, theologians have tried to make sense of it, many of them ultimately concluding that the Trinity is a Mystery best left alone. The rest of us, unaccustomed to theological subtleties, might prefer simply not to think about it: hence Rahner's unitarian worry.

I'm not unsympathetic with either of these moves. But I think we can do a bit better.

Dante beautifully imagines the Trinity as three concentric circles, two of which are like a pair of mutually reflecting rainbows (Irises) and the third like a fiery ring breathed forth by one and by the other. There's

---

41. Rahner, *Trinity*, 10.

an exuberant vitality to the whole as well as utter self-sufficiency and self-fulfillment: abiding in self alone and loving and smiling on self.

This is actually a poetic paraphrase of what Augustine famously wrote: "Each [of the divine Persons] is in each, all are in each, each is in all, all are in all, and all are one."[42]

Yeah, okay. But what the heck does that mean?

Let me conjure up a couple of barbarous sounding (to our ears, anyway) words: the Greek *perichoresis* and its Latin translation *circumincession*. Both of them literally mean "rotation" or "going around," but in Trinitarian theology are invoked to connote the "mutual indwelling" of Father, Son, and Holy Spirit. "I am *in* the Father and the Father is *in* me" (John 14:10). The Trinity is a perichoretic union.

But throwing around fancy words like perichoresis doesn't take us very far, does it? So, let's go a bit further.

Don't think of "union" here as a static, frozen fait accompli. Instead, think of it in dynamically fluid terms. God as a perichoretic union is an unceasing flow of divine essence, such that God the Father forever flows into God the Son and the Son into the Father, mutually giving and receiving in an equal and identical way the very stuff of Godhood: Dante's two mutually reflecting rainbows.

Now think of the eternal flow between God the Father and God the Son, the third fiery ring described by Dante, as the Holy Spirit, that vitality which actually is the mutual giving and receiving of Father and Son.

Here's another way of imaging divine perichoresis: In one of his sermons on the Song of Songs, Bernard of Clairvaux compared the mutual indwelling of Father and Son as a kiss between Lover and Beloved. The Holy Spirit in turn is the spiration or breath exchanged in the divine kiss.[43]

The wondrous thing is that the Trinity isn't something out there in space, way beyond our everyday life. Not at all. Whenever you and I are in-spired by the Holy Spirit, we breathe in some of the same air that connects the Father and Son. Whenever we adore God in prayer or worship, we're mouth to mouth with God—*ad ora* is the Latin root of our "adore"—sharing the divine kiss between Father and Son.

You and I, in other words, participate in the perichoretic union. This recognition should bring us to our knees in awe.

---

42. Augustine, *Trinity*, 214.
43. Bernard of Clairvaux, *Song of Songs*, 46.

This way of thinking about God as Trinity enriches both our understanding of God and our relationship with God in ways that the implicit unitarianism Rahner worries about can't even begin to match. Dante's magnificent evocation of the perichoretic union reminds us of this. But he's not done yet. He has more to say about the Trinity.

Paradise, Canto XXXIII, Part 8: Catch Me If You Can!

> *That circling which appeared in thee to be*
> *Conceived as a reflected light,*
> *By mine eyes scanned some little,*
>
> *In itself, of its own color*
> *Seemed to be painted with our own effigy,*
> *And thereat my sight was all committed to it.*
>
> *As the geometer who all sets himself*
> *To measure the circle and who findeth not,*
> *Think as he may, the principle he lacketh;*
>
> *Such was I at this new-seen spectacle;*
> *I would perceive how the image consorteth*
> *With the circle, and how it settleth there.*

There's a line from Flannery O'Connor's novel *Wise Blood* that sticks with me. It describes Jesus flitting "from tree to tree in the back of [our] mind[s], a wild ragged figure."[44]

For me, Jesus, the God-man, will always remain ineluctable, just out of reach, every so often emerging from the shadows long enough for me to catch a glimpse of him before retreating back into the trees. He'll always be "a wild ragged figure," absolutely beyond churchy domestication. He's not meek and mild, he's not my best buddy, he's not the golden-haired, blue-eyed laughing guy imagined by Sunday School book illustrators.

Here's what he is: a surd, a question mark, a *skandalon* who periodically but unpredictably pounces from the treetops to knock all the theological smugness, all the ecclesial complacency, all the confidence that we've got this Christianity thing nailed down, out of us.

---

44. O'Connor, *Wise Blood*, "Author's Note."

Then, before disappearing again, he whispers, "Catch me if you can!"

But the challenge isn't meant to mock or discourage us. It's a playful but at the same time deadly serious invitation to enter ever more deeply into his enigma instead of pretending that we've cracked the mystery.

It's a surprising fact to some, but makes absolute sense to me, that in all the Paradiso Christ appears but three times, and in each of them Dante's description, although powerful, is achingly nebulous. He offers us fleeting through-the-trees glimpses of the Savior.

The first glimpse is in Canto XIV, in the heavenly sphere of Mars. Dante the pilgrim sees a giant cross, encircled with brilliantly sparkling lights, that "flashed forth Christ." But that's all he conveys. "Here," he confesses, "my memory doth outrun my wit." He can't find words adequate to express the experience.

Sighting number two comes in Canto XXIII, in the sphere of the fixed stars. Over and above "thousands of lamps," Dante sees "one sun which all and each enkindled." Pouring forth from its "living light" is its "shining substance." But the brilliance is so overwhelming that Dante's "poor eyes" could not endure the sight.

The third and culminating appearance of Christ concludes the *Comedy's* final canto. Within the whirling trinitarian circle, an amazed Dante discerns "man's very image." Yet the image is also, at the same time, God the Father's "first reflected light," the Second Person of the Trinity.

These two descriptions, so apparently incompatible, underscore the ungraspability of the Christ-figure: a mirror reflection of the eternal, infinite Father (remember the twin rainbows?) but also a time-bound, finite human.

Ecce Deus. Ecce homo. Catch me if you can.

So we're in O'Connor's tangled forest again. Trying to rationally comprehend the God-man is as impossible as squaring the circle. And yet, as Dante tells us, we hunger to do so. It's true that we can rationally "understand" the definition of incarnation: God the Holy Spirit impregnates a virgin, the messianic Son is born, blah blah blah. The formula can be rattled off at the drop of a hat.

But comprehending it (*comprehendere* = "to take it all in, to intuit its entire complexity")? Forget about it.

Does that mean that this hunger deep within us can never be satisfied? No, as we'll see now that our journey concludes.

Paradise, Canto XXXIII, Finale: At-one-ment

But not for this were my proper wings,
  Save that my mind was smitten
  By a flash wherein its will came to it.

To the high fantasy here power failed;
  But already my desire and will were rolled,
  Even as a wheel that moveth equally, by

The Love which moves the sun and the other stars.

Psychologists have recently put legs on one of the oldest symbols of love, two intertwined hearts. They've discovered that the hearts of mothers and their infants actually beat in unison. Moreover, in a separate study, a similar synchronization was discovered in romantic lovers. "The two will become one flesh, no longer two but one flesh" (Mark 10:7–8).

The same chthonic drive for union that synchronizes the pulses of mothers and infants and romantic partners craves an even deeper intimacy with the divine Source of all that's worthy of love. ("O Plenitude of Grace," as Dante calls God.) This yearning, one that fueled Dante's pilgrimage through hell, purgatory, and paradise, also animates us, even if we often don't recognize it for what it is. At our deepest level, we long for our personal being to unite with the Great Being, to be fused into the Supreme Lover, the Divine Mother, the Universal Womb.

We desire our hearts to beat in tandem with God's. This is the core of the doctrine of the atonement: the at-*one*-ment.

When Dante in the final moments of the *Comedy* sees the image of Christ in the tri-circular Trinity, he realizes his powers of comprehension can't stretch far enough for him to intellectually grasp the paradox of God-manhood. But then Plenitudinous Grace, in a lightning bolt-like flash of inspiration, grants the vision that Dante's imagination or "high fantasy" can't conjure. Things come together in a sudden intuitive grasp of the whole.

Dante's description here is so perfect, isn't it? Like a wheel in perfect balance, he clicks into synchronization with the Love that animates all creation. Think of misaligned gear teeth suddenly snapping into place, or of a glitch in a movie projector that knocks video and audio out of sync suddenly readjusting—or, to return to where we began, think of the hearts of a mother and her child suddenly beating as one: these give you some idea of the mystical union with God Dante finally experiences.

Two become one in a process the church fathers called divinization or *theosis*. At-one-ment. "As thou, Father, art in me, and I in thee, may they be one in us" (John 17:21).

This is the loving synchronization for which we're made, and all of our other loves, each one precious and irreplaceable, are stepping stones to it. This is the ultimate truth Dante the poet graces us with. This makes the long and often perilous pilgrimage into wakefulness and wholeness through which he's guided us more than worth it.

Finis

Works Cited

Anonymous. *The Cloud of Unknowing and Other Works*. New York: Penguin, 2001.
Anselm. *Proslogion*. In *Anselm of Canterbury: The Major Works*, edited by Brian Davies and G. R. Evans, 82–104. Oxford: Oxford University Press, 2008.
Aristotle. *Metaphysics*. Translated by Hugh Lawson-Tancred. New York: Penguin, 1999.
Augustine of Hippo. *Confessions*. Translated by Henry Chadwick. Oxford: Oxford University Press, 2008.
———. *Enchiridion on Faith, Hope, and Charity*. Translated by Bruce Harbert. Hyde Park, NY: New City, 1999.
———. "Homily VII on the First Epistle of John." Translated by John Gibb. In *Nicene and Post-Nicene Fathers*, 7:501–5. New York: Christian Literature, 1888.
———. *Trinity*. Translated by Stephen McKenna. Washington, DC: Catholic University of America Press, 1963.
Bernanos, Georges. *Diary of a Country Priest*. Translated by Pamela Morris. Cambridge, MA: Da Capo, 2002.
Bernard of Clairvaux. *Sermons on the Song of Song*. Translated by Kilian Walsh. Trappist, KY: Cistercian, 2008.
Bhagavad Gita: A New Translation. Translated by Stephen Mitchell. New York: Harmony, 2002.
Calvin, John. *Institutes of the Christian Religion*. Translated by John Allen. Philadelphia: Presbyterian Board of Education, 1813.
Campbell, Joseph. *The Hero with a Thousand Faces*. Novato, CA: New World Library, 2008.
Carroll, Lewis. *Through the Looking Glass*. Ornda, CA: SeaWolf, 2018.
Cicero. *On Friendship and The Dream of Scipio*. Translated by J. G. F. Powell. Liverpool: Liverpool University Press, 2015.
Dante Alighieri. *Inferno*. Translated by John Aitken Carlyle. London: Dent, 1903.
———. *Paradiso*. Translated by P. H. Wicksteed. London: Dent, 1904.
———. *Purgatorio*. Translated by Thomas Okey. London: Dent, 1904.
Dos Passos, John. *U.S.A.: The Complete Trilogy*. New York: Mariner Classics, 2024.
Dostoevsky, Fyodor. *The Brothers Karamazov*. Translated by Richard Pevear and Larissa Volokhonsky. New York: Farrar, Straus and Giroux, 1990.
Eliot, T. S. "Dante." In *Selected Essays*, 237–77. London: Faber & Faber, 1932.
———. "The Hollow Men." In *Collected Poems, 1909–1962*, 77–82. New York: Harcourt Brace, 1991.

WORKS CITED

Emerson, Ralph Waldo. "Self-Reliance." In *Selected Writings*, edited by William H. Gilman, 257–79. New York: Signet, 1983.

Freud, Sigmund. *Beyond the Pleasure Principle*. Translated by James Strachey. New York: Norton, 1961.

Gelb, Arthur, and Barbara Gelb. *O'Neill*. New York: Dell, 1965.

Girard, René. *Deceit, Desire, and the Novel: Self and Other in Literary Structure*. Translated by Yvonne Freccaro. Baltimore: Johns Hopkins University Press, 1976.

Heidegger, Martin. "Letter on Humanism." In *Basic Writings*, edited by David Farrell Krell, 213–65. New York: Harper Perennial, 2008.

———. "The Origin of the Work of Art." In *Basic Writings*, edited by David Farrell Krell, 139–203. New York: Harper Perennial, 2008.

Hobbes, Thomas. *Leviathan*. Indianapolis: Hackett, 1994.

Homer. *The Odyssey*. Translated by Robert Fagles. New York: Penguin, 1996.

Hopkins, Gerald Manley. *Poems and Prose*. Edited by W. H. Gardner. New York: Penguin, 1984.

Hutcheson, Francis. *An Essay on the Nature and Conduct of the Passions and Affections, with Illustrations on the Moral Sense*. Carmel, IN: Liberty Fund, 2003.

Irenaeus. *Against Heresies*. Translated by John Keble. Oxford: James Parker, 1872.

Julian of Norwich. *Revelations of Divine Love*. London: Methuen, 1907.

Justin Martyr. *The First and Second Apologies*. Translated by Leslie William Barnard. New York: Paulist, 1997.

Lewis, C. S. *The Great Divorce*. New York: HarperOne, 2001.

Locke, John. *An Essay Concerning Human Understanding*. Indianapolis: Hackett, 1996.

Lovejoy, Arthur O. *The Great Chain of Being*. Cambridge, MA: Harvard University Press, 1976.

Lucan. *Pharsalia*. Translated by Edwin Ridley. London: Longmans, Green, 1905.

Lucretius. *On the Nature of Things*. Translated by Alicia Stallings. New York: Penguin, 2007.

Marcel, Gabriel. *Homo Viator: Introduction to the Metaphysic of Hope*. Translated by Emma Craufurd. New York: Harper & Row, 1962.

Melville, Herman. "Bartleby, the Scrivener." In *Billy Bud, Bartleby, and Other Stories*, 17–54. New York: Penguin, 2016.

Merton, Thomas. *The Seven Storey Mountain*. New York: HarperOne, 1999.

Milton, John. *Paradise Lost*. New York: Penguin, 2003.

Newman, John Henry. *An Essay in Aid of a Grammar of Assent*. New York: Longmans, Green, 1903.

———. *An Essay on the Development of Christian Doctrine*. Notre Dame, IN: University of Notre Dame Press, 1994.

Nietzsche, Friedrich. *On the Advantage and Disadvantage of History for Life*. Translated by Peter Preuss. Indianapolis: Hackett, 1980.

O'Connor, Flannery. *Wise Blood*. New York: Farrar, Straus and Giroux, 2007.

Otto, Rudolf. *The Idea of the Holy*. Translated by John W. Harvey. New York: Oxford University Press, 1958.

Ovid. *Metamorphosis*. Translated by David Raeburn. New York: Penguin, 2004.

Pascal, Blaise. *Pensées*. Translated by A. J. Krailsheimer. New York: Penguin, 1995.

Peirce, C. S. "Evolutionary Love." In *Philosophical Writings of Peirce*, edited by Justus Buchler, 361–74. New York: Dover, 2011.

Petrarch. *The Life of Solitude*. Translated by Jacob Zeitlin. Urbana: University of Illinois Press, 1924.
Plato. *Euthyphro*. In *The Dialogues of Plato*, translated by Benjamin Jowett, 277–302. New York: Scribner's Sons, 1902.
———. *Ion*. In *The Dialogues of Plato*, translated by Benjamin Jowett, 213–32. New York: Scribner's Sons, 1902.
———. *Symposium*. Translated by Christopher Gill. New York: Penguin, 2003.
Plotinus. *Enneads*. Translated by Stephen MacKenna. New York: Penguin, 1991.
Pope, Alexander. "Eloisa to Abelard." In *The Major Works*, 137–47. New York: Oxford University Press, 2006.
Pseudo-Dionysius. *The Divine Names*. In *The Complete Works*, translated by Colm Luibheid, 47–131. New York: Paulist, 1987.
Rahner, Karl. *The Trinity*. Translated by Joseph Donceel. New York: Crossroad, 1997.
Richard of St. Victor. *The Twelve Patriarchs*. Translated by Grover R. Zinn. New York: Paulist, 1979.
Rousseau, Jean-Jacques. *On the Social Contract*. Translated by Donald A. Cress. Indianapolis: Hackett, 2019.
Rundell, Katherine. *Super-Infinite: The Transformations of John Donne*. New York: Picador, 2022.
Russell, Bertrand. *Autobiography, 1873–1914*. Boston: Little, Brown, 1967.
Sartre, Jean-Paul. *Being and Nothingness*. Translated by Sarah Richmond. New York: Washington Square Press, 2021.
———. *No Exit and Three Other Plays*. Translated by Stuart Gilbert. New York: Vintage, 1955.
Styron, William. *Sophie's Choice*. New York: Vintage, 1992.
Tennyson, Alfred Lord. "The Lotos-Eaters." In *Selected Poems*, 24–29. New York: Penguin, 2009.
Tertullian. *The Prescription Against Heretics*. Translated by Peter Holmes. In *Ante-Nicene Fathers*, 3:243–65. Peabody, MA: Hendrickson, 1994.
Thomas Aquinas. *Summa Theologica*. Translated by Fathers of the English Dominican Order. New York: Benziger, 1948.
Thoreau, Henry David. *Walden*. New Haven, CT: Yale University Press, 2004.
Tillich, Paul. *Dynamics of Faith*. New York: Harper & Row, 1957.
Tolstoy, Leo. *The Death of Ivan Ilych and Other Stories*. Translated by David Magarshack. New York: Signet, 1960.
Vasari, Giorgio. *The Lives of the Artists*. Translated by Julia Conway Bondanella and Peter Bondanella. New York: Oxford University Press, 2008.
Vaughan, Henry. "The Night." In *The Oxford Book of English Verse*, edited by Christopher Ricks, 198–99. New York: Oxford University Press, 1999.
Virgil. *Eclogues*. Translated by David Ferry. New York: Farrar, Straus and Giroux, 2000.
Walters, Kerry. *Merciful Meekness: Becoming a Spiritually Integrated Person*. New York: Paulist, 2005.
Whitehead, Alfred North. *Process and Reality*. Corrected ed. New York: Free, 1978.
Wilde, Oscar. *The Picture of Dorian Gray*. New York: Dover, 1993.
Wittgenstein, Ludwig. *Tractatus Logico-Philosophicus*. Translated by C. K. Ogden. New York: Dover, 1998.

Zamyatin, Yevgeny. "On Literature, Revolution, Entropy, and Other Matters." In *A Soviet Heretic: Essays by Yevgeny Zamyatin*, translated by Mirra Ginsburg, 107–12. Chicago: University of Chicago Press, 1970.

———. *We.* Translated by Clarence Brown. New York: Penguin, 1993.

www.ingramcontent.com/pod-product-compliance
Lightning Source LLC
Chambersburg PA
CBHW022012220426
43663CB00007B/1051